MW00398766

NOVEL SOUNDS

SOUTHERN FICTION IN THE AGE OF ROCK AND ROLL

FLORENCE DORE

COLUMBIA UNIVERSITY PRESS / NEW YORK

Columbia University Press

Publishers Since 1893

New York   Chichester, West Sussex

cup.columbia.edu

Copyright © 2018 Columbia University Press

All rights reserved

Library of Congress Cataloging-in-Publication Data

Names: Dore, Florence, author.

Title: Novel sounds : Southern fiction in the age of rock and roll / Florence
Dore.

Description: New York : Columbia University Press, [2018] | Includes
bibliographical references and index.

Identifiers: LCCN 2017055934 (print) | LCCN 2018002557 (ebook) |
ISBN 9780231546058 (e-book) | ISBN 9780231185226 (cloth : acid-free paper) |
ISBN 9780231185233 (pbk. : acid-free paper)

Subjects: LCSH: Rock music in literature. | American fiction—Southern
States—History and criticism. | American fiction—20th century—History
and criticism. | Rock music—Social aspects—United States. | Rock music—
Southern States—History and criticism.

Classification: LCC PS261 (ebook) | LCC PS261 .D67 2018 (print) | DDC
813/.5409975—dc23

LC record available at https://lccn.loc.gov/2017055934

Columbia University Press books are printed on permanent
and durable acid-free paper.

Printed in the United States of America

Cover design: Will Rigby and the National Humanities Center

FOR GEORGIA

CONTENTS

CODA. NOBEL SOUNDS:
BOB DYLAN'S NOVEL PRIZE
115

ACKNOWLEDGMENTS

It would be reasonable to think that *Novel Sounds* was an inevitable project, that of course I would end up writing a book about the genealogy of rock and roll and literature. After all, the forms of expression developing along these intertwining lines of descent drew me in early on. Growing up the offspring of a Vanderbilt philosophy professor was, for me, a suitable launch for learning how to play songs by Libba Cotten and Memphis Minnie on the guitar. The university setting in Nashville's West End seemed an entirely fitting space from which to travel east down Broadway to hear Johnny Cash play. While earning my English degrees, I spent about as much time in rock clubs as I did in classrooms, close-reading records as attentively as I listened to books. For many years, I expended as much energy composing rock songs as I did writing about literature, and my life in higher education has been, quite as fully, a life in rock music. When I was finishing up the PhD, I took a band to my hometown to play for an independent label; during the years I held a postdoctoral fellowship at NYU, I made a record. While coming up for tenure, I got signed, played a string of dates opening for the Yayhoos, and did showcases at South by Southwest and the Exit/In. Once, over a long weekend between Thursday and Tuesday lectures for an American literature course I was teaching at Kent State, I found myself in the opening bar band for the Blue Highways

Festival in Utrecht, playing in a jet-lagged fog for an encouraging crowd that included Chip Taylor, who wrote "Wild Thing." Underwhelming December royalties statements indicate that my song "Christmas," which I wrote when I was twenty, can be heard by holiday travelers flying on Continental Airlines. In retrospect, *Novel Sounds* does seem an obvious culmination of the life that shaped this work. But this book was never a foregone conclusion. And the joy of having found my way to writing it is matched by profound gratitude to those who, in various ways, helped me piece things together.

For those who came to rock, then, I salute you.

Starting with Post45. Neither this book nor my intellectual life as I know it would exist without this group. I will not try to capture the magic that takes place at Post45 conferences; I will just note here that those two intense days each year have sustained and inspired me for the decade I have been lucky enough to participate. For helping me excavate from early drafts inchoate ideas that later became this book, warm and eternal thanks go to Deak Nabers, J. D. Connor, and Sean McCann in particular. Other members of the Steering Committee, including Merve Emre, Mary Esteve, Loren Glass, Amy Hungerford, Kate Marshall, Deborah Nelson, Anthony Reed, and Michael Szalay, have helped this project along as well, and thanks are owed to each. So many wonderful scholars who came to the yearly meetings improved *Novel Sounds*, including Amanda Anderson, Adrienne Brown, Mark Goble, Richard Godden, Martin Harries, Oren Izenberg, Virginia Jackson, Joseph Jeon, Brian Kane, Mark Katz, Mark McGurl, Karl Hagstrom Miller, Sianne Ngai, Margaret Ronda, and Lytle Shaw. I am grateful to each of these fine thinkers for adding their energies to the exchange.

Elizabeth Mansfield and Robert Newman gave me the extraordinary opportunity to watch my book come to life in two public conferences at the National Humanities Center over the academic year 2016–2017, and I am deeply grateful to both for nurturing and supporting this work. The conversations that emerged enriched and improved what the book became, and I thank the participants here for their contributions, in particular Roddy Doyle, Steve Earle, Peter Guralnick, Todd Harvey, Jonathan Lethem, Greil Marcus, and Richard Thompson. Special thanks to James Revel Carr for managing to get a room full of conference atendees to sing. For generous support of these programs, I also wish to acknowledge the Carolina Performing Arts, as well as the following entities at the University of North Carolina, Chapel Hill: the Department of English and Comparative Literature, College of Arts and Sciences; the Office of Research, Institute for Arts and Humanities; and the Graduate School. In the early stages of *Novel Sounds*, J. D. Connor, Amy Hungerford, and I organized Post45@The Rock Hall, another conference whose discussions enhanced my research. Thanks to Rick Moody and Kevin Young for their contributions, and to Lauren Onkey, who generously made the Rock and Roll Hall of Fame available to us for this event.

I owe a great debt to the National Humanities Center, which provided the space for *Novel Sounds* to come into being. For intellectual rigor and humor, I am grateful to everyone in the inimitable NHC class of 2008–2009, especially Colin Bird, Trevor Burnard, John Doris, Mary Floyd-Wilson, Gregory Maertz, Cassie Mansfield, and Michael Wood. It was an unforgettable year in which serious research and hilarity were combined in just the right proportions. Thanks go to David Bunn, Kim Hall, Benjamin Kahan, Joshua Landy, Charles McGovern, Richard Mizelle, James Mulholland, Ian Newman, Tatiana Seijas, and Blake Wilson as well. These are just a few of the scholars with whom I was lucky enough to exchange ideas in later years at the National Humanities Center.

I am privileged indeed call the Department of English and Comparative Literature at the University of North Carolina, Chapel Hill my professional home. Since 2010, I have been sustained by wonderful mentors and colleagues here, especially Bill Andrews, Bill Ferris, Minrose Gwin, Bland Simpson, Terry Rhodes, and Beverly Taylor, all of whom guided me through institutional hurdles with generosity and kindness. I am happy indeed to be part of a community that includes more amazing colleagues than I can possibly name, among them the likes of Mary Floyd-Wilson and Shayne Legassie.

I completed *Novel Sounds* with the help of a National Endowment for the Humanities Fellowship (2008–2009) and a Fellows' Fellowship (2016–2017), both of which I held at the National Humanities Center;

as well as with a Faculty Fellowship at the Institute for the Arts and Humanities at the University of North Carolina, Chapel Hill (Spring 2013). A grant from the University Research Council at the University of North Carolina, Chapel Hill provided essential support at the end of the project. In addition to the time and space afforded by these fellowships, *Novel Sounds* benefited from the incredible support and community offered by the people who made them run, including Geoffrey Harpham, Robert Newman, John Magowan, Brooke Andrade, Heidi Camp, Josiah Drewry, James Getkin, Joel Elliott, Sarah Harris, Anthony Keyes, Jason King, Joe Milillo, Andrew Mink, Kent Mullikin, Eliza Robertson, Don Solomon, and Lois Whittington. Philip Leventhal provided expert editorial advice and buoyed this work with his enthusiasm. Thanks are due to him, Miriam Grossman, Michael Haskell, and Rob Fellman and to all at Columbia University Press who supported bringing *Novel Sounds* into the fold. I am grateful as well to Emily-Jane Cohen and Stanford University Press and to Eric Lott and J. D. Connor for their incisive and detailed reader reports. Sean DiLeonardi provided impeccable research assistance, and the students in my 2015 graduate seminar "Realism and Sound" engaged these ideas with intelligence, good will, and wit. Haley O'Malley, Kyle Frisina, Daniel Hack, and Susan Scott Parrish at University of Michigan, Ann Arbor, deserve thanks as well, for the wonderful questions they posed during my visit there in Spring 2016. For their kind help with photograph permissions, I also wish to thank Terika Dean, Tanya Singh, and Barbara and Douglas A. Gilbert. A version of chapter 2 was published as "The New Criticism and the Nashville Sound: William Faulkner's *The Town* and Rock and Roll" in *Contemporary Literature* 55, no. 2 (Spring 2014).

I have left plenty for detractors to complain about in spite of input from many fine scholars. That Judith Butler and Dorothy Hale continue to advise me after so many years is a great gift. Their intellectual and personal contributions to this work are deeper than can be adequately expressed, my appreciation more profound than I can say. My good fortune in finding intellectual rapport and friendship with Jennifer Fleissner, Kate Marshall, and Benjamin Widiss cannot be overstated. I am so grateful to each of these excellent humans, both for their kind encouragement and for their astute comments on chapter drafts. For guidance, love, and support, I am grateful to sister supreme Katherine Dore and her amazing family—Paschal, Mary Rives, and Frankie Fowlkes—to Dorothy Clarke, Jill Compton, Chris Erikson (with me every step of the musical journey outlined above, and for part of the institutional one), Cait Fenhagen, Mike Ferrio, Mary Floyd-Wilson, Kate Gilhuly, Tama Hochbaum, Caren Lambert, Maureen Katz, Becky Mode, Cliff Westfall, and Lanis Wilson. Whatever happy fate led me to cross paths with D.G.—true friend, trusted confidant, and chosen sister—must be a force for good in the universe. I trust she knows what she has done to bring this work to fruition, but I mention here my eternal and heartfelt thanks to her.

The list of those who inspired and influenced this work includes Steve Earle and the Dukes. A fair amount of research for this book took place on Steve's bus as I was catching up with his drummer over the decade or so in which *Novel Sounds* was coming into being. What I learned about rock and roll and literature on those trips, in conversations with Steve—and also with Eric Ambel and Kelley Looney—shaped *Novel Sounds* as much as anything. I am forever indebted to Steve, both for having me aboard and for making me feel like family.

As invested as I am in clarifying a relationship that has so deeply structured my life, it seems fitting that I close these acknowledgments with thanks to the rock and roll drummer who is in countless ways my other half. Will Rigby knows better than anyone what demons had to be overcome (and what rock facts had to be righted) to complete this feat of conjoining. For this and for giving me his onlyness, he has all of my tomorrows.

This book is dedicated to one Georgia Katherine Luz Rigby, whose existence to date roughly parallels the time it took to write it. My girl, Georgie, you are the best combination of rock and roll and literature I could ever have imagined. May the wonder and beauty in each—or drawn from elsewhere, as you choose—sustain and enrich you as you make your way into a magnificent future all your own. You are my light, my Luz, and having you in my world makes this work and everything I do infinitely more meaningful.

NOVEL
SOUNDS

0.1 Lead Belly at blackboard singing in a classroom, ca. 1940. Location unknown.

Source: Photograph courtesy of House of Lead Belly, LLC.

INTRODUCTION

Minstrel Realism at the Birth of Rock

Memphis, Tennessee, 1952: Sam Phillips creates the legendary Sun Studio and records the first-ever rock and roll single, "Rocket 88," by Ike Turner's Kings of Rhythm. "Magic," says the rock writer Peter Guralnick of the new sound, achieved with the aid of a broken guitar amplifier, "alchemy."[1] Skip the needle forward a couple of years, to 1954. Elvis Presley records "That's All Right" by African American bluesman Arthur Crudup, also at Sun.[2] In 1957, to advance the needle once more, William Faulkner's novel *The Town* emerges in the midst of public acclaim for his earlier novels, only then first being celebrated as the masterpieces they were afterward considered to be.[3] Although some of the characters in *The Town* do travel from Mississippi to Memphis, following roughly the same geographic route as the road traveled by the Kings of Rhythm, they do not visit Sun Studio while they are there. Nor does Faulkner include any rock in this or any other of his novels. In what follows, I am going to argue that *The Town* is one of a group of 1950s novels that, without even a single rock and roll song in their high-literary pages, were nevertheless profoundly about rock and roll.

"It had a dramatic new sound, an electric sound," the historian Andre Millard says of rock and roll music; Guralnick describes rock in terms more foundational still as "the mystery of sound, the freshness of an idea that was entering the world for the very first time." It was the "vitality and invention of the sounds" made by the early Sun artist Harmonica Frank and others first discovered by Phillips, says the rock writer Greil Marcus, that distinguished this music.[4] By most accounts, rock and roll conveyed a sense of innovation when it first came blasting out of the US South during the 1950s, and it turns out that this phenomenon generated a corresponding literary development as well. Over the decade during which rock and roll came into being, a group of canonical American authors native to rock's birthplace began to produce in their fiction stories about the electrification of oral ballads, expressing in the literary realm key cultural changes that also gave rise to the infectious music being generated in their region.

Faulkner can be counted in this cluster of writers, along with Robert Penn Warren, Donald Davidson, Flannery O'Connor, Carson McCullers, and William Styron. Each of these canonical Southern authors wrote fiction portraying vernacular ballads just as rock emerged. So in 1953 Flannery O'Connor transformed a 1927 blues hit by the Tennessee songstress Bessie Smith, "A Good Man Is Hard to Find," into a short story by the same name.[5] During the same year, Donald Davidson wrote *The Big Ballad Jamboree*, taking his plot from "The Daemon Lover," an ancient English ballad transcribed in Appalachia during the 1920s and later recorded by Bob Dylan. Faulkner's *The Town* (1957) cites the first blues song ever published, "The Memphis Blues," by "Father of the Blues" W. C. Handy, and Robert Penn Warren derived the plot for his 1959 *The Cave* from "The Death of Floyd Collins," a 1925 country hit by the Texas hillbilly crooner Vernon Dalhart. At the decade's end, Styron centered the narrative of his *Set This House on Fire* (1960) around the image of a North Carolina native listening to a 1934 recording of Lead Belly's "The Midnight Special," and, finally, going back to the beginning of the 1950s, Carson McCullers, herself a former pianist, wrote a novella entitled *The Ballad of the Sad Café* (1951). Without mentioning any specific titles, McCullers reproduced in her fiction the same set of ideas that moved these other authors to namecheck specific blues, folk, and country ballads that amalgamated in the creation of rock and roll.

The thematic resonance between 1950s Southern fiction and rock is reason enough to take notice: electrified oral balladry originating south of the Mason-Dixon Line is, after all, one way to describe rock and roll.[6] More striking still, rock and roll can be detected formally in fiction by these authors, in a new aesthetic they created at the birth of rock.[7] The irreverent genre in question developed as a notably hybrid electric form, a blend of blues, country, jazz, swing, and folk. As these merged into rock, Southern authors drew from the same eclectic group of musical genres to create a new brand of realism that, like rock, reconditioned Southern vernacular songs, defining them anew as global, electric, and white. These literary reverberations of rock and roll music, the "novel sounds" of 1950s Southern fiction, coalesced into a subgenre of literature we have not yet identified. Resurrecting this Southern literary tradition as rock came into existence clarifies the surprising but unmistakable influence of rock and roll on the development of the American novel itself.

That this aesthetic emerges in a fictional subgenre created by white authors, many of them incorporating into their fiction songs classified as black, repeats rock's well-known engulfment of black music into white.[8] Just as Presley made Crudup's "That's All Right" his own, Flannery O'Connor, to take a notable but overlooked example of black blues in Southern fiction, absorbed Bessie Smith's "A Good Man Is Hard to Find" into her narrative voice, lifting the title directly for her 1953 story. As relevant is the fact that a white man named Bob Wills originally popularized the hillbilly song ("Ida Red") that inspired Chuck Berry's "Maybellene," the song that launched Chuck Berry's rock and roll career in 1955.[9] And indeed, rock and roll scholars have been at pains to trace in early rock and roll a marked disregard for what the music historian Karl Hagstrom Miller calls the "musical color line."[10] Along with Elvis Presley and Chuck Berry, Ray Charles made his career on forays across that line, recording a number of ballads formerly understood to be white. After recording his first crossover hit, "What'd I Say" (1959)—a song that moved him from the strictly black rhythm and blues markets onto pop charts—Charles cut a version of the 1950 country standard by the white Canadian Hank Snow, "I'm Movin' On," and then surprised executives at his label by putting out *Modern Sounds in Country and Western Music*. This album finds Charles, whose music is rooted in the black church, capitalizing on several songs originally marketed to white listeners, including the 1951 "Hey Good Lookin'" by Grand Ole Opry star Hank Williams. With the extraordinary success of this album, followed by a second country record in 1963, Guralnick notes that Charles had "come up with a new racially mixed audience of hitherto undreamt-of proportions."[11]

With the emergence of rock and roll, Southern blues and hillbilly records that had been coded as black or white were absorbed along with other vernacular forms into aesthetic domains no longer tied in the same way to race or place. The man to whom Faulkner refers as "Professor Handy" in *The Town*, for example, produced several early anthologies of black vernacular music in addition to composing songs. The folklorist William Ferris describes Handy's *Blues: An Anthology* (1926) as "a journey through the black experience," and Handy himself marketed "Memphis Blues"—along with blues music generally—as paradigmatically black expression.[12] By contrast, when Ike Turner's "Rocket 88" came buzzing out of Sun Studio, Southern black musical forms had become available to anyone anywhere via new sound technologies. The very title of this foundational rock and roll song, named after the Oldsmobile Rocket 88, clarifies that rock unmoored its artists from region—the paean to a car clearly celebrating mobility, that which enabled broader access to geographically specific vernacular forms. Southern fiction in the 1950s registers a similar engagement with region as a place from which to withdraw. "To know oneself is to know one's region," says Flannery O'Connor in the age of "Rocket 88's" ascendance. "It is also to know the world, and it is also, paradoxically, a form of exile from that world."[13] Both rock and Southern fiction written at its birth produce this paradoxically grounded yet exiled version of the self—a Southerner but defined only in relief, as against "the world" beyond the South.

RING! RING! GOES THE BELL: ROCK AND ROLL, SCHOOL, AND SOUTHERN LITERATURE

This Southern literary subgenre tied to rock and roll appeared at the very moment the authors who created it were being celebrated as America's finest. Michael Kreyling has aptly dubbed the institutional processes leading to this canonization in the 1950s the "invention of Southern literature."[14] And indeed, Faulkner and his ilk came to enjoy newly elevated status in an expanding and increasingly techno-bureaucratic university culture, a "realm" that Mark McGurl has described as composed "not only" of institutions "but also of technologies, the hard and soft machines in and by which literature comes into being."[15] Southern ballad authors register a sense of the machine ethos McGurl attributes at least in part to university culture, depicting in their novels even paper and pens, the most rudimentary tools that allow for literature, as versions of electronic gadgetry. When technology required for rock's emergence began to materialize—the transistor, the 45-rpm record, vinyl—Southern writers attended anew to the mechanisms of their own work, tweaking the aesthetic in literary domains as well, encompassing as part of their literary project material aspects of their medium.[16] In addition to setting out rock's influence on an American literary form, then, *Novel Sounds* examines university culture to explain why "Southern literature" began to resemble rock, an anti-institutional art form if there ever was one, at the very moment of its institutional ascendance.

Newly attuned to their participation in literature's mechanical processes, these writers created a new realist aesthetic, what I call *minstrel realism*, to present their versions of vernacular ballads. Minstrel realism took shape even as Southern writers were being celebrated for their unique ability to generate difficult modernist literature and, thus, for their ability to remedy what the New Critic Cleanth Brooks described in 1963—just one year before the Beatles made their historic appearance on *The Ed Sullivan Show*—as the "machine-made popular arts."[17] When Brooks published the first book-length study of Faulkner's fiction, also in 1963, he asked, what "can a provincial have to say of any consequence to modern industrial man living in an age of electronics and nuclear power?"[18] Even as the New Critics were claiming Southern modernists as their pretechnological "provincials," these authors were engaged in a machinelike version of fictional representation—a self-conscious construal of their literature as a "machine-made" art, the sort of expression against which Southern fiction was held up as a buffer from the early 1950s to the dawn of Beatlemania and beyond.

In noting rock's influence in literary domains, *Novel Sounds* discovers an aesthetic we have overlooked in Southern fiction, one at odds with the formal difficulty characterizing the Southern Renaissance as it was during this era being celebrated.[19] Perversely eschewing the dense modernist style of that earlier moment, Faulkner and the other authors that *Novel Sounds* examines set about representing their geographic region in a more transparent fictional mode, surprisingly embracing what Theodor Adorno called realism's "passive acceptance of objects."[20] Just as they were being hailed as America's guardians of the high literary, that is, held up as exemplars of literary difficulty, Southern authors were availing themselves of lowbrow aesthetic strategies, creating a literalism in their fiction that expresses the technological ethos of their institutional culture rather than advancing its modernist mission. That they generate this realism in portrayals of vernacular music in particular significantly links their form to sound, and indeed all these authors bring into their novels conspicuous images of sound technology—radios, tape recorders, microphones—creating links between their transparent aesthetic and the emerging commitment to high-fidelity sound that developed with the emergence of the long-playing record in 1948.[21] As sound technologies became better able to reproduce musical performance exactly, Southern novelists began to leave behind the opaque representational strategies of earlier days in their portrayals of vernacular ballads.[22]

But to identify this new turn in Southern fiction as realism only partially describes the aesthetic these authors produced at the birth of rock. By making ballads central to their fictional projects, Faulkner and the rest create what I call minstrel realism, an aesthetic that, like rock's eventual turn to ancient ballads, connects their contemporary genre to the oral tradition of minstrelsy in medieval times.[23] Southern novelists of the 1950s also drew from African American vernacular musical traditions, raising the question of whether and how the fictional kinship between these 1950s novels and ancient minstrelsy engages what Eric Lott and Bob Dylan after him identified as "love and theft."[24] Does the mix of regard for and appropriation of African American forms that characterizes the tradition of blackface minstrelsy Lott has analyzed for us explain this tendency in Southern fiction? Is the meaning of Flannery O'Connor's use of a Bessie Smith song exhausted by acknowledging this tradition?

The institutionalization of Southern literature during the 1950s directly resulted from earlier ideas about vernacular ballads as naturally generated by race. In particular, ballads were understood to spring spontaneously from bodies whose racial essence determined their mode of musical expression. Those literary scholars who during the 1950s anthologized Southern authors or published their stories in influential journals—Robert Penn Warren and Andrew Nelson Lytle, to take two key figures in the establishment of Southern literature—had themselves argued in earlier days that an emerging racial fluidity in the post-Reconstruction years could be remedied by engagement with vernacular ballads. Not all Southern novelists these scholars canonized incorporated ballads into their fiction, but those who did traced in them clues to their own canonization. Focusing on ballads allowed these authors to explore the racial motives governing the institutionalization of Southern literature as a field. It was not only that Southern ballad novelists imitated African American forms because they loved or wanted to steal them, then—however reverent of black singers their white protagonists in some cases seemed to be. More to the point, these authors portrayed ballads from both sides of the color line in order to examine the undoing of the ballad form's racial logic, a cultural phenomenon that was also enabled by radio, as racially ambiguous musical sounds came blasting out of them from across the United States and beyond.

How, more specifically, should we understand these white novelists' use of black ballads, then, if not as an example of love and theft? To answer this question, we need first to acknowledge that when Southern literature was invented amid rock's magical new sounds, it was invented as white.[25] And insofar as the institutionalization of Southern literature was fueled by the idea that ballads coded as white guaranteed white essence, the incorporation into Southern fiction of black vernacular music significantly muddled the institutional project. For Southern literature darlings Flannery O'Connor and William Faulkner to draw blues music into their aesthetic expression was for them to flout their institutional guarantors—to accede, scholarly celebration of their work aside, to the cultural tendencies that enabled not only Elvis Presley's use of "That's All Right" but also Chuck Berry's of "Ida Red." Rock and roll was an interracial genre from the start, after all, encompassing the music of Ike Turner, Little Richard, Chuck Berry, Big Mama Thornton, and other African American pioneers right along with that of white artists like Elvis Presley, Carl Perkins, and Jerry Lee Lewis.[26] And as I have noted, one of the distinctive features of rock was that its artists tended to disregard the racial categories ballads had earlier seemed to require. By similarly drawing on ballads both black and white, Southern ballad novelists exposed a correlation between the field of Southern literature and rock, indeed suggesting that Southern literature, bolstered by archaic ideas about white ballads, was established in part as a corrective to rock and roll. Southern writers of the era disobey this implicit mandate, offering up racial indeterminacy in their fiction instead, perversely charting the demise of that which their work was intended to restore.

O'Connor's white grandmother finds herself the robotic mouthpiece of African American blues singer Bessie Smith; Warren's Appalachian balladeer from Tennessee becomes a Jewish media mogul in New York; Styron's Cass finds his Virginia roots in Italy while listening to a scratchy Lead Belly 78; *The Town*'s Southern gentleman Gavin translates Handy's "Memphis Blues" into learning how to close-read poetry at Harvard. Such are the Southerners found in this fiction written at the birth of rock: exiles connected to their region via ballads coded as Southern, unspecific citizens of the world for whom the institutional preservation of old Southern ballads comes to take the place of a geographically specific birthright to create them. These writers demonstrate that Southern literature was already obsolete at the moment of its institutional apotheosis, suggesting that if "Southern literature" ever existed at all, it was by the 1950s a nostalgic defense against the sense that Southerners inhabit an increasingly interracial, virtual, and global space.

This claim corresponds with arguments made by scholars of Southern literature like Scott Romine and Martyn Bone, who have acknowledged the role of media—if not rock specifically—in creating a "mechanically reproduced South." The South in these accounts is an "indistinct and simulated" region that exists beyond geographic location.[27] Bone asks of the region's evolving lack of identity, if "'the South' ceases to be a distinctive socioeconomic geography, what happens to 'Southern literature'?"[28] Scholarly accounts of what Romine and Bone describe as "post-southern" literature in the postwar moment share with one another this interest in whether and how a Southern literature exists past the moment at which Southern Renaissance writers were "either dead or past their creative peaks," to put it in the terms offered by the scholar of Southern literature Richard King.[29] *Novel Sounds* does not address the question of whether a distinctively Southern literature survived midcentury globalization so much as it analyses the broader cultural milieu that gave rise to this question.

Why indeed was Southern literature invented just when the South seemed to be disappearing, along with every other place, into electronically transmitted signals? The central claim of *Novel Sounds* is that the attachment to an idea of Southern literary authenticity in the university bears a crucial relation both to rock's interracial origins and to the transfer of the indelibly Southern sounds of Muscle Shoals, for example, heard on the Rolling Stones' 1971 *Sticky Fingers*, to voices originating in other locales—to British rockers, say.[30] The eponymous 1964 debut album by the Stones also included tracks by several eminent African American bluesmen from Mississippi—Rufus Thomas, Jimmy Reed, and Willie Dixon—and these songs became weirdly inverted specimens of Southern black vernacular when Jagger delivered them back into the United States as artifacts of a British and notably white "invasion."[31] One year before that, sounds of the South were readily given to the Beatles as well, in their version of Alabama-born Arthur Alexander's "Anna," found on their first album release, *Please Please Me* (1963). In addition to undoing ballads' racial essence, the incorporation of ballads into Southern novels at the birth of rock registers the coming globalization so-called British Invasion rockers brought to fruition a decade later, simultaneously affirming and invalidating the idea of the provincial that Southern writers had been held to embody. Even as the ballad form marked these authors as Southern from within the institution, then, the construal of vernacular music as electric in their pages signaled the South's disappearance into the virtual realms traversed by rock and roll.

DEFENSELESSLY FATUOUS: JAMES BALDWIN, RALPH ELLISON, AND THE BLUES

And what about 1950s fiction portraying blues that was written by those who were legally barred from the rooms in which this institutionally sanctioned form originated? Is *Invisible Man* "profoundly about" rock too? If so, did rock and roll influence this classic of the African American novel tradition in the same way that it shaped the aesthetic of that celebrated paradigm of Southern literature, "A Good Man Is Hard to Find"? Both Ellison and James Baldwin wrote about black vernacular music during these years: think of Trueblood's spirituals in *Invisible Man* (1952), for example; or *Go Tell It on the Mountain* (1953), whose very title is derived from a spiritual popularized by Fisk University's Jubilee Singers. Baldwin's "Sonny's Blues" (1957), about a heroin addict who drops out of school to pursue jazz, is no less a fictionalization of proto-rock forms than "A Good Man Is Hard to Find."[32] So why not describe these works as minstrel realism too? Because neither Ellison nor Baldwin was writing under the aegis of Southern literature as that category was then being institutionalized, these authors' aesthetic and social commitments differed from those of the writers *Novel Sounds* studies. Baldwin's status as a New Yorker would be an obvious reason for not claiming him as a Southern author, even if through his lineage he might legitimately be called Southern by inheritance, a point bolstered by the many flashbacks to the South in his debut novel. But it is neither geographical lineage nor physical location that distinguishes Baldwin's approach to musical fiction from that taken by Flannery O'Connor. More important than his regional identity, Baldwin was an African American author without a college degree. And just as relevant, Ellison earned his BA at a historically black college, Tuskegee University. Although they shared with Southern white writers an interest in vernacular music, Baldwin and Ellison approached their topic having been denied entry into the white university culture, the access to which is registered virtually everywhere in Southern fiction. Ellison's scathing portrayal of the institution's uses of black balladry in *Invisible Man* clarifies his distinct approach: Trueblood's singing of "primitive spirituals" for the entertainment of white "officials" at a black college is a form of racially specific debasement in *Invisible Man*, linked to the brutal electrocution that Ellison portrays as the gateway to black education.[33]

It is these institutional considerations, not racial essence or geographical origin, that account for literary distinctions that emerged along the color line in 1950s ballad fiction. Within the postwar university system, after all, white Vanderbilt professors solidified decades of educational advantage by producing literary anthologies that only included white authors.[34] As the white ballad writers valorized in these anthologies began to adhere to the dictates of a new brand of realism, Ellison and Baldwin took rather a different tack. Baldwin specifically railed against fiction that hews too closely to what he described as the "cage of reality." In his 1949 essay "Everybody's Protest Novel," Baldwin famously broke ranks with his mentor Richard Wright, claiming that Wright's Bigger Thomas resembled Harriet Beecher Stowe's sentimental rendering of Uncle Tom. Baldwin describes both as "badly written" protest fiction, arguing that their realism amounts to a debasement of humanity. For him it is the absence of "paradox" in particular that prevents the possibility literature enables—"that our lives shall be other than superficial."[35] One way to describe Baldwin's critique of Wright would be to say that it indicates a refusal of fictional principles Southern writers embraced in the 1950s, including Cleanth Brooks's noted valorization of "the language of paradox" itself.[36] Black writers, excluded from the white university culture in which modernism was celebrated, produced an antirealist fictional aesthetic, in Ellison's case modeled in part on early novels by Faulkner.[37] The position of the African American author writing about music or anything else clarifies that the white writers *Novel Sounds* analyzes were afforded the opportunity to engage in a literary form of slumming and to express this institutional advantage by thumbing their noses at the very practices that launched and sustained their careers.

"The blues is an impulse," wrote Ellison in a 1945 review of Wright's *Black Boy*, an "autobiographical chronicle of personal catastrophe expressed lyrically."[38] Black musical forms did not indicate racial indeterminacy for either Ellison or Baldwin as they did for Southern white writers. These African American authors instead claimed black vernacular forms as part of their aesthetic legacy in the years leading up to the Civil Rights Act of 1964, specifically aligning themselves with blues and jazz to affirm black citizenship—to clarify political rights by elevating the worth of black aesthetic traditions devalued not just by university culture but by society at large. In 1963, Baldwin made known his view on blues in a complaint about inane versions of the blues, sung, "God help us," by white people, "sounding . . . so helplessly, defenselessly fatuous that one dare not speculate on the temperature of the deep freeze from which issue their brave and sexless little voices."[39] Unlike Faulkner and O'Connor, for whom black blues rendered race less distinct, for both Baldwin and Ellison, the blues signified blackness. And it was in the same year, 1963—when the Beatles unveiled their version of Alabama black vernacular with "Anna"—that LeRoi Jones (later Amiri Baraka) published *Blues People: Negro Music in White America*, in it arguing that both blues and jazz demonstrate how crucially influential African American music had been in American culture generally. Black music, Jones argued, should be understood as the "orchestrated, vocalized, hummed, chanted, blown, beaten, scatted, corollary confirmation of" the history of "Afro American life."[40] As white Southern novelists were finding in black blues a tool for producing cheeky transgressions of their institutional privilege, a privilege they continued to enjoy, African American novelists were holding up the genre as a precedent for aesthetic self-determination.

SOUTHERN NOVEL, ROCK NOVEL

One way to grasp rock's influence on postwar Southern fiction is to consider portrayals of music in American novels written before rock came
into existence. Such a comparison might begin with W. E. B. Du Bois's
The Souls of Black Folk (1903), which, while not strictly a novel, famously
included the score of noted African American spirituals as epigraphs to
his chapters, describing them as "some echo of haunting melody from
the only American music which welled up from black souls in the dark
past."[41] The invocation of black voices from a dark past was clearly on
Faulkner's mind when he decided to title *Go Down, Moses* (1942) after one
of these spirituals, and that novel too should be considered among those
on the long list of pre-rock ballad fiction in American literature.[42] Unlike
the subgenre *Novel Sounds* examines, ballad fiction written before the
birth of rock valorizes the natural in its portrayals of human voices singing vernacular songs, exemplifying exactly the rhetorical links between
race and voice that postwar Southern writers would undo. While surely
Southern fiction about ballads extends this tradition as it evolves from
the early twentieth century and moments prior (Homer's *The Odyssey* is
neither a novel nor a ballad, but was it not sung?), Faulkner and others
writing under the auspices of Southern literature at the birth of rock
responded to rock's detachment of the ballad from race and place by
exposing, rather than covering over, the ballad's technical operations.

Eudora Welty's 1941 story "Powerhouse," composed after Welty
attended a concert given by the jazz piano virtuoso Fats Waller, provides
an instructive point of comparison. Like O'Connor, Welty is moved to
bring a song by Bessie Smith into her story, in Welty's case the 1928
recording "Empty Bed Blues." But whereas O'Connor collapses the grandmother's voice into the mechanical recording of Smith's, as I will show in
chapter 3, Welty valorizes the hyperbolically bodily voice of Powerhouse,
the live singer, noting so visceral a sign of his orality as the "bubble" that
"shoots out on his lip." His bodily presence is meant to contrast Welty's
chosen Smith recording, which the author depicts as emanating weakly

from a "burnt-out-looking nickelodeon." "Of course you know how he sounds—you've heard him on records," says Welty's narrator. "But still you need to see him."[43] No such relief in live performance or oral forms exists in O'Connor's "A Good Man Is Hard to Find," in which the mouth emerges only to be collapsed into its robotic substitute. Evolving along with the dramatic new electric sounds of rock music, Southern ballad fiction is part of a general tendency in postwar American fiction—McGurl calls it "high literary *techne*"—to align literature with technology, and the readings that follow show how these authors collapse novels with sound technology in particular to achieve that alignment.[44]

Returning to the question with which *Novel Sounds* opens, we might ask: Really? *The Town* and these other 1950s Southern novels are about rock and roll? No "Rocket 88" appears in these pages, no "Hound Dog," no "Maybellene." How can they be about rock? Fast forward to fifty years after the birth of rock, to the era in which rock was said to die.[45] The rock and roll in 1950s novels is easier to see from that vantage, in retrospect—clearer when we trace it backward from what I have elsewhere called the "rock novels" of the contemporary moment.[46] In the early twenty-first century, at rock's putative death, one finds an explosion of fictional references to historical rock bands and their songs, and the authors portray these in strikingly literal terms. So, in *The Fortress of Solitude* (2003), to take a paradigmatic example, we find Jonathan Lethem glossing the consciousness of Bob-namesake Dylan Ebdus with the lyrics of one-hit-wonder Wild Cherry's "Play That Funky Music" (1976) when he is a teen. The somber "Another Green World" (1975) does the job later in his life, Brian Eno's intellectualized rock the better to match a more mature Dylan's complex existential emotions.[47] Also apposite here are Dana Spiotta's *Eat the Document* (2006), a novel whose title she took from Bob Dylan's unreleased documentary (from his 1966 tour) with the same name; and Lorrie Moore's story "People Like That Are the Only People Here: Canonical Babbling in the *Peed Onk*," from her collection *Birds of America* (2010), in which a bereft mother sings the Animals' 1965 "We Gotta Get Out of This Place" to comfort her infant, who is strapped down to a hospital bed after a cancerous tumor has been removed from his tiny body.

The presence of these undigested rock songs in novels written at the death of rock makes more vivid the subtler signs of rock in fiction written at its birth. They allow earlier fictional forays into electrified ballads to come into view as marking an early phase of the rock novel. Recognizing this trajectory enables us to count as part of an evolving tradition representative examples of the rock novel: from the 1960s, Harlan Ellison's *Spider Kiss* (1961) and Thomas Pynchon's *The Crying of Lot 49* (1964); from the 1970s, Don DeLillo's *Great Jones Street* (1973); and from the 1980s, Brett Easton Ellis's *Less Than Zero* (1985) and Roddy Doyle's *The Commitments* (1987). *Novel Sounds* provides a prehistory for this development, revealing that what appeared to be a brand-new aesthetic category in the decades around the year 2000 had in fact been developing since rock's beginnings. This tradition thus also illuminates an overlooked institutional genealogy that begins in Southern fiction and ends in the global novel, for if rock novels belonged to Southerners during the 1950s, by the year 2000 they had become available to millennial citizens of the world. Inveterate New Yorkers Jonathan Lethem and Colson Whitehead; Mumbai-born Salman Rushdie; Manila's Jessica Hagedorn; Dublin's Roddy Doyle; Hanif Kureishi, Englishman of Pakistani descent; the Norwegian Karl Ove Knausgård; and Hari Kunzru, British-born son of a Kashmiri Pandit: all took up the form with a new fervor as rock began to die.[48] By the turn of the twentieth century, the "place" Moore's rock-savvy mom wants to "get out of" could be anywhere. Readers of *Novel Sounds* hoping to find clarification on what counts as Southern literature proper will find instead the beginnings of a story about how its institutional values came to be extended into global domains.[49]

LEAD BELLY'S CHANNELS: FOLKLORE AND THE NEW CRITICISM BEFORE ROCK AND ROLL

To rewind again, tracing this story backward once more, to the era from which 1950s Southern authors and rock and rollers alike drew their ballads, we find institutional precedent for the overlap between high-literary culture and popular music. I have noted that ballad fiction written in the decades before the 1950s tended to promote oral singing over the "burnt-out" sounds, as Welty called them, emanating from jukeboxes. This tendency corresponded with an institutional conception of the literary as rooted in vernacular song that evolved in the 1920s and 1930s, an idea that persisted even as electric microphones were replacing acoustic horns in musical recording—and as pioneers in the American music industry were dividing vernacular music along racial lines into "hillbilly" markets and "race records."[50] It was these early ideas about vernacular music, generated by the very scholars who would later canonize Southern literature, that paved the way for an astonishing event that took place in 1934. On December 28 of that year, attendees of the Modern Language Association's annual meetings in Philadelphia were invited to a Friday night "smoker," a social gathering listed in the MLA program featuring "Negro Folksongs and Ballads, presented by John and Alan Lomax, with the assistance of a Negro minstrel from Louisiana." At a panel held the next day on popular literature, John Lomax gave the talk "Comments on Negro Folk Songs (illustrated with voice and guitar by Negro convict Leadbelly [sic] of Louisiana)."[51] And so it was that in 1934, the African American folksinger and twice-convicted murderer Huddie Ledbetter, also known as the "King of the Twelve-String Guitar," performed as the "Negro minstrel from Louisiana" at the largest gathering of literature scholars in the world.

"Two Time Dixie Murderer Sings Way to Freedom," reads a 1934 headline covering Lead Belly's MLA appearance in the African American newspaper *Philadelphia Independent.*[52] One year prior, Lomax had discovered Lead Belly in an institutional space quite distinct from the literary rooms into which the performer would soon be introduced—at the Louisiana State Penitentiary, also known as Angola, where he was serving time for murder.[53] Lomax secured Lead Belly's release from prison, hired him as servant and driver, and took him on a tour of American colleges that included a stop at the MLA meetings in Philadelphia.[54] It was on the basis of Lomax's recordings of Lead Belly in Angola, captured by a device Lomax described as an "instantaneous aluminum recording machine," that the governor of Louisiana agreed to pardon Lead Belly.[55] And while it is striking indeed that Lead Belly's acoustic music would justify judicial exoneration, his presence at the Philadelphia meetings raises questions about another acquittal as well: what cultural pardon in 1930s America gained Lead Belly entrance to the all-white rooms at the MLA? What was an African American singer who dropped out of school at the age of fourteen to play guitar in Texas juke joints doing with an entirely white group of literature scholars in a conference room in Philadelphia, three decades before the passage of the Civil Rights Act?

The guitar-slinging "two time Dixie murderer" could "sing his way to freedom" because even as race and hillbilly records were making vernacular ballads more widely available on shellac 78s, scholars of literature were celebrating the social function of the ballad as an oral form. In 1930, a group of twelve Vanderbilt professors published *I'll Take My Stand*, a book of essays lamenting the waning influence of Southern values on American culture generally. *I'll Take My Stand* advanced the case for what Andrew Nelson Lytle called "ballets" as a remedy for this decline, and Lytle's admiration for the ballad form involved a worry about sound technology in particular.[56] Southern farmers should "throw out the radio and take down the fiddle from the wall," he declares. If for Lytle the problem was radio, for Donald Davidson it was the manufacture and distribution of records that caused cultural erosion. Lamenting in particular the "shop-girl" who listens to "a jazz record while she rouges her lips," Davidson argues that the "magnificent possibilities for distributing art became appalling opportunities for distributing bad art." The South is a model for changing what the distribution of jazz records has destroyed, says Davidson, because the region "has been rich in folk-arts, and is still rich in them—in ballads, country songs and dances, in hymns and spirituals." The "shop-girl" should throw away race records and radio, should cease listening to jazz and return to her own white ballads, ballads preserved in the geographical enclaves Davidson describes as "mountain fastness and remote rural localities."[57] Agrarians imagined that a return to ballads from the British Isles, those that had been preserved in "mountain fastness," would allow Southern values to be restored to national prominence.

Lytle embellished this call to "throw out the radio," moreover, with a racial epithet about a hidden African American in "the woodpile," clarifying that the call for pretechnological music is inextricable from a commitment to white dominance.[58] Amid its messages about "ballets," *I'll Take My Stand* included complaints about the end of slavery, including Robert Penn Warren's declaration, "Let the negro sit beneath his own vine and fig tree."[59] Davidson's worry about record distribution and the spread of jazz carries with it a similar anxiety about the spread of black cultural forms into white spaces, a segregationist view that he expresses in his writings about ballad collecting as well. In 1934, Davidson wrote of a trek with his Vanderbilt colleague George Pullen Jackson into rural Georgia to find Sacred Harp songs, described by Jackson as "white spirituals":

> As for Dr. Jackson's argument that the Negro spirituals derive ultimately from the white spirituals, I thought as I listened that no one acquainted with the controversy between those who argue for a white origin and those who hold out for an exclusively Negro origin could remain unconvinced in the light of Sacred Harp performance. . . . Doubtless the Negro had adapted them in his peculiar way, but he had first of all taken his songs from the source where he had got his Bible, his plow, his language.[60]

During the 1930s, the author and ethnographer Zora Neale Hurston made forays into rural locations to collect African American folk ballads, and Hurston's recordings clearly formed part of what Daphne Brooks describes as an effort to "put black voices on the (scholarly) record."[61] But Davidson's "mountain fastness" indicates the opposite impulse, the designation of a natural refuge away from the reach of black sounds. The affirmation of "ballets" in *I'll Take My Stand* emerges as inextricable from this segregationist message, and Davidson associates ballads with national purity as well when he later writes that Sacred Harp spirituals are examples of "native American culture" originating in the British Isles. For Davidson, ballads found in mountain fastness confirmed links between white Southerners and their ancestors from England and Scotland.[62] His rejection of music with an "exclusively Negro origin" in 1934 clarifies that his goal was in part to establish racial essence through the ballad form and to make a claim for white superiority in opposing the phonograph. Lead Belly's presence at the MLA registers this segregationist valorization of the oral.[63]

We find a link between these ideas about ballads' racial origins and the later claims about poetic form that framed the invention of Southern literature. Eight years after declaring that "the negro" should "sit beneath his own vine and fig tree," Warren edited the influential New Critical tome *Understanding Poetry* with Cleanth Brooks. Along with poems by John Donne, William Shakespeare, T. S. Eliot, and John Keats, Warren and Brooks include a sampling of ballads in this text, most of them ancient Scottish and English instances of the form. But among these, remarkably, we also find one that Lomax recorded Lead Belly singing at Angola before bringing him to the MLA: "Frankie and Johnny."[64] Warren and Brooks do not credit any source for "Frankie and Johnny." But no matter how they learned of it, whether from Lomax's recording or some other source, it is striking indeed that the same ballad captured the notice of Lead Belly, Lomax, and the New Critics alike. For reasons that John Guillory has explained, the New Critics attributed to literature the power to unify secular culture, and they traced this power back through Eliot's modernist verse to Donne's metaphysical poetry.[65] This New Critical program of poetic repair, as articulated in another of the important New Critical works, Brooks's influential 1947 *The Well Wrought Urn*, involved showing students how to appreciate the "miracle of which the poet speaks" by learning to make "the closest possible examination of what the poem says as a poem."[66] Donne's "The Canonization" is a good place to start, so Brooks's title, taken from the poem, suggests. But what should we make of the appearance in *Understanding Poetry* of a Lead Belly tune alongside "The Canonization"? How shall we understand the idea that poetry's "miracle" can be found in a Lead Belly ballad, particularly in light of Warren's opinions about "the negro"?

New Critics construed ballads as the original buffer against what Brooks called machine-made arts because of their imagined connection to the human voice. "Poems like 'Frankie and Johnny' or 'Jesse

James,'" explain Warren and Brooks in *Understanding Poetry*, "narratives to be sung that sprang from unknown sources and are transmitted by word of mouth, and that may experience alteration in this process, are usually called *ballads*."[67] It was just one year before the Beatles made their historic appearance on *The Ed Sullivan Show* that Brooks wrote his lament about "the machine-made popular arts of our time." The "pressure of the popular arts today," Brooks opined, "as exerted through cheap fiction, Tin Pan Alley, the movies, the radio, and now television makes what Wordsworth faced in 1800 seem very mild indeed."[68] "Frankie and Johnny" qualified for inclusion in *Understanding Poetry* because unlike a Tin Pan Alley song—and in starker contrast to the rock songs broadcast on television during the era in which Brooks launched this later complaint—it seemed to have hatched from something like "mountain fastness." As a ballad thought to originate in uncorrupted space, "Frankie and Johnny" had been "transmitted," or so it seemed, by "word of mouth."[69]

"Frankie and Johnny" is one of two American ballads Warren and Brooks include in *Understanding Poetry* (the other is "Jesse James"), and of the ancient English and Scottish ballads it includes I note here "The Daemon Lover" and "Sir Patrick Spence" because each, as we shall see, made their way from literary into rock and roll domains. As with "Frankie and Johnny," Warren and Brooks offer no source for these ballads, but they had been compiled before. "Sir Patrick Spence," for example, can be found in print as early as 1765, in the first ballad collection in the English tradition, *The Reliques of Ancient Poetry* by Bishop Thomas Percy. In the dedication of *The Reliques* to the Countess of Northumberland, Percy describes the ancient ballads he anthologizes as the "rude songs of ancient minstrels," urging the countess to understand them "not as labours of art, but as effusions of nature, showing the first efforts of ancient genius."[70] Along with rest of the ancient ballads in *Understanding Poetry*, "Sir Patrick Spence" can also be found in the ten-volume anthology *The English and Scottish Popular Ballads* (1882–1898), compiled by the literature scholar Francis James Child. Child based his anthology on Percy's work, absorbing ideas about the ballad as natural expression from Percy's era. In his preface to *The*

English and Scottish Popular Ballads, in particular, Child distinguishes between "spontaneous products of nature" and the less authentic "works of professional ballad makers" in terms that echo Percy's.[71]

In Percy's moment, then, "Sir Patrick Spence" and ballads like it were understood to be paradigmatically unmediated. Indeed, Percy construes minstrels' voices as entirely embedded in nature—as if ballads move directly from nature through the balladeer's mouth to the ear of anyone who might hear. In her examination of eighteenth-century ballad collections, Susan Stewart argues that ballads evoke the "entire aura of the oral world—such a world's imagined presence, immediacy, organicism, and authenticity."[72] Analyzing the same tendency, Maureen N. McLane demonstrates how this aura is assigned even in transcription and suggests that the ballad's oral status creates an illusion of direct contact with singing bodies.[73] Later uses in rock of the ballad form would overtly parody the ballad's imagined connection to the body. This is one way to understand Fairport Convention's 1960s updates to ancient ballads, with rock drums and roiling electric guitar added to acoustic versions of ancient ballads they had learned from the British folk masters Ewan MacColl and A. L. Lloyd.[74] Rock would eventually draw ancient ballads one way—Fairport Convention recorded an acid-rock version of "Sir Patrick Spens" (taking the ancient spelling) for their third album; Dylan recorded "The Daemon Lover" in 1961, a fact I examine more closely in chapter 1.[75] But in the 1930s New Critics were still caught in these earlier ideas. In their definitions of the vernacular as the original literature, that is, Warren and Brooks held to a backward-looking definition of the ballad, one that emphasized its natural features. It was on this basis that the ballad was included in New Critical textbooks dividing high-literary from "machine-made popular arts" and on this basis as well that ballads were taken to guarantee racial essence.

Davidson's idea that ballads are preserved in "mountain fastness" brings into the era of early electroacoustic recording Percy's "effusions of nature," and *Understanding Poetry* as well contains remnants of the notion, residual even then, that "rude songs" arise directly from nature.[76] In the 1938 volume this emerges as an assertion that sound technology spoils what "word of mouth" enables. Extending Lytle's call eight years earlier to "throw out the radio," Warren and Brooks argue that radio interrupts poetic "experience." "We like a poem," they proclaim, "not because it gives us satisfaction of our curiosity or because it gives us an idea we can 'carry away with us', as people sometimes put it, but because the poem itself is an experience":

> We can illustrate by a comparison to a football game. If a person listens to a radio report of a game, he may really have more accurate infor- mation about it than if he were present. And when the game is over, he will know the exact score. But if he has his choice he will probably take the trouble, and spend the money, to go to the game itself. He does this because the game is a richer experience. The score and the statistics of the game come to him, if he watches it, not as bare facts, but in terms of action.[77]

Radio provides "accurate information" that we can "carry away"; poetry creates "experience." Modulating from football game to poem, Warren and Brooks present the ballad as exemplifying poetic "experience." If "we like it at all," they explain, "we like it because of its particular nature as experience."[78]

To elaborate their ideas about ballads in general, Warren and Brooks turn to "Frankie and Johnny." The "mere fact, as a fact, that a woman in the slums shot her sweetheart Johnny," they explain, "is of little interest to us." Rather, they argue, if "we enjoy hearing 'Frankie and Johnny' sung, we do so because of something more than the statistical impor- tance of the subject."[79] Opposing poetic experience to radio suggests that the "more" to which they refer is the presence of an unmediated singing body. It is the physical "enjoyment" of a singer's voice in the listener's ear, it seems, that constitutes this surplus, this "more" that cannot be "carried away" as radio "carries" away. "Mountain fastness" is destroyed by radio; the sensory pleasure associated with the live voice in the bal- lad indicates that both geographic and bodily boundaries are intact. A ballad that captured the attention of the folklorist Lomax as essentially black thus also helps New Critics explain poetic experience. The African American balladeer hovers, then, as a figure of corporeal integrity in the New Critical claim that literary experience can deliver a miracle.[80] Warren and Brooks do not mention race in this discussion of "Frankie and Johnny." But by rooting poetry in the ballad's mythic bodily wholeness, Warren and Brooks clarify that "understanding poetry" means inheriting features of the Agrarians' segregationist logic.[81]

Lomax brought versions of these literary ideas about oral ballads with him into the Louisiana State Penitentiary when he went there to record Lead Belly singing "Frankie and Johnny." In his introduction to the Lead Belly anthology Lomax published two years after that visit, he explained why Lead Belly's songs qualified as folk. The reasons he gives resemble those given by Warren and Brooks for designating ballads as poetry: songs like "Frankie and Johnny" created an idea of unmediated transmission—fulfilled an ideal of smooth passage between mouth and ear, sensory enjoyment without interference from technology. "His eleven years of confinement," wrote Lomax, "had cut him off both from the phonograph and from radio," and the "songs learned by 'word of mouth'" qualified for the anthology. The idea that Lead Belly had been isolated from media extended even to a claim about his exposure to paper. Lomax claims that he "saw no printed page of music, either in his prison cell or in his home."[82] As for the New Critics, so for Lomax: literary value depended on unmediated transmission between human bodies. That the racially segregated black space within the prison guaranteed for Lomax the same purity Davidson found in the Southern hills clarifies the links between Agrarian mountain fastness and institutional segregation, suggesting that Davidson's idea of natural enclosure is in fact a figure for the sequestering of rooms like those at Angola—or at Vanderbilt—from blackness.

While Southern Agrarian Lytle was issuing his mandate to "take down the fiddle from the wall," then, Lomax was recording and archiving musicians who were doing just that. The similarity between these two projects seems perhaps surprising, but in fact champion of the folk Lomax had plenty of institutional credibility. Over the academic year 1906–1907, he took some time away from taping the music of convicted murderers in prisons to seek insights from literature scholars in the hallowed halls of Harvard University. Lomax worked under the tutelage of George Lyman Kittredge, principally a Chaucer scholar but head of the American Folklore Society as well and editor of its journal.[83] This set of interests was not anomalous: folklore and literature were elements in a single endeavor at Harvard during these years—in 1904 Kittredge held posts as president at both the Modern Language Association and the American Folklore Association. Kittredge had worked under Child, moreover, bringing out the final volume of *The English and Scottish Popular Ballads* after Child died.[84] Lomax's time at Harvard surely explains why we find him comparing "Home on the Range" and other American ballads to "Beowulf" in the introduction to his 1910 *Cowboy Songs*: "If his life of isolation made [the cowboy] taciturn, it at the same time created a spirit of hospitality, primitive and hearty as the mead-halls of Beowulf."[85] American ballads retain an "Anglo-Saxon ballad spirit," Lomax explains:

> Out in the Wild, far-away places of the big and still unpeopled West—in the cañons along the Rocky Mountains, among the mining camps of Nevada and Montana, and on the remote cattle ranches of Texas, New Mexico, and Arizona—yet survives the Anglo-Saxon ballad spirit that was active in secluded districts in England and Scotland even after the coming of Browning and Tennyson.[86]

Those unspoiled by print culture are for Lomax the best contemporary source of a literature still tied to a "ballad spirit": "Illiterate people, and people cut off from newspapers and books, isolated and lonely folk—thrown back on primal resources for entertainment and for the expression of emotion—express themselves through somewhat the same character of songs as did their forefathers perhaps a thousand years ago."[87] The ideas in Lomax's later collection of Lead Belly's songs are rooted in the belief, found here as well, that folk ballads like Lead Belly's are the modern replica of ancient minstrelsy. This notion can be traced directly to Harvard scholars immersed in medieval literature.

The preface to *Cowboy Songs* was written by another of Lomax's mentors at Harvard, Barrett Wendell, whom Mark McGurl notes also taught some of the earliest composition classes to encourage creative writing. This may explain why Wendell's endorsement of Lomax sounds so much like the later injunction within creative writing programs to "write what you know."[88] "It is the sense, derived one can hardly explain how," argued Wendell of the ballad in *Cowboy Songs*, "that here is the expression straight from the heart of humanity; that here is something like the sturdy root from which the finer, though not always more lovely, flowers of polite literature have sprung."[89] The valorization of unlovely "expression straight from the heart" involves a conception of authentic voice we can trace back to "rude songs of ancient minstrels." This preface ends with Wendell's observations about Lomax visiting his American literary history class at Harvard to read ballads aloud from *Cowboy Songs*. Extolling the way in which the students' "cheerless progress of a course of study" was altered by these ballads, Wendell's preface concludes, "I commend them to all who care for the native poetry of America."[90] Lomax's ballads thus entered the world carrying Harvard's imprimatur—"Frankie and Johnny" was authorized as poetry even before Warren and Brooks included it in *Understanding Poetry*.

Heading into prisons and remote communities to record Lead Belly and other vernacular musicians, then, Lomax carried out in the field a version of the cultural work New Critics were performing in university classrooms. And as it turns out, this legitimation involved a sleight of hand in which technology was purged from the ballad, erased from its construal as a raced form. Lead Belly's qualifications were rooted in Lomax's claim that he had been "cut . . . off both from the phonograph and from radio," as we have just seen, and "Frankie and Johnny" qualified as poetry in *Understanding Poetry* because it had been transmitted by "word of mouth." But the 78s from whose spinning grooves "Frankie and Johnnie" emanated were in circulation before Lomax arrived at Angola— and before the publication of *Understanding Poetry* as well. In 1928, OKeh Records recorded "Frankie," a version of the song by Mississippi John Hurt, an African American farmer, releasing it that year as a race record. When OKeh's scout Tommy Rockwell found Hurt, he was hoping "Frankie" might replicate the commercial success of Mamie Smith's 1920 "Crazy Blues," the first blues song ever recorded.[91] But Columbia Records had two years earlier put out a hillbilly version of "Frankie and

Johnny," a recording by the group Charlie Poole and the North Carolina Ramblers called "Leaving Home," this one aimed at white buyers.[92] When Lomax arrived at Angola, "Frankie and Johnny" had already been sold as a sound recording on both sides of the color line.

"Frankie and Johnny" had already lived a life in and as shellac by the time Lomax arrived at Angola to capture it as a ballad spontaneously emerging from Lead Belly's black body.[93] During the 1940s, Lead Belly let on that he had been influenced by the white cowboy singer Gene Autry's records, but this information is nowhere to be found in any of Lomax's earlier promotional materials.[94] What "Frankie and Johnny's" mediated status suggests is that although Lomax promoted Lead Belly's music as Exhibit A of black folk—including "Frankie and Johnny" in a section of his Lead Belly anthology entitled "Negro Bad Men," for example—the racial status of his songs is far from clear. Indeed, there is no guarantee that Lead Belly did not learn "Frankie and Johnny" from a "white" record. The readings of vernacular songs in *Novel Sounds* demonstrate a correlation between Lomax's assertions about "folk" and the contemporaneous institutional understanding of literature, exposing the racial basis of purely formal claims about the literary. No matter how "Frankie and Johnny" may have sounded at the MLA (if in fact Lead Belly performed it there), the excavation of "Frankie and Johnny" as ultimately a media artifact clarifies that in both fields, racial essence was a technological effect produced and enabled by the material life of songs.[95] A 1935 *Time* newsreel depicting Lomax and Lead Belly as stiffly acted, costumed versions of themselves first meeting at Angola crystallizes the contradictions entailed in vernacular music of the 1920s and 1930s: the reel, its poorly lit actors scripted into marked racial stereotypes, produced bodily authenticity but as ghostly cinematic illusion.[96] No recording of "Frankie and Johnny," no print version of the tune—not even this obviously bogus *Time* newsreel—seems to have altered the view that "Frankie and Johnny" carried forward the purely oral traditions of ancient minstrels into the 1920s and 1930s. Even in rock's prehistory, then, decades before "Rocket 88" launched, vernacular music was involved in the transmission of a virtual South, engaged, just as rock would be twenty years later, in disconnecting ballads from race and place.

As we shall see, the obscured technological origin of apparently oral ballads became a key topic for Southern writers in the 1950s, and as they explored the electrification of ballads in their own moment, they presented the vernacular as originating in an ever receding bodily origin. The chapters that follow show Lead Belly making crucial appearances in Southern novels at the birth of rock: in Donald Davidson's 1954 *The Big Ballad Jamboree*, for example, and in William Styron's 1960 *Set This House on Fire*. Familiar conceptions of the distinction between high and low culture, a topic I take up in the coda to this book, would lead us to understand these depictions as scandalous violations of literary protocol. But in fact the midcentury portrayals of the vernacular to which *Novel Sounds* attends avow traditional conceptions of literature that predate even the New Critical champions of these authors. By the time rock and roll was born, that is, ballads had been understood as a form of literature for centuries, and Lead Belly already held a place in literary domains on the basis of that history.

UNDER THE SIGN OF THE FIDDLE

In chapters focused on portrayals of the key sound media whose evolution led inexorably to rock and roll—magnetic tape, radio, the book, and vinyl—*Novel Sounds* shows how Southern fiction about vernacular music exposes the high literary too as ultimately a mechanical art, even as it emerges under the sign of Lytle's fiddle on the wall. *Novel Sounds* presents these arguments in four chapters, the first a reading of magnetic tape found in novels by two former Agrarians—contributors, no less, to *I'll Take My Stand*—Donald Davidson's *The Big Ballad Jamboree* (1954) and Robert Penn Warren's *The Cave* (1959). Chapter 2 examines the book as sound medium in Faulkner's *The Town* (1957), and chapter 3 analyzes overlaps between radio and fiction in short stories by two women, Carson McCullers's *The Ballad of the Sad Café* (1951) and Flannery O'Connor's "A Good Man Is Hard to Find" (1954).

The final chapter provides an analysis of the record in William Styron's *Set This House on Fire* (1960), and my coda extends these readings to an argument about what the *New Yorker* editor David Remnick described as an "astonishing and unambiguously wonderful thing," Bob Dylan's win of the 2016 Nobel Prize in Literature.[97] Books might on first glance seem unlike the other media in this grouping, but by unraveling the figural symbiosis between sound media and the high literary in these novels, I show how Southern authors portray their own printed paper as virtualizing the South right along with rock's sound technologies. As such, a surprising idea emerges from Southern ballad fiction: just as surely as record or radio, the book too generates novel sounds in the age of rock and roll.

One of the rationales given for the conferral of this prize is that Dylan was "a great poet in the grand English tradition."[98] Whether or not one agrees with this assessment, surely it makes sense to claim that poetry belongs in a study of rock at midcentury—that there is an obvious kinship between rock songs and poems.[99] *Novel Sounds* leaves study of that meaningful topic to others, addressing instead the question of why an apparently unrelated form, the novel, became such an important genre for exploring rock and roll at its birth. Insofar as it makes explicit some of the prevailing ideas about the novel and technology during the 1950s, Ian Watt's 1957 *The Rise of the Novel* provides some clue. Writing at the birth of rock along with the novelists *Novel Sounds* examines, Watt argued that the novel was defined by its "formal realism." What Watt meant by this was that the novel extends in its very form the modern philosophical construction of the individual, advancing along with René Descartes and John Locke "the position that truth can be discovered by the individual through his senses."[100] The centrality of senses comes across in the novel, Watt maintains, because of all genres the novel most successfully creates "a full and authentic report of human experience."[101] The novel's verisimilitude derives from this elevation of the senses.

But even as Watt asserts the importance of human sensory experience to the novel's function, he also suggests that the sense of reality novels create is an effect of print technology:

The impersonal authority of print is complemented by its capacity for securing a complete penetration of the reader's subjective life. The mechanically produced and therefore identical letters set with absolute uniformity on the page are, of course, much more impersonal than any manuscript, but at the same time they can be read much more automatically: ceasing to be conscious of the printed page before our eyes we surrender ourselves entirely to the world of illusion which the printed novel describes. This effect is heightened by the fact that we are usually alone when we read, and that the book, for the time being, becomes a kind of extension of our personal life—a private possession that we keep with us in our pocket or under our pillow, and that tells of an intimate world of which no one speaks out loud in ordinary life.

(198)

For Watt arguing in 1957, then, just after Elvis had his hit with "Heartbreak Hotel," the novel had made its contribution to the modern idea that the sensory body is central somewhat paradoxically: via aspects of the medium that would shut down senses. Bodily senses become important because of the novel's technological capacity to make readers "surrender" them—to make readers abandon the "conscious" knowledge of the "printed page before our eyes."[102] Writing at the same time that Southern fiction and rock came into existence, Watt makes explicit an idea that clearly engaged Faulkner and other Southerners writing novels about vernacular music: the idea that the novel is a uniquely technological medium.

The claim that novel readers abandon "consciousness" before the printed page in order to experience the novel's "illusion" as real can be understood as a version of what the media theorists J. David Bolter and Richard Grusin described in 1999 as the domain of the "virtual": "Virtual reality is immersive, which means that it is a medium whose purpose is to disappear."[103] Although discussions about the virtual have tended to focus on so-called new media and digital arts, however, Watt's observations suggest that they are just as relevant to the novel, understood even in 1950 as a medium producing this very effect.[104] Mark Goble makes the apt observation that the tendency to identify as media only forms that emerged in the late twentieth century and afterward can be traced to a persistent idea of modernism as disconnected from its historical context.[105] *Novel Sounds* joins other literary scholarship—like McGurl's *The Program Era: Postwar Fiction and the Rise of Creative Writing* (2009), Goble's *Beautiful Circuits: Modernism and the Mediated Life* (2010), Mark Wollaeger's *Modernism, Media, and Propaganda: British Narrative from 1900 to 1945* (2006), and Kate Marshall's *Corridor: Media Architectures in American Fiction* (2013)—that seeks to disentangle the opposition between a modernist aesthetic and media.[106] The observations about the novel's emergence as technology in *Novel Sounds* correspond with Marshall's assessment of "genre noisiness" in the American modernist novel; with Wollaeger's identification of modernism and propaganda as "proximate information practices operating within a system"; with Goble's insistence on "the power of media technologies" as "already" modernism's "own"; and with McGurl's description of the novel as a "meaning-bearing gadget."[107] While the work by Goble, Wollaeger, and Marshall identifies in the modernist aesthetic traces of the media imagined as anathema to it, *Novel Sounds* examines later versions of this apparent division, like *The Program Era* focusing on the moment of modernism's institutionalization.

The novelists in *Novel Sounds* exploit the paradox Watt unreflectively expresses about the book as medium, dramatizing the way in which the image of a provincial unravels, portraying live singing voices that reduce to electrical signals. We might link these voices to those the media theorist Jeffrey Sconce identifies as "voices in the void"—radio voices, as Sconce puts it, "still corporeal" yet "bathing in the waves of the wireless sea."[108] Whether or not we agree with Watt that it is mechanized print which produces the novel's sensory body in the novel's "world of illusion," his interest in the technological basis for the novel's sensory experience matches 1950s Southern writers' desire to expose their own high-literary productions as, after all, forms of media. Essentially "connected with the medium of print," as Watt pointed out, the novel is distinguished from other literary forms precisely in that it was never oral.[109] Perhaps these Southerners reached for the novel, then, because writing about music at the birth of rock called for it, required a literary genre that had always used machines to sing. What seems clear is that these authors gleaned that their work bore a crucial relation to the musical forms that also became rock and roll. The increasing electric buzz of the ballad form was in any case for them a provocation to create their own novel sounds.

1.1 Original audiotape of Robert Penn Warren's 1964 interview
with Martin Luther King Jr.

Source: Photograph by Mona Frederick. Courtesy of Mona Frederick and the
Robert Penn Warren Center for the Humanities.

1

FUGITIVES AND FUTILITY

Agrarian Ballad Novels in Bob Dylan's Moment

I n 1916, the English musicologist Cecil P. Sharp and his assistant Maude
Karpeles traveled to the mountains of Tennessee, Kentucky, and North
Carolina to see whether there were ancient English ballads still being
sung in isolated communities of the US South.[1] There were. In the North
Carolina mountain town of Allanstand, Mary Sands, a forty-four-year-old
woman pregnant with her tenth child sang a seventeenth-century ballad
for them entitled "The Daemon Lover."[2] As she sang, they transcribed,
taking down with pencil on paper the tune's words and music. Sharp
and Karpeles published Sands's version of this ballad, along with several
others, in Sharp's 1917 *English Folksongs from the Southern Appalachians.*[3]
The "national type," Sharp says in his introduction to *English Folksongs,*
"is always to be found in its purest, as well as in its most stable and permanent form, in the folk-arts of a nation" (xxxv). The Appalachian folk
ballads, Sharp declares, "would quite correctly be called English" (xxxiv).
Half a century later, Bob Dylan recorded this ballad during his second
recording session ever, for Columbia Records in New York.[4]

Between Sharp's 1916 written transcription of "The Daemon Lover"
and the 1961 taping of this song in Columbia's studios, two former Fugi-
tives wrote novels based on ballads: Robert Penn Warren takes his plot
for *The Cave* (1959) from the 1925 hillbilly ballad "The Death of Floyd
Collins," and it is none other than "The Daemon Lover" that Donald

Davidson adapted for the novel he wrote in 1953, *The Big Ballad Jamboree* (1996).[5] These former Agrarians, both pioneers of the New Criticism, wrote their ballad novels in the midst of rock and roll's dismantling of the racial classifications guiding earlier reception of ballads, and both authors eschew the interracial practices defining 1950s rock by incorporating into their fiction ballads whose racial origins matched their own. Warren's choice, "The Death of Floyd Collins," was a 1925 hillbilly tune recorded in the era of "Ida Red" and aimed at the same listeners; Davidson's English "The Daemon Lover," renamed "The House Carpenter" when it migrated to the United States in the mid-nineteenth century, dates to 1685.[6] Both Davidson and Warren wrote about ballads to explore the decades-old claim that literature originates as music. Whereas Davidson chose "The Daemon Lover" to consolidate and affirm a white Southern literary tradition, Warren's fictional rendition of "The Death of Floyd Collins" dramatizes that very move gone awry.

I have noted that "The Daemon Lover" appears in *Understanding Poetry* and that by the time Warren and Brooks decided to include it, this ballad had already been collected in both Percy's 1765 *Reliques* and Child's *The English and Scottish Popular Ballads* (1882–1898). Davidson's seventeenth-century ballad thus bears the mark of poetry as he and his Vanderbilt colleagues had defined it during the 1930s. "The Death of Floyd Collins" does not. On the contrary, Warren seems to have chosen this ballad to contrast his earlier designations of poetry as pure "experience" indicating "word-of-mouth" transmission. As we shall see, both authors depict a breakdown in the division between bodies and machines that validated racial essence in this earlier claim, but for Warren, this resonance with rock's racial crossings was part of a conscious reassessment of his earlier stance on race. Davidson was less in control of how changing racial ideology came into his fiction, so the surprising appearance of the technological in figures intended to erase any trace of it in *The Big Ballad Jamboree* emerges as a return of the repressed. And whereas Dylan's "The House Carpenter" formed part of a detour into vernacular folk ballads that fed his later return to rock and roll, Davidson's became part of a segregationist political agenda, one that emerges in *The Big Ballad Jamboree* as a symptomatically didactic affirmation of ballads' earlier racial categorizations.

"The Death of Floyd Collins" was written in imitation of a traditional English song resembling "The Daemon Lover." Hardly "permanent and stable" expression of an English past, this tune was instead whipped up in 1925 by a professional disaster ballad hitmaker immediately after the widely publicized disaster on which it was based: the slow death of a white Kentuckian by the name of Floyd Collins.[7] Collins got stuck in a cave while scouting for tourist attractions on his land, and over the next two weeks he suffocated to death as rescuers worked to dig him free. Nightly radio reports broadcast this grim ordeal, and as rescuers worked a massive crowd gathered outside the cave to hear the up-to-the-minute reports from the *Louisville Courier-Journal* reporter William ("Skeets") Miller. "Families gathered expectantly beside their radios each evening," writes one of Collins' chroniclers, "to catch the latest installment of what amounted to a running suspense story."[8] Just after Collins died, the ballad was commissioned by Polk Brockman at OKeh Records, "a scrappy businessman," as Miller describes him, a pioneer of the "first major field recording expedition conducted by a phonograph company."[9] Brockman enlisted as singer for the tune the Texas crooner Vernon Dalhart, a man who had gone from singing Tin Pan Alley in New York to recording the first million-selling country music song, another disaster ballad called "The Wreck of the Old '97." "The Death of Floyd Collins" quickly became a hit.[10]

Twenty-four years after Collins's death, Warren reproduced the story of his fellow Kentuckian in *The Cave*, moving the setting from Kentucky to Johntown, a fictional city in the Tennessee mountains.[11] Warren makes other changes to the original as well, most notably blending the historical event with the ballad it inspired and melding Collins and Dalhart into a single character—the fictional ballad singer Jasper Harrick. In Warren's version of the story, Skeets Miller also becomes the Vanderbilt dropout Isaac Sumpter, and Warren portrays him as fabricating meetings with the suffocating Jasper to relay to the public, preventing the actual rescue. Along with its overt commercial origins in the 1920s, the media sensationalism surrounding this event sets the song apart from

"The Daemon Lover." The remote origins of the older ballad could more easily be claimed as conforming to Agrarian ideas about "mountain fastness," and as we shall see, Davidson appears to have chosen it precisely because it confirmed Southern links to British whiteness. Warren surely selected "The Death of Floyd Collins" because it did not, and I am going to show here that he drew its impure status into *The Cave* to create a correspondingly awkward prose that fails to fulfill the promise of Southern whiteness.

THE NOVEL GOES ELECTRIC: DAVIDSON, DYLAN, AND THE *ANTHOLOGY OF AMERICAN FOLK MUSIC*

Two years or so before Davidson began work on *The Big Ballad Jamboree*, Cecil Sharp's assistant Maude Karpeles returned to the Appalachian hills to gather more songs for a new edition of *English Folksongs from the Southern Appalachians*. Although for this trip Karpeles ditched her pencil and brought a tape recorder instead, she complained in the updated 1951 volume about what such advancement had done to the ballad form by midcentury. "Roads and electricity have brought 'civilization' to the mountains," she opines in her preface, adding that "radio, which by now operates in nearly every mountain home, has let loose a flood of 'hilly-billy' and other popular music, and this is gradually submerging the traditional songs."[12] Davidson evinces a similar concern about what is called in *The Big Ballad Jamboree* "whangin' and bangin'," which refers to the corroded sound of traditional Appalachian music incorporating electricity.[13] In Davidson's novelistic setting in the North Carolina hills, ballads of the sort Sharp and Karpeles had gathered in Appalachia are presented as transforming into noisy buzzing as sound technology corrupts oral music. Davidson seeks to intervene in the historical developments his narrative represents with this music-based novel itself, bringing "The Daemon Lover" into *The Big Ballad Jamboree* to model a form of midcentury cultural production that reconnects to Southern region in the age of rock and roll.

To accomplish this, Davidson allegorizes "The Daemon Lover," in which the Devil seduces a woman away from her carpenter husband and "babies three." Davidson retells this as the story of a ballad scholar named Cissie Timberlake who is lured away from her boyfriend Danny MacGregor by a bootlegging ballad singer named Buck Kennedy. Danny is a hillbilly star who models himself on the Grand Ole Opry's own Hank Williams—"Burl Ives can't hold a candle to Hank Williams" (54), Danny tells Cissie—and Davidson portrays the electrified music Danny plays as ethically compromising. The novel opens with Cissie returning home after studying Child ballads at college, and for the rest of the novel she instructs Danny in the ways of the ballad form as they trek through the mountains with her tape recorder. Danny learns from Cissie that the ballads their grandparents taught them came from England and Scotland, that these same songs can be found in Child's collection, and that they matter because, as she says, "little as you think it, Danny, ballads are art too. Art music!" (54). Cissie informs Danny that his band the Turkey Hollow Boys is a bunch of "hillbilly howlers" (21) and that his "noisy" music sounds like nothing more than "whangin' and bangin'" (19). The idea behind taking up so much of the narrative with Danny's lessons is that Davidson's reader too will undergo a version of reeducation via the Child ballads, gleaning from "The House Carpenter" what Danny learns from Cissie. Along with Danny, the reader is exposed to ideas about how the ballad is high culture, including a college lecture in which "The House Carpenter" is compared to Shakespeare (192), and these ideas come to fruition at the end of the novel, when a group of white folk singers performs "The House Carpenter" at the eponymous jamboree. The allegorical version of "The Daemon Lover" ends averting the tragedy in the tune as links between Southern regional forms and high literature are restored.

As part of this restoration, Davidson portrays Lead Belly as a negative inspiration for Cissie to take Buck on the road. If even black balladeers can make an impact, one of her mentors points out, Buck will surely succeed as a folk hero:

If John Lomax could go all around the country with Leadbelly—with old Leadbelly [*sic*], a convicted criminal and jailbird—and present him in concert, think of what our beautiful and capable Cissie . . . can achieve with a real mountain singer like Buck Kennedy, with his wonderful repertory of ancient ballads.

(124–25)

Cissie tells Danny that Buck is "a perfect example of the true folk-singer . . . the genuine article, unspoiled by civilization" (100), and her discovery of his tunes promises to make her career. Buck's ballads are passed down through his mother, and it is clear that Davidson means to portray him as the sort of singer Sharp and Karpeles hoped to meet, a balladeer whose repertoire of Child ballads connects him via family genetics to the British Isles. Danny and Cissie know these ballads too, but because Buck has never left the mountains he confirms the South's "mountain fastness." Davidson suggests that Buck's ballads will therefore draw Danny backward from the electric "whangin' and bangin'" to whiteness, and the novel is caught up in this logic as well. Danny and his electric music will connect with region via Buck's oral singing, and the reader experiencing the Southern novelist's version of "The Daemon Lover" will be similarly guided via these same ballads. At the close of the novel, Danny is installed as an instructor at the local college, qualified for the post not because of his education, which for him terminated at the end of high school, but by his musical links to a white past in the British Isles. *The Big Ballad Jamboree* entirely collapses the inheritance of white vernacular ballads with institutional literary expertise, presenting in Danny a dialectical merging of uneducated balladeer and university professor.

But acoustic ballads in *The Big Ballad Jamboree* end up slipping into electrical noise, and there is a sense of confusion throughout the novel about how to square Cissie's tape recorder with her commitments to oral traditions. So, when she and Danny turn on the machine to record the dulcimer played by their neighbor Mrs. Parsons, Cissie's tape recorder makes "a little quiet humming sound" (65). The acoustic dulcimer then hums as well, as if absorbing the electronic sound: a "little lonesome tune was shaping up on that one string, above the humming and twanging of the other strings that backed it up." When Danny notes that the "pleasant humming sound went with the little old woman and the smell of ashes and the turkey-feather duster that hung by the fireplace" (68), he clearly intends the hum to indicate the archaic sound of the dulcimer. But the hum of the machine precedes it, merging with the "lonesome tune" emanating from the dulcimer, as Davidson succumbs to portraying the acoustic instrument, too, as a machine:

> She was tuning the dulcimer, softly, using a ten-penny nail to turn the wrought iron keys that stood straight up from the head. She put a nail through a hole in the keys and twitched the corners of her mouth as she tuned and listened. It was a very old dulcimer, I could see, not made like any I could remember, because it had an extra soundbox raised above the tapered body, and the strings ran along that on to the fretboard, where the frets were just pieces of wire, set in somehow. And it was a four-string dulcimer, and all the strings were fretted, none open. The head of the instrument ended in a carved scroll, very lovingly whittled out and finished.
>
> (67–68)

The "iron keys," the nail, the pieces of wire: this acoustic instrument's rudimentary features also liken it to a simple machine, and Davidson creates an inadvertent elision in his narrative. As nail and wire expose the dulcimer's technological essence, the tape recorder disappears into the acoustic sound it records, so that the "loving" dulcimer's archaic hum incorporates the medium of its transmission into its own acoustic presence. The recording bleeds into the live performance of the song, placing at an impossible remove the oral world that Cissie hopes her recordings will capture.

And where the oral eludes, the racial guarantees maintaining a clear distinction between Buck and Lead Belly fail. The breakdown comes in a startling affirmation in *The Big Ballad Jamboree* of Ku Klux Klan violence against the white criminal Buck. Cissie is an instructor at the college as well, and like Lomax at Harvard she brings Buck to campus to sing for her ballad class. When it becomes clear that Buck's bootleg liquor sales to college students might endanger Cissie's academic career, Danny and his friend Wallace rush to protect her reputation. Wallace suggests delivering Buck a "good whuppin," but Danny is concerned: "You mean Ku Klux him? . . . Folks go to jail for that. It would jest make things worse" (186). Wallace responds, "We ain't gonna dress up in sheets and all that rot. It's out of date" (186). Out of date Klan violence was not. In 1951, the KKK bombed integrating neighborhoods in Miami, killing the leader of the NAACP, Harry T. Moore, and his wife, Hariette V. Moore. In 1957, Klansmen murdered Willie Edwards by forcing him to jump to his death off a bridge into the Alabama River. The Klan-backed murder of NAACP field secretary Medgar Evers rocked civil rights activists in 1963. Nearer to the scene of *The Big Ballad Jamboree*'s writing, Nashville's Hattie Cotton Elementary School was blown up by the KKK leader John Kasper. This took place in 1957, just after Nashville's public schools enrolled nineteen African American first-graders in whites-only schools.[14] In the midst of persistent Klan violence against African Americans, then, Davidson aligns punishment against an errant white balladeer with racial brutality against African Americans. But the wires have crossed in this narrative: the acoustic hum merges with electricity, and vernacular music fails to restore what electric guitar "whangin'" undoes. Buck is blackened, and racial indeterminacy erupts into an explicitly segregationist narrative.

If for Davidson English and Scottish ballads preserved in the hills are the musical indication of an essential Southern whiteness, how should we understand Bob Dylan's interest in the same repertoire? It was just a few years after Davidson wrote *The Big Ballad Jamboree* that Dylan began learning ancient Scottish and English ballads like "The House Carpenter," and he was at the same time matriculating in the school of Lead Belly, admiring his songs well enough to pen the line, "Here's to Cisco an' Sonny and Lead Belly too," just one year after he recorded "The House Carpenter."[15] The symbolic crossover that associates Buck Kennedy and Lead Belly in Davidson's novel presents an obvious contrast to Dylan's intentional melding of Lead Belly tunes with ancient ballads, for example on his 1962 debut album *Bob Dylan*, which includes songs by early African American blues artists like Blind Lemon Jefferson (Lead Belly's mentor) and the pianist Curtis Jones alongside his arrangements of the traditional Scottish "Pretty Peggy-O" and "Man of Constant Sorrow."[16] Dylan's second album, *The Freewheelin' Bob Dylan* (1963), follows suit in bringing ballads forward into rock's interracial present, this time with original compositions mixing black and white ballad traditions. "Masters of War," for example, was based on the ancient English tune "Nottamun Town," and Dylan acknowledged that "Blowin' in the Wind," also on this album, reworks a slave spiritual: "I took it off a song called 'No More Auction Block,'" he said in a 1991 interview.[17]

Tracing the threads back from Elvis Presley and Chuck Berry to the musical origins of rock in a racially segregated past, Dylan delivered ballads into a present whose racial lines rock had already breached, explicitly flouting the ballad's earlier racial categories even as he delved into the songs that earlier confirmed them. While Davidson sought and failed to move the needle back to a more racially divided musical moment, Dylan embraced the mixture, building upon rock's practices to create songs of racial protest: "Oxford Town," on the 1963 *Freewheelin'*, for example, which narrates the University of Mississippi's integration; "The Death of Emmet Till," about a fourteen-year-old African American boy murdered for speaking to a white woman, recorded for *Freewheelin'* but released on volume 6 of Folkways' 1972 *Broadside Ballads*; and "Only a Pawn in Their Game," Dylan's lament about the death of Medgar Evers, on the 1964 *The Times They Are a-Changin'*. These early 1960s recordings show Dylan's interest in tracing ballads across the color line developing into full-blown political protest songs, a practice that culminated in Dylan's performance of "Only a Pawn in Their Game" as an opener for Martin Luther King Jr.'s "I Had a Dream" speech at the 1963 March on Washington.[18]

The very same ballad was employed by Davidson in his futile effort to draw Southern literature in the rock era back toward white dominance and by Dylan en route to the March on Washington. And while for Davidson "The House Carpenter" was meant to return him to a moment when Southerners could imagine "throw[ing] out the radio," Dylan's version of the tune was recorded on his path toward the embrace of a Fender Stratocaster at the 1965 Newport Folk Festival.[19] One other midcentury appearance of "The House Carpenter" explains how these contrasting versions of the ballad close the gap between literature and rock. The version of the tune in question, recorded in 1930 by a white Tennessee banjo player named Clarence Ashley, emerges in 1952 on Folkway Records' *Anthology of American Folk Music*.[20] The *Anthology* gathered together a selection of obscure recordings from the filmmaker Harry Smith's extensive collection of 1920s and 1930s 78s, many of them originally commercial ventures that had flopped in their day.[21] Along with blues and other vernacular forms coded both black and white, the *Anthology* includes several ancient English and Scottish ballads, like *Understanding Poetry* presenting 1920s and 1930s American ballads alongside ancient ones. It turns out that the *Anthology* includes both "The Daemon Lover" and "Frankie and Johnny"—Hurt's 1928 rendition "Frankie" appears along with Ashley's "The House Carpenter"—just as *Understanding Poetry* had. That we find these songs in both collections is striking. While Brooks and Warren had sanctioned both of these ballads as literature in 1938, the *Anthology* ensured that they would also be taken into the emerging hybrid form coming to be known as rock and roll.

The *Anthology* had a profound impact on American popular music: the folklorist Robert Cantwell describes it as the "enabling document" of the American folk revival, and Greil Marcus maintains that it was the source for Dylan's *Basement Tapes*.[22] In noting the "presence of Smith's music in Dylan's," indeed, Marcus describes the *Anthology* as the "secret language," indeed as a "lingua franca," among early rock artists.[23] The *Anthology* "came to reverberate through rock music," as the historian David Suisman puts it, in the years after its appearance.[24] "The House Carpenter" is thus a link in the chain connecting recorded music in the 1920s and 1930s to rock and roll. There is some controversy about the source for Dylan's "The House Carpenter," but it is clear that Dylan was well acquainted with the Smith *Anthology* when he recorded it.[25] Taken up in the establishment of the high literary in *Understanding Poetry*, then, "The Daemon Lover" crosses over via the *Anthology* into rock and roll, and this ballad stands as a common genealogical origin from which both literature and rock spring. Noting the glee with which Harry

Smith celebrated the indeterminate race of the singers on the *Anthology*, Marcus quotes Smith as exulting: "It took years . . . before anybody discovered that Mississippi John Hurt wasn't a hillbilly"—before it was understood, that is, that John Hurt was black.[26] Given that the Smith *Anthology* was released just as Davidson was writing *The Big Ballad Jamboree*, it is perhaps no surprise that Davidson's depiction of Buck's "The House Carpenter" would involve a figural collapse into black vernacular. If even "The Daemon Lover" could be drawn into rock's crackly buzz, after all, what ballad could escape it?

WHAT DID I SAY? WARREN'S WITHERED BALLADEER

The Cave emerges between the two works Warren wrote to sort out his changing attitudes on race, *Segregation: The Inner Conflict of the South* (1956) and *Who Speaks for the Negro?* (1965). The latter book, published one year after Dylan performed "Only a Pawn in Their Game" at the March on Washington, evinces Warren's interest in African American historical figures, some of whom also inspired Dylan: *Who Speaks for the Negro?* includes interviews with both Martin Luther King Jr., for example, as well as with Medgar Evers's brother, Charles. These publications demonstrate Warren's increasing distance from the views his former colleague Davidson continued to espouse, and indeed the portrayal of ballads we find in his 1959 *The Cave* aligns Warren with Dylan more readily than with Davidson. Rather than as an embrace of black ballads, however—which after all describes Warren's 1930s inclusion of "Frankie and Johnny" in *Understanding Poetry*—in *The Cave* Warren's updated views emerge in the ballad's failure, as he portrays it, to generate a Southern literary tradition. Hardly the unadulterated attempt to move ballads backward that Davidson's novel was, neither do we find in Warren's novel the explicit political outrage expressed in Dylan's protest songs. Instead, *The Cave* presents its commensurability with the changin' times as white guilt.

Warren's novel about a family of white ballad singers in the Tennessee hills depicts a break within its lineage. "For thirty years," we find out early on in *The Cave*, "hero of all the hillbillies," Jack Harrick, had regaled live audiences all over East Tennessee with his acoustic music: "Old Jack had dragged jugs dry, whipped his box till folks fell down from dancing, cracked jaws with his fist like hickory nuts under a claw hammer, and torn off drawers like a high wind in October stripping a sycamore to bare-ass white."[27] Warren's older ideas about ballads can be detected in the portrayal of Jack's hyperbolic bodily music, the "whipping" of his acoustic guitar, here called his "box." Jack's eldest son, Jasper, whose ballad performances the narrator identifies as paradigmatically lyric, a singing alone "to the solitude" in the mountains (317), extends Jack's vernacular into the next generation. But the youngest Harrick, Monty, is entirely disconnected from this tradition. Hatched from the era in which the car is a "floating juke box" (150), Monty is a pseudo-balladeer, a mountain singer who wears a "farmer's hat" (7) but only for effect, "unfarmerishly" (217), and who sings not into the mountains but into the mirror. Monty's girlfriend articulates in stark terms the corruption Warren means to convey when she praises his singing thus: "It was real pretty . . . as good as radio. Or even TV" (29).

Warren portrays jukebox, radio, and television as separating Monty from the culture his blood should have guaranteed, and he emerges in *The Cave* as disconnected from that which would have earlier rooted him to a place from which white balladry naturally emerges. Paradoxically, Warren shows these media also making that balladry available to Monty, allowing him to learn and adopt the hillbilly practices formerly considered part of his essence. The musical expression Davidson presents as springing deep from within Buck Kennedy's mountain self emerges in *The Cave* as something else entirely—a transferrable art form derived from imitating radio and TV. Here in Warren's ballad novel we can detect a version of the cultural changes that gave rise to rock and roll, the departure of vernacular forms from Southern region that return to reaffirm a new Southern essence. Monty's balladry confirms his regional identity, but in a dialectical form in which the dispossession O'Connor describes as "exile" constitutes repatriation. Warren's Monty resembles

Mick Jagger, whose delivery of Mississippi delta blues back to America as its own black vernacular was similarly enabled by the globalizing forces that first took it away.

The detachment of ballads from region that allows for this transfer of Southern vernacular forms works the other way around in *The Cave* as well. While white Southerners in Warren's fictional world may take on the cultural practices formerly imagined to be essential to their white being, they can adopt other ones just as well. Isaac Sumpter, for example, begins the novel as the son of Johntown's local Baptist preacher and a reader of John Keats, and Warren portrays him as having studied literature at a college "down in Nashville" (100). Son of a preacher and beneficiary of Agrarian teachings, this mountain boy nevertheless finds himself a Jewish media mogul in New York at *The Cave*'s end. Warren accomplishes this surprising identity switch by presenting the genealogies of Isaac's Bible-thumping relatives and the ballad-singing Harricks as intertwined. As the novel unfolds, we learn that before marrying Jasper's mother, Celia, Jack had impregnated a woman named Mary Tillyard and refused to marry her. Isaac's father, the preacher MacCarland Sumpter, then stepped forward to marry the pregnant Mary and stand in as the baby's father. After the wedding, the child of her union with Jack is born dead. But Mary becomes pregnant again, this time by her preacher husband "Brother Sumpter," and although this baby survives, now it is she who dies in childbirth. Isaac is the offspring of Mary and MacCarland Sumpter. In thus portraying Isaac as half-brother to a deceased baby whose father is Jack, Warren produces a skewed lineage in which the Vanderbilt student is almost a balladeer's son, but not quite. In *Understanding Poetry*'s conception of ballads, John Keats's poem "Ode to a Nightingale" is heir to "The Daemon Lover." And as we shall see, Warren figures the racial implications of this literary inheritance in the broken bloodline leading from Jack to Isaac. That Isaac's blood connection to Jack is skewed precipitates a corresponding break in the relation between poetry and ballads that Isaac would have studied at Vanderbilt.

This Vanderbilt-trained reader of Keats is well versed, Warren implies, in the lessons of *Understanding Poetry*. And as a child from the

Appalachian Mountains, Isaac is also well poised to learn from reading Keats how to "experience" oral poetry in the same way he experiences his native Southern ballads. Warren rewrites the messages of *Understanding Poetry* in *The Cave*, however, revising them to portray bodily experience as ultimately unavailable. So, when Isaac first appears, we find him "propped on the bed on a summer afternoon, mumbling the poetry of Keats" (93). Isaac's father enters Isaac's tiny "hot-box of a room" (101) and apologizes for interrupting Isaac's "studying." Isaac replies that he is "reading," not "studying," and complains, "'There's not much to do . . . except read—this— . . . This shit'" (94). He calls it shit, but just after his father leaves the room Isaac reads the poem aloud—it turns out to be "Ode to a Nightingale"—and experiences what Brooks called the "miracle":

> He stopped again. He closed his eyes. A cool sweetness was dewing into the darkness of his breast. It was as though something that had mattered was, slowly, not mattering. He did not know what it was that was not mattering, because the cool dew fell in his darkness, or what made that cool dew suddenly begin to fall so sweet, but he did know that if he stirred, if he even drew a single breath, the dew might cease to fall, the *not-mattering* would again be that dark, grinding *mattering* which was every breath you drew. So he held his breath, as long as he could, letting himself slip loose into the coolness of that dark dew fall.
>
> (98)

Warren's narrator briefly takes on the poem's iambic pentameter: "He stopped again. He closed his eyes." Here, incorporating Keats's poetry into his prose style, Warren creates the apparent suggestion that this novel too will fall into line with balladry, will connect backward through "Ode to a Nightingale" to that original form of poetic experience. Like Davidson, Warren inserts his own novel into the literary genealogy elaborated by the Agrarians and extended into the 1950s by the New Critics.

But the "Ode's" miraculous effect quickly evaporates as realist description takes over: "*Oh, yes they do! They tread you down*" (99), says Isaac, doing away with the iamb and transforming Keats's poetic language into banal dialogue. This shift occurs as just one instance of many in Warren's construal of Southern literature as generally banal. There are many, for example, when the narrator explains that Monty's hat is "the kind that bends over tobacco plants at suckering time, over the hoe in the corn patch" (7). Drawn into Monty's simulation of a ballad singer, striking the posture of a Southern writer but in prose intended not to measure up, Warren's narrator enacts the rupture from Southern racial essence he depicts both in Monty's balladry and in Isaac's failure to retain the poetic iamb. Warren opens *The Cave* with the sound of Jack's acoustic guitar and ends it with a "big clanging chord that filled the room" (403), positioning *The Cave*'s narrative between images of acoustic guitar sound to trace Southern literature's roots back through the poetry of John Keats to Southern ballads. But as I have noted, "The Death of Floyd Collins" hardly signifies the "word of mouth" he earlier identified as essential to creating "experience" that cannot be carried away, and Warren seems to choose it for just this reason. This ballad's failure as a tenable literary origin for the Southern novel exposes uncertainty at the heart of the literary field Warren was at that moment helping create.

Looking more closely at the acoustic guitar in *The Cave*'s first few pages, we find out early on that this novel, published several years after white people had started listening to Chuck Berry in significant numbers, will not portray acoustic music as delivering the experience Warren argued ballads would guarantee in *Understanding Poetry*. The guitar at *The Cave*'s opening, "propped over" a pair of boots outside the mouth of the cave where Jasper has left it before becoming trapped inside (4), does not even make audible sound, instead producing a visual image of sound when a "ray" of sun "strikes the strings to a glitter," as the narrator puts it. In the image, "you think that the glitter might almost be sound, so startling it is, a single guitar chord stabbing the afternoon silence" (4). When "the ray of sunlight strikes the glitter off the guitar strings," the narrator explains, "you hear it like a big *whang*" (5). In Warren's figure here, seeing the "glitter" sunlight makes on guitar strings produces the sound of a "stabbing" guitar chord. Warren's figural prose thus accomplishes something like what the electric guitars delivering "Back in the U.S.A." produce: a sound that is not exactly an acoustic guitar's but one "like" it. The visual image of the acoustic guitar as "almost" its own sound, moreover—as a visual image "like" a guitar "*whang*"—portrays the sensory experience in this story world as a little off, and the human body in it is correspondingly disarranged.

When the guitar does achieve sound, it comes in a "thin sweet note" that "vibrates spookily from the one string," and it is caused by a "jay bird's heel" having "plucked"it (7). The narrative modulates to a more realistic mode as the sound emerges, and the realism construes the guitar sound as now part of an organized sensory experience: the hearing of an acoustic guitar note instead of the vision of one that resembles sound. At the same time the guitar makes its sound, however, we find parodic hyperbole in the idea that acoustic instruments are harmonious with nature. (Really?, Warren wants us to ask: A jay bird's heel?) The move into realist description is thus a move away from the idea of music as natural, and indeed this hyperbole morphs immediately into the suggestion that acoustic music has been supplanted by the awful sound of electricity in the drone of locusts:

> Then the silence is over. The locusts begin again, for this is the year of the locust. In fact, there has not been silence at all, for the air has been full of a dry, grinding metallic sound, so penetrating that it has seemed, paradoxically, to come from within the blood, or from some buzz saw working fiendishly away at the medulla oblongata. It is easy to forget that it is not from inside you, that glittering, jittering, remorseless whir so much part of you that you scarcely notice it, and perhaps love it, until the time when you will really notice it, and scream.
>
> (4)

The electricity that marks the narrative's turn to realism here indicates an abandonment of poetic figuration, and this seems also to abolish Warren's earlier conception of poetry's roots in oral music. As the listener's body comes into proper sensory arrangement, that is, the idea that oral ballads confirm bodily wholeness is paradoxically disrupted by the discovery that electricity already inheres in nature. Realism emerges as rock and roll's narrative mode.

Warren creates yet another version of disconnected prose in this Southern ballad novel, another kind of writing whose distance from any literary origin allows the writer completely to abandon his Southern identity for another kind of self. Just before Isaac commences the coverage of Jasper's entrapment that will both launch his career and kill Jasper, he sees in the mirror an image of himself as a "stage Jew": "He shrugged, dropped his hands, palms outward, in a parody of the classic gesture of the Jew's resignation and irony, and repeated, in the accent of the stage Jew: 'Ikey—Little Ikey'" (100). While learning how to read Keats at Vanderbilt, we discover, Isaac was romantically entangled with another A student, one Rachel Goldstein, and his affiliation with her gives people the impression that he is Jewish. A classmate asks Isaac to dinner at the Jewish fraternity, and Isaac suddenly realizes, "*He thinks I am a Jew. The son-of-a-bitch thinks I am a Jew like him*" (120). It then dawns on Isaac that Rachel too thinks he is Jewish, and "Goldie," as she is called, confirms this. "Well, I'm not," he says (123). "Oh yes, you are, Ikey-Baby," says Rachel, "for I've made you one—I've made you an Honorary Jew and that's the very best kind. You're the honorablest Honorary Jew that ever was, and I love you to total distraction" (123).

Rachel is a sculptor, and while at Vanderbilt, Isaac absorbs his artistic practices from her rather than from New Critical texts. But Isaac does not find his voice by adopting her craft. Instead he learns to express himself in the same way Monty is trained to sing ballads: by imitating culturally specific practices. Rachel helps Isaac get his start as a writer for the Nashville newspaper through family connections, and the editor ends up liking Isaac's humor. The editor "knew," we are told, that "the squirt was pretty good. What he didn't know was that if you laughed at Goldie Goldstein when she laid into a tale, you were very apt to laugh when you read a column by Isaac Sumpter" (116–17). Isaac emerges from Vanderbilt having learned to read, then, but as a close-reader of Goldie's Jewish self, not of poetry. Isaac adopts Rachel's "Jewish" humor just as Monty learns ballads.[28] Rachel eventually berates Isaac for sleeping with her friend, and in their breakup she calls him a "bleeding, clod-hopping, Honorary-Jew Bible-thumper" (131). But by the end of the novel there is nothing of the "Bible-thumper" left. Indeed, when we last see Isaac it is in the elevator in his New York office of "Big Media" (370–71), where he hears "someone whisper," "Yes, that's Sumpter, yes that's Mr. Sumpter, yes, that's the great Ikey, *and, hearing that, would curl his lip in a deep, mysterious, ironic satisfaction, for he was Ikey, Little Ikey, and it didn't do any harm to be called Ikey in the world of Big Media*" (371). Isaac is all "Honorary Jew" by the end of *The Cave*, his natural connection to Scottish ballads now an addiction to scotch, "the most famous product of Scotland" (372). This Southerner who reads Keats ends not as a balladeer who takes down his fiddle from the wall, then, nor as a Southern novelist. Instead, he becomes a self-hating Jew cut from the same cloth as characters found in another 1959 publication, Philip Roth's *Goodbye Columbus*.[29]

Isaac can become "Ikey," it is suggested—he can exchange one white ethnic identity for another—because he has the proper technology. The "first-rate tape recorder" he orders, "large size, field type, play-back, and about twenty spools of tape, small spools" (232), is the obvious cause of his disconnection from the mountains. But as we have seen, when Isaac first appears in *The Cave*, he is engaged not with a tape recorder but with a book. As he reads "Ode to a Nightingale," the volume of Keats's poetry turns into a medium resembling a radio:

> Isaac Sumpter held a second-hand copy of the Cambridge edition of *The Complete Poetical Works and Letters of John Keats* in his hand, the cover an ugly pebbled red with gold stamping flaking off, the paper of the page the color of cheap hygienic tissue, the format double-column, with an offensive, blurred, too small type face like deploying ants.
>
> (93)

Keats's poetry in this moment is reduced to the physical book in which it is printed, exactly the fear articulated by Brooks when in *The Well Wrought Urn* he decried the tendency to "explain the miracle away in the process of reduction which hardly stops short of reducing the 'poem' to the ink itself."[30] Rather than creating "experience," as Warren argued poetry would in *Understanding Poetry*, here "Ode to a Nightingale" is shown to have been carried away via the book as radio carries away. The book's material features render Keats's poems "hygienic tis-sue," a "double-column" pattern of the type in which they are printed. The "sweetness" in the poetry's meaning becomes an "ugly" thing with a "pebbled" surface that can "flake" off, the words on the page "deploying ants." The reference to insects here recalls the electric-guitar locusts at the beginning of the novel, incorporating the "metallic grinding" into Keats's words in the association. The miraculous transcendence of "experience" gives way to an encounter with a physical medium that swarms with nonhuman life.[31] The sociologist Richard A. Peterson has argued for the importance of transistor radios to the rise of rock and roll, noting that in 1954 "hundreds of thousands of cheap, light-weight, compact transistor radios" from Japan flooded the American market.[32] In 1959, it was clear both that nobody would be "throwing out the radio" to "take down the fiddle from the wall" and that it was the media forms in which rock was delivered, not books, that were entering the rooms of homes in the East Tennessee hills. The term "hot-box" likens Isaac's room to a radio, and the sounds emanating from it, Isaac's "mumbling" of Keats's poetry, become versions of radio voices. Crucially, moreover, the image is one of infinite regress: the "voice" emitted through the "hot-box" originates not in Isaac's mouth but, moving backward, in the "typeface" on paper, small and antlike. The book emerges here too as a version of sound technology, a medium displacing the human mouth.

Neither Warren's interest in black ballads nor the revisions to Agrar-ian logic he advances in *The Cave* ever fully translated into a valoriza-tion of black literature. We can look to *Understanding Fiction*, perhaps the most influential of the New Critical tomes he edited with Brooks, to see this. *Understanding Fiction* included not a single black author until 1979. For all Warren's attention to civil rights, then, on some level his commitment to the whiteness of Southern literature persisted. First published in 1943 and reprinted in 1959 and 1979, *Understanding Fiction* finally included stories by James Baldwin and Ralph Ellison only in its last edition. And even then, the history of Warren's involvement with these authors suggests that the logic guiding the inclusion brings forward the racial presumption ballads made obvious in earlier days.

When Warren left Yale to gather material for *Who Speaks for the Negro?* fifteen years before, he interviewed both Baldwin and Ellison, carrying a tape recorder with him to capture, in his words, "something, first hand, about the people, some of them anyway, who are making the Negro Revolution what it is." The book is not "a history," he says, or "a sociological analysis," but "a transcript of conversations." Warren explains, "I want to make my reader see, hear, and feel as immediately as possible what I saw, heard, and felt."[33] Toting his tape recorder into the South to create "transcripts" that would make the reader "see, feel, and hear" black cultural leaders, Warren seems buoyed by John Lomax, seeking from interviews given by Baldwin and Ellison that which Lomax had in earlier decades found in "Negro folk" music. Whether or not Warren would acknowledge Lomax's influence, his post-taping inclusion of the black "voice" in *Understanding Fiction* carries into contemporary literary contexts assumptions from New Critics' surprisingly musical past.

The introduction for *Who Speaks for the Negro?* includes a recanting of Warren's earlier defense of segregation in *I'll Take My Stand.* I am suggesting that even here we find traces of the Agrarian ideas guiding Warren's inclusions of Lead Belly in *Understanding Poetry.* Warren acknowledges "that in the real world I was trying to write about, there existed a segregation that was not humane."[34] To illustrate the effect of this inhumanity on him, Warren recounts his memory of "an oak tree that stood by the decrepit, shoe-box-size jail" in "the little town in Kentucky where I was born and raised":

> When I was a child I scarcely ever passed down that street . . . without some peculiar, cold flicker of feeling. The image of that tree which I still carry in my head has a rotten and raveled length of rope hanging from a bare bough, bare because the image in my head is always set in a winter scene. In actuality it is most improbable that I ever saw a length of rope hanging from that tree, for the lynching had taken place long before my birth. It may not, even, have been that tree. It may, even, have been out in the country.

(11)

We find a "rotten rope" in *The Cave* as well, when Jack stares out of the window. His eyes "fill with tears" at the sight: "He looks out the window. There is the white oak in the yard, the remnants of rope yet hanging from it where he had once put up a swing for his boys. No, for his older boy, years ago. How long did it take a piece of rope—good rope too—to rot?" (5). When the rope comes up again, the narrator explains that Jasper's mother "knew that Jasper would be swinging there right this minute if the rope weren't rotten, if only [Jack] hadn't put up rotten rope" (202). This "rotten" rope recalls the lynching rope from *Who Speaks for the Negro?*, and the image of Jasper "swinging" from it as he suffocates underground construes the media's response to his ordeal as a lynching. More like Davidson, in the end, than on first glance it appears, Warren also produces a white balladeer who is subject to the tradition of violence against African Americans. For Davidson this racial blending takes place in spite of his novel's refutation of rock's version of racial integration. Things are only slightly different with Warren if Jasper's lynching indicates Warren's version of racial inclusivity. If for Warren, that is, the logic goes like this: just as African Americans must be included in literature anthologies as authors of literature per se, and not as "Negro folk" balladeers, so too the loss that expresses itself as Jack's withering white vernacular can be understood as a lynching.

In 1964, the year Warren published *Who Speaks for the Negro?*, the Elvis Presley film *Viva Las Vegas* emerged, and it featured a twitchy Ann-Margret dancing in a room full of white people as Elvis sings his version of "What'd I Say." In 1977, two years before Warren and Brooks finally managed to anthologize Baldwin and Ellison in the third edition of *Understanding Fiction*, Ray Charles hosted the television show *Saturday Night Live*. The members of the band who had originally played on the 1959 recording of "What'd I Say" were corralled for this episode to perform the song with Charles once again. Before this inaugural group of early rockers tears into their version, however, the cast member Garrett Morris starts off a skit with Charles in which he plays a slimy agent trying to persuade a black progenitor of rock and roll music to sell his song for four hundred dollars. The band in question, "The Young Caucasians," is a khaki-clad group of ultrawhite singers—the comedians

Dan Aykroyd, John Belushi, Jane Curtin, Bill Murray, Laraine Newman, and Gilda Radner—and they hope to record Charles's early rock hit for their upcoming album, *Shades of White*. Sporting argyle vests and supercilious soda-jerk smiles, the members of the Young Caucasians present their hyperbolically white version of "What'd I Say" to Charles, altering the lyric as they sing to enunciate each word painfully, so that "What'd I Say" becomes "What Did I Say." Recalling Baldwin's reference to the "brave and sexless little voices" of white people singing blues, this searing satire of white appropriation suggests that rock's interracial crossings—of the sort we find in *Viva Las Vegas*, for example—had not fulfilled the civil rights aims forthrightly expressed by Dylan in the early 1960s. Warren's gesture of inclusion similarly falls short. Surely this must be the conclusion if the message he gleaned from Ray Charles and Chuck Berry was that the image of lynching was transferrable to white victims of technology.

2.1 William Faulkner at the microphone, being taped at the University of Virginia, 1957.
Ampex Portable operated by by Frederick Gwynn and Joseph Blotner.

Source: Photograph courtesy of University of Virginia Visual History Collection, Special Collections,
University of Virginia Library and Faulkner at Virginia: An Audio Archive.

2

NEW CRITICAL NOISE IN MUSIC CITY

Thomas Pynchon's William Faulkner

About halfway through William Faulkner's *The Town* (1957), a young garage mechanic from Ohio bursts into protagonist Gavin Stevens's office and throws a book of John Donne's poetry at him. Matt Levitt, the mechanic, is dating a girl named Linda Snopes, and he has gleaned that the middle-aged Gavin intends to steal her away with the gift of a book containing Donne's poetry. After Matt "shoots" the book "so that the ripped and torn pages came scuttering and scattering out across the desk," he beats the shit out of the older man.[1] The "ragged claws" in Eliot's "Love Song of J. Alfred Prufrock" don't "scutter," they "scuttle." But Faulkner creates this sonic image, focusing his reader on the sound of the paper in the shift from "scuttling" to "scuttering," in order to call to mind Eliot's poem. We know this because he also depicts Gavin as filled with "a thousand frantic indecisions" (205), eating peach ice cream (188), and wearing his trousers rolled (214). Thomas Pynchon's Mucho Maas later offers a way to understand this moment in *The Town* when he provides a reading of rock and roll songs like the Beatles' 1963 "She Loves You." "The songs," Mucho says in Pynchon's 1965 *The Crying of Lot 49*, "it's not just that they say something, they *are* something, in the pure sound. Something new."[2]

Hang on—Pynchon? The Beatles? Aren't we talking about William Faulkner? Why consider a work by a Southern "provincial" in relation

to the overtly technological *The Crying of Lot 49*? Those who canonized Faulkner as the patron saint of Southern literature looked to the
older Agrarian claims about "Negro folk," John Donne, and T. S. Eliot
to bring into a postwar present the restorative powers of the ballad
form, and Gavin is cut from this cloth, not Pynchon's.[3] A Mississippian
attuned to songs by "Father of the Blues" W. C. Handy, Gavin grows
up to become a close-reader of Donne, and Faulkner indeed presents
Gavin as a walking New Critical anthology.[4] The author's own infamous
public objections to racial integration, moreover—Faulkner added his
voice to the call to "go slow"—suggest that Gavin's leap from Handy
to Donne is meant to affirm the racial clarity that ballads before rock
and roll seemed to assure.[5] But Gavin fails in his endeavor to impart
Agrarian values to the young white people of Jefferson, and in broad-
ening the scope of our reading to territories west of Mississippi, and
to a moment just a few years later, we can begin to understand why.
When considered alongside *The Crying of Lot 49*, *The Town* comes to
seem less Agrarian and more rock novel—comes to appear as part of
an emerging contemporary style that drew from rock and roll rather
than resisting it, a style whose reciprocity with rock the Beatles-loving
Mucho Maas would make more obvious in retrospect.[6] Donne's poems
"scutter" as paper because in 1957 they are more like rock songs than
like poetry; what they "say" becomes the sound of pages because in
the age of rock and roll, poems "*are* something," even bona fide poems
like those celebrated by the New Critics. While Gavin hopes Linda will
"make the closest possible examination" of the Donne poems and generally follow Brooks's directives, this scene indicates the dominance of
a new form of reading. Marshall McLuhan would make this practice
official in 1964, in his announcement that "the medium is the message,"
encapsulating in 1964 what Faulkner was beginning to express in rock's
inaugural decade.[7]

   Like Faulkner, the Southern literary scholar Louis D. Rubin diagnosed
the Agrarian plan as outmoded in his introduction to a new edition
of *I'll Take My Stand*, brought out in 1962. There, Rubin complained
that the "suburbs of Nashville, Richmond, Charleston, and Mobile are
scarcely distinguishable from those of Buffalo, Trenton, Indianapolis,

and Hartford," adding, "Andrew Lytle's suggestion that the Southern Farmer throw out the radio and take down the fiddle from the wall has not been followed; instead the radio has been replaced by the television set."[8] Catherine Jurca has charted the emergence of the suburban whiner in the postwar American novel, but Rubin's comments suggest that the suburbanization of the US South warranted a particular lament, one marked by changes in Southern music—the phenomena that in 1950 led one disc jockey to dub the Agrarians' home "Music City, U.S.A."[9] As rock and roll became dominant across the country, the Nashville from which Lytle and Davidson issued their writings about ballads mutated into a broadcast town, a virtual Southern city generating electric sounds that could be experienced anywhere.[10] *Novel Sounds* began with the claim that Faulkner's *The Town* is about rock and roll, and in what follows we will see that *The Town* portrays ballads in the same way rock delivered them to the world: as electrified, as disconnected from Southern region, and as racially ambiguous. In a world where ballads are celebrated in these ways, Faulkner suggests, reading necessarily becomes a different practice.

As late as 1966, in his introduction to a collection of critical essays on Faulkner's earlier fiction, we find Robert Penn Warren validating Faulkner the man with recourse to Agrarian ideas. Arguing that it was only when universities started admitting GIs with no background in formal education that people began to grasp Faulkner's difficult work, Warren aligns Faulkner with genius cultivated outside of bureaucratic university culture:

> I do not know what force the college classrooms of the country exerted in making or breaking literary reputations, but in the period of the late thirties and early forties, when professors of American literature and the then new-fangled American Studies were often inclined to speak of Steinbeck's *In Dubious Battle* and of Howard Fast's *Citizen Tom Paine* in the tones of hushed reverence once reserved for the works of Sophocles, Faulkner had received short shrift. After the War, with the horde of returning GI's, the process backfired. As one GI put it to me, "I been robbed!" He reported that in the good university where he had

pernoctated before the call to arms, his class had dedicated six weeks to *The Grapes of Wrath* and thirty minutes to Faulkner, being long enough to allow the professor to document from *A Rose for Emily*, the only work investigated, that Faulkner was a cryptofascist. Such young men immersed themselves in the work of Faulkner with ferocious attention. As far as I could determine, they had little of that kind of romantic disillusion that was reputed to have been common after World War I. They were motivated, rather, by a disgust for simple, schematic, two-dimensional views of the world. Many of them had had, first hand, a shocking acquaintance with the depths and paradoxes of experience, and now literary renderings that did not honor their experience were not for them.[11]

GIs who speak in Southern vernacular—"I been robbed"—can best understand Faulkner, Warren reasons here, because like him they are unspoiled by formal education. Unencumbered by institutional baggage, those newly afforded a university education by the GI Bill of 1946 grasped "depths and paradoxes" in Faulkner's work because they had lived and not studied them. Warren was a Rhodes Scholar who had graduated from Vanderbilt University summa cum laude; when he wrote this introduction, he was teaching at Yale.[12] He nevertheless ratified Faulkner's literary stature according to the anti-institutional protocol he inherited from ideas about the ballad—according to an idea, that is, that the vernacular is a kind of genius that develops naturally, outside of institutional culture. Here, I want to suggest, are echoes of the ideas about ballads that Warren had advanced almost thirty years earlier. Warren framed Faulkner as escaping the "new-fangled" bureaucratic ideas generated in the "good university," construing him as a version of the "rude minstrel" himself, a dialectical merging of balladeer and literary expert, like Davidson's Danny MacGregor. Two years after the Rolling Stones returned Mississippi blues vernacular to the United States as a global form, Warren was still moving the needle backward, validating Faulkner's pen by giving it the status of the fiddle.

Gavin's gift to Linda aligns him with the New Critics in quite literal terms, and his ties to the literary lineage originating in Nashville emerge again when Donne's "well wrought urn" turns up as a kitschy object in the suburban living room of Linda's mother, Eula. Here, Gavin finds a "trivial spurious synthetic urn" (221), not a "well wrought" one, and this object makes Gavin apoplectic. In what Gavin views as the diminished world of the suburban South, urns are not what Brooks hoped they would be but the material detritus of a formerly high culture. No longer lofty ideas, the urns here are made of "the stuff the advertisements don't tell you is better than silver but simply newer" (220). Gavin refuses the coffee held in the urn, crying, "I don't want anything! I'm afraid!" (223). The room is spurious too, straight out of an advertisement in a "photograph from say *Town and Country* labeled *American Interior*, reproduced in color in a wholesale furniture catalogue" (221). The obvious decline from "well wrought" to "synthetic" leads Gavin to the admission, "*I have lost*" (220). He experiences the synthetic nature of suburbia as a personal attack: "the coffee, the low table, the two intimate chairs—was an assault not on the glands nor even just the stomach but on the civilized soul or at least the soul which believes it thirsts to be civilized" (220). Brooks's worry about miracles in the postwar era is legible in Gavin's sense that whatever has led to the valorization of a synthetic urn will also attack his soul.

Even after *The Town*'s publication—indeed, after the author's death in 1962—Faulkner's career was being advanced according to the ideas his blues-educated, Donne-reading protagonist embodies. Yet with its kitschy urns and fake silver, the image of Eula's living room does not invite links to African American vernacular music or the poetry of John Donne. Rather, *The Town*'s suburban Jefferson seems an earlier version of "Kinneret-Among-The-Pines," home of the literary reader Oedipa Maas and her rock and roll disc jockey husband Mucho. Pynchon's suburban living room, like Faulkner's, contains a close-reading protagonist, and like Gavin, Oedipa searches for literary meaning in a world in which it seems no longer to exist. Faulkner thus perversely flouts rather than reaffirms the institutional ideas that sustained his career. No surprise, perhaps, that New Critics deemed *The Town* a failure. Brooks found himself "tempted" to "advise the reader simply to omit reading *The Town* and move from *The Hamlet* directly to *The Mansion*." The problem with

The Town as Brooks saw it was its "failure in tone," and he lamented some "tenuous" episodes in the plot as well. Lytle, too, described the tone as off and the narrators as "flat," adding that Faulkner made "an error in strategy" in trying to "make comedy out of an epical subject." In a more contemporary instance of the tendency to understand *The Town* in terms of his earlier, better work, Michael Kreyling describes Gavin as a "windbag Quentin Compson who survived Harvard in 1910 to become a garrulous clown."[13] And Kreyling's point is apt. In what follows, however, I will demonstrate what happens when we remove *The Sound and the Fury* as the dominant point of reference. Considered in relation to contemporary issues, like the emergence of suburbia or the *Brown v. Board of Education* decision, *The Town* begins to seem less like a weakened version of earlier Faulkner—a lame instance of Southern genius—and more like part of a global move toward contemporary literary form, into a new literary terrain that is just as connected to rock and roll as it is to Donne.

Sit-ins on West End Avenue, protests over the expulsion of James M. Lawson Jr. from Vanderbilt's divinity school: Rubin was right. By the early 1960s, things in Nashville had changed since the Agrarians took their stand there. The suburban South was also, notably, a racially integrating South.[14] For the New Critics, Faulkner's oeuvre continued to demonstrate the lasting power of Agrarian ideas in this context, not least of which was the idea that refusing technology would allow for the maintenance of clear racial distinctions. To "throw out the radio and take down the fiddle from the wall" was to move away from technology to the pastoral "woodpile": "That is the nigger in the woodpile," as Lytle put it, "keep the machines turning!"[15] Lytle's figure was residual, even in 1930, when race records already circulated widely. A concealed African American person is degraded in the epithet, returned by it to the brutalizing racial hierarchy for which Agrarians expressed nostalgia. The "woodpile" undoes technology in Agrarian terms, restoring the technological present, as Brooks hoped Faulkner's work would in the 1960s, to a provincial moment before technology held sway. And within *The Town*, W. C. Handy's essential blackness marks this previous moment. The physical conflict between Matt and Gavin at first appears to replicate this view of technology and thus to reiterate its regressive racial message. Gavin's nephew Charles was present for Gavin's beating by the younger man, and it is Charles who tells the story:

> He didn't, he didn't seem to hit hard, his fists not travelling more than four or five inches it looked like, so that it didn't even look like they were drawing blood from Uncle Gavin's lips and nose but instead wiping the blood onto them; two or maybe three blows before I could seem to move and grab up Grandfather's walking stick where it still stayed in the umbrella stand behind the door and raise it to swing at the back of Matt's head as hard as I could.
>
> "You, Chick!" Uncle Gavin said. "Stop! Hold it!" Though even with that, I wouldn't have thought Matt could have moved that fast.
>
> (190)

Matt can get in "two or maybe three blows" "before" Charles can even "seem to move." Like the instantaneous reading of Donne, as we shall see, this machinelike speed construes Matt as an enemy of the Southern provincial and links good literature to a South unspoiled by machines or free black bodies. That Matt is an Ohio transplant in Mississippi is not incidental here: New Critics thought that the poetic "miracle" would be preserved only if American cultural authority could be wrested away from readers like Matt—replanted in spaces where the sounds of W. C. Handy's blues might still be heard as verifying Donne.

Faulkner links Matt's physical dominance to technology's encroachment on the South's natural beauty, and on first glance, this seems to align the narrative with New Critics. But the trouncing of the Harvard graduate by an auto mechanic belies New Critical orthodoxies, in part because it allegorizes a sense that their project is futile. Matt has read the Donne book, but Faulkner makes the point that he does not need to open it to do so. Matt reads the poetry instantly—experiences it as a transparent object—and this is meant to contrast the way Gavin learned to read literature as an undergraduate at Harvard. Matt clobbers Gavin, I submit, because by 1957 Faulkner believed that Matt's version of instant reading had become the dominant one. In his assessment of popular culture in Faulkner's fiction, William Brevda argues that in *The Town* Faulkner portrays technology as morally corrosive—that the "artificial" glow of neon signs in particular "casts the world in a false light."[16] Although Faulkner obviously associates the mechanic with technology in this scene, however, he also mechanizes Gavin, his close-reader. Matt says to Charles, "Nice going almost; too bad your uncle telegraphed it for you" (190). Although Matt is pegged as a product of the "age of electronics," Gavin reproduces machines too, here telegraphs. In the act of making Charles's physical maneuver obvious, Gavin also engages in the creation of transparent meaning, the kind for which New Critics believed his earlier novels would provide an antidote. Gavin's "telegraphing" renders the instances of technology in *The Town* more ambivalent than we have allowed and prevents any stark opposing of literature to technology.

Gavin's purpose for visiting Eula in her living room is to persuade her to allow Linda to attend schools "up East" (218)—to rescue her from this cheap, middle-class setting in which close-reading is outmoded. To get Linda away, Gavin must not only provide her with poetry by Donne but also engage in what he calls the "constant seduction of out-of-state school brochures" (287). Gavin sends Linda catalogues for these schools in order to entice her to go somewhere so that she can learn to close-read—to Radcliffe, ideally, which Gavin notes is "practically Harvard" (214), or to "Bennington and Bard and Swarthmore" (213). Before arriving, Gavin imagines what he will say to Eula:

> *There they are, the smart ones, the snob ones. We have been fair, we gave you your chance. Now, here is where we want to go, where you can help us go, if not by approval, at least by not saying no;* arranging for the other catalogues to reach her then: the schools which would not even notice what she wore and how she walked and used her fork and all the rest of how she looked and acted in public because by this time all that would be too old and fixed to change, but mainly because it had not mattered anyway, since what did matter was what she did and how she acted in the spirit's inviolable solitude.
>
> (211)

Here, Gavin projects a version of the South into spaces outside of the region entirely, removing it from Mississippi to be reconstituted in university classrooms "up East." It is the "spirit's inviolable solitude," moreover, that the university will allow Gavin to give Linda, a version of the retrenched provincial status associated with Faulkner himself. Gavin's Agrarian view thus renders the conception of the South guaranteed by the ballad portable. The South in this world becomes an abstract practice, a matter of technical skill—"the South," but something to be experienced in spaces beyond it.[17] To return to *Understanding Poetry*, we might note that the South here becomes something we can "carry away" as radio carries away. New Critical practices in *The Town* end up resembling the sound technologies from which Warren and Brooks meant to distinguish them.

And so Gavin's plan for restoring Linda requires that she leave Mississippi—as he had in attending his own school "up East"—undoing regional specificity by construing the South as a formal practice unmoored from particular geographical coordinates. The withdrawal into Radcliffe, moreover, is achieved by means of a consumer desire enabled by the technological ethos Gavin wants Linda to escape. In this world, where urns in sonnets have given way to "spurious" ones in suburban rooms, Gavin's postulation of spiritual solitude dissolves into the magazine-ad-reading, radio-saturated culture that makes of the New Critical reader an ordinary consumer. Gavin imagines how he must appear to Flem, as "even more of a danger" than Matt, "persuading the girl herself to escape beyond the range of his control . . . showing her where she could go seek images and shapes she didn't know she had until he put them in her mind" (285–86). Gavin hopes that these "images and shapes" will be the miraculous images of the verbal icon, but Faulkner makes it clear that they are more like photographs in "out-of-state school brochures." In *The Town*'s world, New Critical poems share something of the commercial gloss in the advertisement for Flem and Eula's tacky furniture. Faulkner's transparent representational mode, moreover, aligns his putatively New Critical novel with the brochures. How else are we to take Faulkner's decision to allegorize—to portray Gavin as eating peach ice cream? Like his alignment of poems with magazine-ad photos, this sort of transparency indicates the author's decision to contradict New Critical orthodoxy.

The Town resembles Matt's Donne, not Gavin's, and Faulkner indeed rejects the modernist protocols of reading that he attributes to Gavin. Take, for example, the portrayal of Coca-Cola in *The Town*. As Gavin watches Charles deliver the Donne book to Linda from his office window, he considers how he might time things right to create a "chance" encounter with Linda at Christian's drugstore:

> and then I thought how if I had only thought to fill a glass with water, to count off slowly sixty seconds, say, to cover the time Skeets McGowan, the soda squirt, would need to tear his fascinations from whatever other female junior or senior and fill the order, then drink the water slowly to simulate the coke.

(207)

What characterizes Faulkner's symbolic mode here is not "occlusive stylistics," as Godden has aptly described the earlier style, but something more like what Jean Baudrillard would later call the hyperreal.[18] The Coke here refers to an idea of water, not to the thing itself, and so this simulacrum, to borrow another of Baudrillard's terms, emerges as the synthetic form to match the synthetic substance. Coca-Cola originated in Georgia, moreover, but its logo rapidly spread across the globe after it was trademarked in 1944, eventually rendering it what the historian H. W. Brands calls "the first truly global consumer item and the most valuable product name on the planet."[19] While simulacra, Coke, and rock all mark the shift from Faulkner's formerly modernist prose, and surely from the South itself, all emerge as elements in *The Town*'s contemporary, global aesthetic.

The South is thus portrayed in *The Town* as a region that to preserve must be left, and the narrative proceeds in a correspondingly mobile way. In contrast to the heavy historical referentiality of an early classic like *The Sound and the Fury*—indicated by the Civil War monument, for example—in *The Town*, time flies. The narrators make constant reference to acceleration. The Snopeses, led by the ascendant Flem, "accrete"

(8) into and instantly "appear" (5) in Jefferson. I. O. Snopes at first seems "doomed to immobilization" (37) but quickly transforms into a "dust-cloud travelling fast along a road" (38). Wallstreet Panic Snopes accelerates four years of elementary school by completing them in one (127), and Flem takes up the position as superintendent of the town's public works "suddenly and without warning" (9). Eula's youth seems erased rather than succeeded by her daughter Linda's, since Gavin simply transfers his desire from mother to daughter, as if they occupy the same generation. In the names as well—Montgomery Ward, Wallstreet Panic, and I. O.—Faulkner collapses distinct eras within a progression into a single generation. The names are transparent references to moments in a "survey," Mauri Skinfill calls it, of "American commercialism"—but, we will add, moments depicted in *The Town* as emerging all at once.[20] This simultaneity is evident as well when Charles explains that Flem's water tower is not a "monument" but a "footprint" (3) and then explains what this means: "A monument only says *At least I got this far* while a footprint says *This is where I was when I moved again*" (29). In including Charles's gloss of what the narrative term "footprint" is intended to mean, Faulkner dispenses with the need for close-reading. Godden teaches us that Faulkner's early work "demands that the reader attend closely" (4). But in collapsing interpretation into narrative, Faulkner creates in *The Town* a feeling of instantaneousness—something more akin to what Matt experiences when he sees the Donne book. Our great Southern modernist is engaged in something new with this novel: the design, along with the other authors *Novel Sounds* examines, of a realist aesthetic. In the process of flouting his formerly difficult style, Faulkner produces his readers as versions of the mechanic.

Why give the Snopeses such obvious names? With these, Faulkner suggests that transparent signs mark his new technology-inspired version of narrative time. The transparency of the brand name, whether Coke or Montgomery Ward, both indicates the South's geographic dispersal and exemplifies the symbolic mode of a perpetual now. This aligns *The Town* less with *Absalom, Absalom!* or *The Sound and the Fury* than with an experience of time that Norman Mailer described in "The White Negro" as the "enormous present." In this essay, also published in 1957,

Mailer infamously advanced the figure of the "hipster." As the title of his essay suggests, white hipsters sought in blackness ways to exist in what Mailer described as the "bleak scene" of the postwar moment.[21] Michael Szalay has argued that the era is crucially defined in terms of the idealization of blackness found in Mailer's essay, identifying "a range of predominantly white fantasies about hip" that "have animated the secret imagination of postwar liberalism."[22] With reference to Robert Penn Warren's 1965 *Who Speaks for the Negro?*, Szalay has also shown how crucial an understanding of Mailer's notion is to the New Critical project. That the "enormous present" Mailer describes is the proper milieu for white idealizations of "the negro" goes some way in explaining how Faulkner's early portrayals of racial fluidity in the South were altered in the postwar context. The aesthetic we find in *The Town* developed along with a changing racial landscape, and the demise of Jim Crow that *Brown v. Board of Education* marks occurred amid anxiety, well founded or not, that a culture hospitable to rock and roll might contribute to bringing about racial equality.

Regarding the "occlusive stylistics" in the early novels, Godden argues that the density in Southern fiction of the 1920s and 1930s derives from a "labor trauma" in which whites are exposed as "blacks in whiteface."[23] *The Town* opens with a story Faulkner published in 1931 about two African American workers who undercut the authority of their white boss, and indeed the shifting racial hierarchy Godden describes as emerging in the modernist era seems at first relevant to *The Town* as well. But this later novel's aesthetic fails to command from its readers the solitude in reading that Gavin hopes Linda will find reading Donne, and the inhabitants of Jefferson in *The Town* therefore emerge as more like the "white negroes" of Greenwich Village than Southerners newly traumatized by the changes to labor relations that took place decades earlier. The "eternal present" in which Faulkner ensconces Jefferson can be found in any suburb, as Rubin later observed, and *The Town*'s confluence with an aesthetic more aligned with mechanics than with poets indicates a new version of whites as "blacks in whiteface," one that would come to be associated with Bob Dylan's "minstrel-boy" appropriations.[24]

In its overt mention of rock and roll songs, *The Crying of Lot 49* makes obvious what Faulkner more subtly intimates in *The Town*: that the racial clarity W. C. Handy and by extension John Donne were to guarantee no longer obtained in the age of rock and roll. Mucho's boss Funch makes this explicit when he complains that Mucho has become "generic" (114)—that he "hasn't been himself." Oedipa asks, "And who . . . pray, has he been, Ringo Starr? . . . Chubby Checker? . . . the Righteous Brothers?" (114). With reference to this list of rock and rollers both black and white, Pynchon's characters indicate that as the new suburban aesthetics demand different reading practices, they produce different subjective positions for their readers as well. "When those kids sing about 'She loves you,' yeah well, you know, she does," to return to Mucho's exultation. "She's any number of people," he adds, "all over the world, back through time, different colors, sizes, ages, shapes, distances from death but she loves. And the 'you' is everybody" (117). His generic self crucially includes "different colors," and Mucho celebrates this kind of racial merging as a feature of life in the rock era. Even if Pynchon is making fun of Mucho's rock-inspired commitment to civil rights here— which he surely is, since listening to the line in an ad, "rich chocolatey goodness," brings him the same groovy sense of oneness with the color brown—the rock song is portrayed as enabling Mucho to be more than white; in letting "she loves you" speak for him, Mucho can be the "you" that is "everybody." Robert Penn Warren seems to have been dead serious when he portrayed his white balladeer's decline as a lynching. Pynchon is more critical. For him, Mucho's drug-induced embrace of rock clarifies how easily racial inclusion can slide into apolitical appropriation.

Gavin, ever backward, instead seeks solitude in reading. Toward the end of *The Town*, he drives to Seminary Hill and looks down at Jefferson from above. Faulkner describes Gavin's experience there as a "perusal" (316), and his reading consolidates the sort of solitary subject whose undoing, Mucho suggests, is marked by rock music:

And you stand suzerain and solitary above the whole sum of your
life beneath that incessant ephemeral spangling. First is Jefferson, the
center, radiating weakly its puny glow into space; beyond it, enclosing

it, spreads the County, tied by the diverging roads to that center as is
the rim to the hub by its spokes, yourself detached as God Himself
for this moment above the cradle of your nativity and of the men and
women who made you, the record and chronicle of your native land
proffered for your perusal in ring by concentric ring like ripples on
living water above the dreamless slumber of your past.

(315–16)

Gavin is a reader here, "perusing," glossing the town, "record and chronicle" of his "native land." In keeping with the verbal icon—that New
Critical mainstay, a conception of visual and verbal meaning "handled
all at once"—this reading is not linear, not left to right.[25] Gavin sees the
town and its history in a single instant; Jefferson's moments in time are
visible simultaneously from a solitary, "suzerain" place.

The idea of Jefferson as the "center" of a "wheel" whose "spokes"
lead to the county renders the town for which this novel is named an
archaic image of mobility. And that wheel immediately gives way to
the suggestion of faster electronic media in the wheel of a film pro-
jector. Almost instantly, Gavin's experience of the whole image all at
once, his "perusal," becomes sequential viewing of a "panorama." As
he gazes out across the town's concentric circles of history, from "the
rich alluvial river-bottom land of old Issetibbeha, the wild Chickasaw
king" (316), to "where Frenchman's Bend lay beyond the southeastern
horizon, cradle of Varners and ant-heap for the northwest crawl of
Snopes" (317), his reading in "inviolable solitude" comes to resemble a
cinematic experience:

And you stand there—you, the old man already white-headed . . . and
pushing forty, only a few years from forty—while there rises up to
you, proffered up to you, the spring darkness, the unsleeping darkness
which, although it is of the dark itself, declines the dark since dark is
of the little death called sleeping. Because look how, even though the
last of the west is no longer green and all of the firmament is now
one unlidded studded slow-wheeling arc and the last of earth-pooled
visibility has drained away, there still remains one faint diffusion, since

everywhere you look about the dark panorama you still see them, faint as whispers: the faint and shapeless lambence of blooming dogwood returning loaned light to light as the phantoms of candles would.

(317)

Jefferson's history is "proffered" "ring by concentric ring," but here that literary simultaneity is contrasted with the linear progression of a movie plot. Faulkner's description of cinematic experience using natural images—as a "panorama," that is, in which a "diffusion" of "loaned light" remains in darkness—alters the terms of reference, so that nature here is cinema's vehicle, not the other way around. America's great modernist produces media technology as nature's referent—an aesthetic mode Fredric Jameson associates with postmodern form, the "hysterical sublime."[26] In the transposition, cinema, paradigmatically social, comes to underpin an image of solitary reading in mountain fastness, and the very idea of solitude is shown to devolve into an originary media experience resembling Mucho's with the radio. Here, as with "She Loves You," the solitary "you" becomes an "everybody," an "everybody" produced by ballads' departures from both place and race. And the reversal in Pynchon, in which the solitary becomes generic in rock and roll, exposes the racial dimension of the technological collapses in *The Town* as well. Just as Gavin's view of the verbal icon in solitude finds an origin in the social experience of cinema, so by extension is the reader's solitude grounded in media technologies. The suggestion Faulkner creates is that reading *The Town* is more like Mucho listening to the Beatles than it is like Gavin hearing W. C. Handy perform live—or than reading Donne.

Mucho's boss Funch calls Oedipa "Edna" because, as Mucho explains, this is how it must be said "allowing for the distortion" of the sound produced by taping for radio (114). This comment casts Oedipa's already distorted name in terms of sound technology. Like Gavin, Oedipa is engaged in a quest driven by the hope for a literary haven outside of mass culture, but her vaguely Oedipal search for literary truth leads toward the disappointing revelation of a mere sound—"Edna." Pynchon's novel too thus produces a version of literary reading in which close-reading is after all superfluous. Indeed, Pynchon takes the critique of literary protocol one step further, portraying the Beatles acolyte Mucho telling Oedipa that "the human voice" is "a flipping miracle" (117), bringing New Critical orality into his parody of reading, updating the conception of "voice" for a technological era. And we can read backward from *The Crying of Lot 49* to *The Town* from the word "flipping" too, to view earlier commitments to black vernacular voice like Gavin's to W. C. Handy as a harbinger of the coming British Invasion. Mucho is referring in this moment to the human voice as radio has altered it, to the voice as detached from bodies—the voice as a physical thing broken down into its "synthetic" elements: "basic frequencies and harmonics, with all their different loudnesses" (116).[27] The noisy "scuttering" pages in *The Town* perform similar work, previewing Oedipa's radio voice, transforming the oral Donne into media. "Scuttering" is the distorted "scuttling," after all, just as "Edna" is the distorted Oedipus, and no less than Mucho's radio, Gavin's book produces meaningful literary signification as devolving into its own surface sound.

"When those kids sing about 'She loves you,'" explains a hallucinating Mucho, parroting the Beatles' lyrics, "yeah well, you know, she does." Mucho explains here that it is popular songs that do away with the need for reading. "The songs"—we return once again to Mucho's proclamation—"it's not just that they say something, they *are* something, in the pure sound. Something new" (118). Brooks worried about the trends that were leading to this idea: In *The Well Wrought Urn*, he complained about the prevailing tendency to "explain the miracle away in the process of reduction which hardly stops short of reducing the 'poem' to the ink itself" (xi). That Brooks's fears are confirmed in *The Crying of Lot 49* is no surprise, but reduction afflicts readers in *The Town* as well, as we have seen, and in its world the book of poetry is a thing. Charles recounts how Gavin and Linda met at "Christian's drugstore after school while Linda ate another banana split or ice-cream soda," and he notes seeing the "last book of poetry Uncle Gavin had ordered for her lying in the melted ice cream or spilled Coca-Cola on the marble table top" (180). Here, Faulkner casts poetry by Donne as sticky paper, pages that "*are* something." Sticky pages, radio; "The Canonization," "She Loves Me." *The Town* was understood as Southern literature, even if Brooks declared it bad Southern literature, and its life as Southern fiction depended on its presumed connections to poetry by John Donne and to blues songs by W. C. Handy. In comparing the Donne book to radio, and in explicitly thematizing the process of *The Town*'s own institutional verification, Faulkner means to clarify that poetry can be counted among the "machine-made popular arts."

The revelation that New Critical solitude in reading is fundamentally elusive is reiterated in a surprising display of electric music toward the end of *The Town*. The failure of the verbal icon to restore the miracle to a technological age means that technology, with all of its attendant racial indeterminacy, has prevailed. Gavin's experience of reading on the hill is portrayed as a moment of close-reading; Faulkner depicts the institutional equating of literary "perusal" with an experience of "mountain fastness" in the Southern hills—that which in 1930 Lytle claimed "ballets" would provide. But the experience falls apart immediately, in the end resembling the moment Oedipa gazes down at San Narcisso and sees in the suburban sprawl of California the image of a "circuit card" in a radio and is reminded of her husband spinning rock records at the radio station (14). Although mountain fastness should link Faulkner's novel to ballads, Gavin's view of Jefferson links "the town" to the electric pulses of radio:

There is a ridge; you drive on beyond Seminary Hill and in time you come upon it: a mild unhurried farm road presently mounting to cross the ridge and on to join the main highway leading from Jefferson to the world. And now, looking back and down, you see all Yoknapatawpha in the dying last of day beneath you. There are stars now, just pricking out as you watch them among the others already coldly and softly burning; the end of the day is one vast green soundless murmur up the northwest toward the zenith. Yet it is as though light were not being subtracted from earth, drained from earth backward and upward into that cooling green, but rather had gathered, pooling for an unmoving moment yet, among the low places of the ground so that ground, earth itself is luminous and only the dense clumps of trees are dark, standing darkly and immobile out of it.

This hyperbolically poetic moment seems to deliver the kind of iconic experience no longer available in the rock and roll world occupied by Oedipa—or, for that matter, to *The Cave*'s Monty Harrick. But even as Faulkner constructs the lovely literary image of "gathering" natural light, tying his own poetic narrative to the Donne contained in the unopened book, he also reduces light to its physical essence, describing it as a concrete substance that "drains" and "pools" on the earth.

As Gavin watches the stars, "fireflies" emerge, and Gavin describes them as the "Mississippi child's vernacular," tying Faulkner's poetic narrative back through Donne to Handy's blues. The visual image of "vernacular" fireflies fittingly becomes sound: "myriad and frenetic, random and frantic, pulsing; not questing, not quiring, but choiring as if they were tiny incessant appeaseless, cries, words" (315). The verbal icon was always rooted in the ballad, always linked to the experience of live oral performance. But the sound is reduced here, like the pages of the Donne book—"questing" becomes "quiring," then "choiring"—so that Gavin's experience of words, like Mucho's, devolves into a surface meaninglessness. The vernacular Mississippi "voices" turned electric pulses refer to Handy, to be sure, but they can also be read as "rude minstrel" Faulkner's ballads. As the flashing lights become "cries" and then "words," they make Gavin's iconic reading an experience of listening, of hearing a ballad that *Understanding Poetry* led him to expect would be acoustic. But the "cries" and "words" originate as "pulses" of light, flickers whose "myriad and frenetic, random and frantic" movement makes them electric, a version of the ants and locusts we find in Warren's *The Cave*. Again, the relation between nature and technology has been reversed, so that the origin of the vernacular sound is revealed to be technology, "tiny voices" emerging from "pulsing" and "frenetic" lights in the Southern hills. The verbal icon is thus electric sound, and Handy's mouth vanishes into broadcast voices. Here, as Gavin experiences in a breached mountain fastness a corrupted version of that which he hoped Donne would create for Linda at Radcliffe, reading the Donne book becomes a version of listening to rock and roll. It seems that Marshall McLuhan, defector from literary close-reading and godfather of media studies, more clearly explains Faulkner's gesture than the New Critical ideas that led to his canonization. The view of Jefferson fails to affirm New Critical claims that Southern literature is rooted in oral ballads, instead demonstrating that the medium is the message.

3.1 Aunt Harriett McClintock at the microphone with John A. Lomax Sr.,
Mrs. Ruby Pickens Tartt, and Aunt Harriett's "great-grands" children in background,
at crossroads near Sumterville, Alabama, November 3, 1940.

Source: Photograph by Ruby T. Lomax. Photograph courtesy of Library of Congress,
Prints and Photographs Division, Lomax Collection.

3

THE BALLAD'S GENDER

Femininity and Information in Georgia

Toward the end of Carson McCullers's *The Ballad of the Sad Café* (1951), the character Marvin Macy returns from jail with an acoustic guitar and performs the bodily act McCullers is construed by her title as also performing: he sings. A few years later, Flannery O'Connor published another musically informed story, "A Good Man Is Hard to Find" (1953), which she named after a 1927 hit for "Empress of the Blues" Bessie Smith, also entitled "A Good Man Is Hard to Find."[1] McCullers and O'Connor wrote these music-based fictional works just as rock and roll's electrified sounds were first emerging: *The Ballad of the Sad Café* was published the same year "Rocket 88" was released; "A Good Man Is Hard to Find" was anthologized right around the time O'Connor's fellow Georgia native Ray Charles recorded "I Got a Woman" for Atlantic.[2] It had been a decade or so since Warren and Brooks had explained that we "enjoy" hearing the balladeer's voice in person because of "something more than the statistical importance of the subject," drawing Andrew Lytle's call to abolish the radio and "take down the fiddle from the wall" into definitions of literary form.[3] In creating obvious parallels between the songs depicted within these stories and the stories themselves, both *The Ballad of the Sad Café* and "A Good Man Is Hard to Find" appear to enter the rock and roll era affirming this retrograde conception of ballads.[4]

But the singing in *The Ballad of the Sad Café* and "A Good Man Is Hard to Find" is not pleasurable—none of the characters "enjoy" it—and so the relation between these fictionalized balladeers and their Agrarian precedents is skewed. Macy's voice, for example, is "wet and slimy, as he always had too much spit in his mouth," and, even more disgusting, the "tunes he sang glided from his throat like eels."[5] In O'Connor's story too we find a balladeer associated with a "wet and slimy" creature resembling the eels in *The Ballad of the Sad Café*—this one a snake that appears at the end of O'Connor's grim little tale, at the moment the Misfit kills the grandmother on the side of the road. In what follows, I am going to show that the displeasure indicated by these serpentine creatures aligns the ballads in these stories, and by extension the stories themselves, with the "statistical importance" reviled by New Critics. Warren and Brooks anthologized stories by McCullers and O'Connor in *Understanding Fiction*, and O'Connor was mentored at the Iowa Writer's Workshop by Lytle.[6] As we shall see, however, both *The Ballad of the Sad Café* and "A Good Man Is Hard to Find" seem to have been crafted with the perverse intention of demonstrating radio's ubiquity, not "throwing" it out. McCullers and O'Connor indeed update the Agrarian conception of "ballets" in their stories, redefining it to fit the emergent terms of what Marshall McLuhan would later describe as "information" in "the electric age."[7]

Were we inclined to bring psychoanalytic categories to bear in this reading, we would perhaps observe that the presence of these serpentine ectotherms also appears to confirm claims that the voice is phallic. Roland Barthes speculates that the "thrill" enabled by the singing voice is produced by an illusion of direct contact with the body, by the fantasy of connection between listeners and the singer's deepest bodily "cavities."[8] In fact, Barthes argues, the pleasure delivered by the voice is created symbolically, by the "phallic stature" of "the Father," not the elusive body itself.[9] The slimy creatures associated with oral singing in these stories, a Barthean reading might go, literalize this phallic aspect of the voice. And the presence of phallic imagery in musical fiction by women might invite special note, might lead to the supposition that by virtue of their bodies Southern women writing in the postwar moment bore a particular relation to this gendered aspect of the voice. Allowing that speculations about the phallus cannot exhaust the cultural meanings surrounding these snakes and eels, the readings that follow nevertheless show that these institutionally sanctioned women viewed the ballad form as decidedly male, and their depictions of serpentine voices mark this view. In their cheeky embrace of radio as a feature of their high-literary craft, both McCullers and O'Connor set out to mock this gendered feature of their institutional milieu.

THE BALLADEER AND
THE INFORMATION HIGHWAY

We have seen how Faulkner's *The Town* is illuminated by a consideration of Pynchon's *The Crying of Lot 49*. *The Ballad of the Sad Café* and "A Good Man Is Hard to Find" look clearer as well from the vantage of 1960s ideas, in particular McLuhan's claims about information technology. The term "communication," explains McLuhan in *Understanding Media*, the 1964 publication in which he declared that "the medium is the message," has "had an extensive use in connection with roads and bridges, sea routes, rivers, and canals, even before it became transformed into 'information movement' in the electric age."[10] Couriers on roads emerge in *Understanding Media* as the bodily origin of the "information movement," the first, physical version of broadcast—the means by which messages were transmitted.[11] The "increased speed of information movement by means of paper messages and road transport," McLuhan explains, was simply the "ever faster movement of information by couriers on excellent roads" (90). Pausing briefly to again consider 1950s Southern fiction through the lens of *The Crying of Lot 49*, we note in Pynchon's symbolic scheme a history of communication that precisely accords with McLuhan's. Pynchon's allegory of miscommunication in *The Courier's Tragedy*, in particular—the wildly convoluted play in which couriers traverse roads to deliver lethal messages—presents couriers as originating the more overt technological forms of communication that suffuse almost all aspects of Oedipa's world.

The Ballad of the Sad Café begins on a "miserable main street" (3) and ends at the "Fork Falls highway," a road with "rough places" (70) in need of repair, and the events of "A Good Man Is Hard to Find" similarly unfold while its characters are in transit on highways and "hilly" dirt roads with "sudden washes" and "sharp curves on dangerous embankments" (124). We might look to *The Crying of Lot 49* for contrast and claim that the peripatetic singers in these short works by Southern women are not couriers at all but artists whose "ancient genius" places them in the tradition of traveling minstrels that informed the Agrarian conception of ballads in *Understanding Poetry*. But it makes more sense to understand the roads in the stories by both McCullers and O'Connor as versions of those traversed in *The Crying of Lot 49*. These Southern women indeed produce genealogies in their stories that resemble Pynchon's, suggesting that the stories themselves have followed the same route as "information movement in the electric age." In spite of the favor they found with the New Critics, that is, these women were engaging ideas in the early 1950s that McLuhan would make explicit a decade later. In following this strain of thought, moreover, McCullers and O'Connor locate Southern fiction along a continuum—one that they suggest begins not with phallic corporeal wholeness but with feminine forms of archaic communication.

The speaker in Bessie Smith's version of "A Good Man Is Hard to Find" opines, "my man's treating me mean," and O'Connor finds in this a precedent for portraying the grandmother as once similarly attached to a man with whom romantic relations do not end well. To entertain her bored comic-book-consuming grandchildren, who are slapping each other as they travel rapidly along a Georgia highway, the grandmother spins her tale about this man. Edgar Atkins Teagarden, the grandmother says, brought her a watermelon every Saturday "with his initials cut in it, E.A.T."[12] Miscommunication ensues: "Well, one Saturday, she said, Mr. Teagarden brought the watermelon and there was nobody home and he left it on the front porch and returned in his buggy to Jasper, but she never got the watermelon, she said, because a nigger boy ate it when he saw the initials, E.A.T.!" (120). O'Connor means to associate the grandmother's tale and Bessie Smith's song, and the watermelon image emerges in the comparison as inheriting from the legacy of racism found in Davidson's characterization of the jazz record. In the logic here, mechanical reproduction of the blues hit produces the same conditions for consumption as the watermelon. O'Connor raises the specter of a searing racial stereotype: as the watermelon is to the African American child, so Bessie Smith's replicated voice is to black listeners. Figuring race record as watermelon seems an unambiguous fulfillment of the Agrarians' demeaning vision for a white Southern literature originating in natural Southern enclosures.

How, then, shall we understand the African American child's reading, to which O'Connor conspicuously likens the white children's perusal of comic books? As an affirmation of the racist image within which he appears? Or, on the contrary, as a salutary description of the emerging interracial reading public? In addition to its likeness to the Bessie Smith song, the watermelon expresses Edgar's courtly intentions. As his white Southern expression, we might say, the watermelon is Edgar's text, naturally rooted in the "ballet." Springing spontaneously from his white body, his courtly feeling is white, and the etching signifying that feeling—his signature, no less—is therefore white as well. But the African American child's reading divorces the watermelon from its intention, and this allows him to take it into his body. Hardly affirming Edgar's whiteness, as Davidson hoped literature grounded in ballads would, here the Southern text is up for grabs—transferrable, as rock and roll was, to black bodies. As racial ambiguity emerges, moreover, so too does a confusion over gender, and these are intertwined: as the watermelon becomes a Bessie Smith song, the masculine position it occupies in this courtship narrative is compromised. The white ballad singer is both feminized and blackened by the watermelon image, then, and this transaction crucially involves a collapse of the ballad-text into an artifact of sound technology.

O'Connor thus mocks rather than extends the racial guarantees promised in the Agrarian argument, presenting Southern literature as, like rock, available for cross-racial exchange. Lest we take this rocklike racial ambiguity as an affirmation of rock and roll per se, however, we note here O'Connor's savage portrayal of an actual rock song, "Shake, Rattle, and Roll," performed as "rock, rattle, and roll" by the damaged delinquent

Rufus Johnson in "The Lame Shall Enter First," as he profanes the memory of a child's dead mother by singing the song—snapping fingers and swinging hips—while dressed in her corset.[13] Nor should this figural merging in the fiction be confused for political intention, since just as "What'd I Say" was released to an interracial audience of unprecedented magnitude—five years after *Brown v. Board of Education* was decided—the university-bred O'Connor refused to meet with James Baldwin in Georgia. "Might as well expect a mule to fly as me to see James Baldwin in Georgia," she wrote to her friend Maryat Lee.[14] O'Connor's figural associations belie her adherence to racist norms in the decision not to meet Baldwin, and so perhaps whatever irrepressible force pulled both African Americans and whites across the color line to form rock and roll also structured literary forms—even those marshaled to quell its ambiguous sound.

"When she told a story," O'Connor's narrator explains of the grandmother, "she rolled her eyes and waved her head and was very dramatic" (120). Why do the grandmother and Edgar part? O'Connor's narrator does not offer details, but the grandmother's "dramatic" delivery of the tale construes it as the white Southern lady's bodily version of Bessie Smith's mechanically reproduced song. As Edgar's "ballet" ends up inside a black body, though, the grandmother's story of a "good man" seems to belong to Bessie Smith, and O'Connor elides distinctions crucial to the establishment of the institutional field that claimed her. In *Understanding Poetry*, recall, poetry is that which is not "carried away": "We like a poem not because . . . it gives us an idea we can 'carry away with us' . . . but because the poem itself is an experience."[15] And the experience of poetry, as we have seen, originates as whatever "more than statistical importance" oral ballads can deliver. This distinction is reiterated in "The Intentional Fallacy," first published in 1946, in which Wimsatt and Beardsley explain why "poetry differs from practical messages." Messages, they declare, "are successful if and only if we correctly infer the intention. They are more abstract than poetry."[16] With Edgar present, the watermelon is like the book of Donne's poetry in *The Town*; Edgar's medium is his message, the gift of watermelon transparently legible as chivalry even without attention to the letters etched into its rind. When the African American boy reads it as text, however, something not intended is conveyed, and it is the African American reader who thus makes watermelon's message less "abstract," more poetic. New Critical logic seems on first glance reversed here, as the black child makes the white man's media into literature. But the child also clearly turns the artist's signature into a message, and in the end the scene blurs New Critical distinctions. The grandmother's likeness to Bessie Smith similarly muddles the relation between poetry and messages—and, by extension, between ballads and information. She is the type of a Southern storyteller whose art is grounded in ballads and who creates expression that cannot be "carried away" from her body. But as a traveler along the highway, she is also a body whose rapid movement disconnects her oral expression from place, hurling it, along with rock and roll, forward toward information.

O'CONNOR'S TYPEWRITER

The collapse of the grandmother's oral voice into Smith's mechanical one becomes explicit toward the end of the story, when the grandmother suddenly finds herself parroting the Misfit's philosophy—"'Maybe He didn't raise the dead,' the old lady mumbled, not knowing what she was saying and feeling so dizzy that she sank down in the ditch with her legs twisted under her" (132). As she begins to take on the murderer's voice, the Misfit takes on hers, speaking, the narrator says, in a "high voice" that seems to belong to her (132). O'Connor ends her story with the suggestion that the gospel-singing Misfit's words are hers; the grandmother and her singing killer exchange voices. This collapse occurs in the exposure of her tall-tale-telling oral voice as ultimately also mechanical:

Alone with the Misfit, the grandmother found that she had lost her voice. She wanted to tell him that he must pray. She opened and closed her mouth several times before anything came out. Finally, she found herself saying, "Jesus, Jesus," meaning, Jesus will help you, but the way she was saying it, it sounded as if she might be cursing.

(131)

The word "Jesus" resembles the watermelon, a word carried away from the body, a body whose voice becomes "lost" to it. The grandmother's oral expression turns out to be robotic gesture, the mechanical opening and closing of a mouth—more blues recording than live ballad. Conceptually, the grandmother seems at first to be the inverse of the blues singer's recorded voice as it comes into the story: Smith, a sound with no mouth; the grandmother, a mouth with no sound. As sound begins to emerge from the grandmother's moving mouth, however, and as the grandmother notes its disconnection from her, we recognize it as cursing and so belonging to the Misfit—as if indeed his sound is broadcast from her mouth. Giving her short story the title of a race record figures the Southern author's putatively more literary form as resembling a radio.

As the grandmother's mouth moves mechanically to emit someone else's voice, the suggestion arises that O'Connor's story too is a mechanical version of the author's mouth broadcasting Smith's voice. We might say that the grandmother's robotic mouth refers to O'Connor's fingers at the typewriter, troubling the Agrarian idea of Southern fiction as originating in bodily wholeness. "I been most everything," the Misfit tells the grandmother just after they hear the shots that kill Bailey and his son (129). I have mentioned that O'Connor includes "gospel singer" among the Misfit's odd jobs. His status as one who sings becomes quickly enmeshed with his status as one who signs: "I said long ago," the Misfit explains to the grandmother, "you sign you a signature and sign everything you do and keep a copy of it. Then you'll know what you done and you can hold up the crime to the punishment and see do they match" (131). With the reversal of a single letter, the bodily singer becomes a duplicating signer, and the literary pun reduces to a typo. O'Connor alters a single letter, that is, making of her close reader a proofreader, altering the fruits of her own labor to construe watermelon as race record and author as necessarily tethered to machines.

Just before the Misfit shoots her, the grandmother makes a final utterance: "Why you're one of my babies. You're one of my own children!" (132). She vocalizes this claim to maternal status when she touches the Misfit on his shoulder on the shoulder of a dirt road. Shoulders come up again in relation to "Pitty Sing," the startled cat whose errant leap from the grandmother's valise to the driver's shoulder causes the car accident that leads to the family's grisly fate.[17] The shoulder of the road, the cat's leap to a shoulder, the grandmother's maternal touch. These shoulders indicate not so much symbols as a circuit, standing as uniform stations through which there is physical movement. In their association with roads, these shoulders belong to communication; they are a vestige of the electronic information literary figuration will become—or, more precisely, of the electronic information that O'Connor's story suggests that literary figuration is already. One way of describing the central coincidence of "A Good Man Is Hard to Find"—the grandmother leads her family to an encounter with the killer she reads about in the newspaper at the beginning of the story—is as a move backward from electronic information to bodily communication, a retreat from the "ever faster" movement represented by newspaper to a firsthand encounter with a balladeer in "mountain fastness." We might remember Lomax when we consider the grandmother in this way, and, noting again that the killer identifies himself as a "gospel singer," we might read the encounter at the end of O'Connor's story as redefining the cultural milieu in which Lomax's discovery would become relevant to literature professors at the MLA. We have seen that the "rude songs" Lomax imagined he was finding in Lead Belly's oeuvre was confirmation of Thomas Percy's view that literature originates as musical "effusions of nature." "A Good Man Is Hard to Find" rewrites this cultural script, locating the balladeer on the side of the road, inserting the vernacular into a new narrative that blurs art with communication and, eventually, literature with rock.

The circuit turns physical movement between shoulders into something resembling pulses, then, and the maternal gesture, the touch that comes with identification of the Misfit as one of her "babies," depicts both biological reproduction and mechanical replication as electrical. In this firsthand encounter, balladeers are associated with the body O'Connor construes as the first firsthand—the original, the mother. The grandmother's maternal touch indeed traces a progression from electronic communication backward to the maternal conduit that precedes roads, to the mother's body, here construed as an image of archaic communication. But the maternal touch feels to the Misfit like a snake, making him spring "back as if a snake had bitten him and shot her three times through the chest" (132). This phallic creature emerges at the site where the distinction between balladeer and courier breaks down, where once more the Misfit's voice is found in the grandmother's body. His phallic song, that is, seems here to have been relocated, depicted as making a perilous emergence from her feminine radio mouth. As the exchange of Bessie Smith's voice with O'Connor's unravels Agrarian rhetoric about race, it seems, the substitutions thus enabled call the balladeer's masculinity into question at the same time. The phallic snake—a balladeer's voice construed as male—also originates as a baby in a woman's body.

ERRANT FEMININE SONG FRAGMENTS

Singing bodies and the literary turn out to be inextricable from electricity in *The Ballad of the Sad Café* as well, and firsthand encounters with singers in McCullers's novella too fail to produce the experience *Understanding Poetry* assigns to those listening to ballads. *The Ballad of the Sad Café* depicts the joyous rise and awful decline of a thriving café in a cotton-mill town where repetitive labor makes of the workers, described as "spinners," miserable automatons who think "only of the loom, the dinner pail, the bed, and then the loom again" (10). McCullers populates this story with bodies mechanized by repetitive labor—broken and in need of physical remedy: in addition to Cousin Lymon's "crooked little legs" and "warped chest" (7), his skin is "yellowed by dust," and there are "lavender shadows beneath his eyes" (7). Stumpy McPhail's "red face" and "dainty, purplish hands" (4); the protagonist herself, the excessively tall (12) Miss Amelia, with her crossed eyes (3) and "bony knees" (56)—all indicate the decrepit state of bodies in this world dominated by the mill. The live performance of the ballad by the singers on a chain gang that takes place at the novel's end is presented as reparative. The interracial group—"twelve mortal men, seven of them black and five of them white boys" (71)—sing as they literally repair a "certain dangerous place" (70) on the "Forks Falls highway" outside of town, and the danger they are employed to prevent by fixing the road seems linked to these broken bodies, as if the mechanical damage the prisoners are employed to prevent has already been inflicted on them:

> There is a guard, with a gun, his eyes drawn to red slits by the glare. The gang works all the day long, arriving huddled in the prison cart soon after day break, and being driven off again in the gray August twilight. All day there is the sound of the picks striking into the clay earth, hard sunlight, the smell of sweat. And every day there is music. One dark voice will start a phrase, half-sung, and like a question. And after a moment another voice will join in, soon the whole gang will be singing. The voices are dark in the golden glare, the music intricately blended, both somber and joyful. The music will swell until at last it seems that the sound does not come from the twelve men on the gang, but from the earth itself, or the wide sky. It is music that causes the heart to broaden and the listener to grow cold with ecstasy and fright. Then slowly the music will sink down until at last there remains one lonely voice, then a great hoarse breath, the sun, the sound of the picks in the silence.
>
> (70–71)

The "sweat" in the scene of singing roots the song in the singers' bodies, the ballad in the authenticating body of the balladeer. On first glance, these prisoners' "somber and joyful" ballads seem versions of "Frankie and Johnny" in *Understanding Poetry* or Lytle's fiddle on the wall: music capable of creating transcendence. By causing "the heart to broaden" or the "listener to grow cold with ecstasy and fright," the singers seem to carry out the recuperation of the bodies threatened by the "dangerous place" on the highway. But the music is embedded in the sound of the tools the prisoners wield as they are forced at gunpoint, themselves the guard's tools, to transform the "earth" into highway. The "sound" of the prisoners' "picks striking into the clay earth" precedes and concludes the ballad, as if the sound of making the highway is a sound in the song. The picks appear to constitute the ballad's refrain, emerging as its beginning and as the end into which the musical notes disappear. Even as the voices seem to repair bodies in this figural sense, the singers literally repair the highway that will end up being, we are meant to assume, a conduit to future bodily harm.

The New Critics posit the body at the origin of poetry in the figure of the balladeer; McLuhan makes the same claim for communication, describing the body of a courier traveling on the road as the origin of electronic information. Recalling the New Critical dictum that poetry is less "abstract" than "practical messages," we can understand McCullers's image here as a collapsing of the two. Communication and poetry coincide at their origin, that is, in a firsthand encounter with the body in which singing is shown to be inextricable from roads. More precisely, McCullers's image construes the bodily singing that gives rise to poetry as involving tools, the very tools that produce the conduit enabling archaic bodily forms of communication. With the sounds of the picks as part of the song, it is as if the ballad that emerges from the mouths creates the highway, supplies the tools for the electronic information that the highway will eventually become. And balladeers already contain technology within their bodies. "The music will swell," the narrator explains, "until at last it seems that the sound does not come from the twelve men on the gang, but from the earth itself, or the wide sky." The authenticating bodily presence indicated by the balladeers transforms into disembodiment—the "earth and sky" generate the music, now something like radio voices, "voices in the void," to return to Sconce, not emerging from mouths.[18]

To emphasize the point that her own literary contribution flows from this originary mediation, McCullers portrays physical space in *The Ballad of the Sad Café* as situated around paper. The cotton mill around which the town springs up obliquely associates the labor of its inhabitants with papermaking, but the mass of files in Miss Amelia's office makes paper's importance explicit:

> This office was a room well-known, in a dreadful way, throughout the county. It was there Miss Amelia transacted all business. On the desk was a carefully covered typewriter which she knew how to run, but used only for the most important documents. In the drawers were literally thousands of papers, all filed according to the alphabet. The office was

also the place where Miss Amelia received sick people, for she enjoyed
doctoring and did a great deal of it. Two whole shelves were crowded
with bottles and various paraphernalia. Against the wall was a bench
where the patients sat. She could sew up a wound with a burnt needle
so that it would not turn green. For burns she had a cool, sweet syrup.
For unlocated sickness there were any number of different medicines
which she had brewed herself from unknown recipes.

(16)

This story called a "ballad" contains at the physical center of the town
created by a cotton mill an image of "thousands of papers." These paper
files literalize the mediated status of ballads figured in the singers at the
novel's end. The image of the author's machine at the center as well, the
"carefully covered typewriter," involves McCullers's craft in Miss Amelia's. Even though McCullers traces her story back to the ballad form,
then, her aim is to call attention to the legacy of mediation Davidson
denies.

What should we make of the "bottles" that "crowd" the shelves? These
seem distinctly out of place in this space, with its typewriter and cache
of "copies." Miss Amelia cures inhabitants of her town with the medicine
contained in the bottles, and so they resemble ballads—like the song at
the end of the story, these bottles contain that which repairs the bodies
damaged by the mill. The medicine might be understood as a metonym,
then, a figure in which the ballad's curative power symbolizes the ballad
itself. Since the recipes are "unknown," the undocumented status of the
recipes is brought into the metonym as well, and the figure thus perfectly exemplifies the cure New Critics imagined unmediated ballads
might effect on broken humans—in this story, on the puffy faces, purple
skin, and "unlocated sickness" of the repeating spinners. We discover
early on that Miss Amelia possesses a "passion for lawsuits and the
courts," engaging in "long and bitter litigation over just a trifle" (5). As
a doctor, however, she is an artist, charging "no fees whatsoever" and
creating "hundreds of cures from her great imagination" (16). Drawn
from her "imagination" and linked to an oral world without documents,
indeed, Miss Amelia's medicine is her art—her curative bodily poetry,

her ballad. Unlike the thousands of papers and the typewriter, which literalize mediation of the story itself, the medicine is entirely figural. As a metonymy among impenetrable things without referents, that is, the medicine figures figuration itself, what Richard Godden calls the "occlusive" stylistics of the earlier moment in which Southern literature's invention was grounded. But rather than suggesting that McCullers's story should be aligned with earlier Southern stylistic tendencies, the metonym seems placed near paper to expose its proximity to the literal.

The one child Miss Amelia treats in the narrative's time frame does not get well. Her "medicine" inebriates the child, in fact, and he exits the café draped over his father's shoulder with a "puffed-up" and "very red" face (41). The comingling of the essentially unmediated art and the "thousands of papers" in the office resembles the image of the balladeers on the chain gang. Tools do not extend but meld with voices there, and the description of bodily singing renders them indistinguishable from radio voices. Similarly, these apparently archaic files—the bottles—end up as like the alphabetic filing system they seem to contrast: both files and bottles contain that which produces "puffed-up" faces. In another of McCullers's depictions of paper, we discover why this might be. Bodily art, she suggests, cannot undo the sickening perpetrated by the mechanical arts, because humans are already mediated; paper can be found inside of her spinners, defining paper as a core feature of their being:

It is known that if a message is written with lemon juice on a clean sheet of paper there will be no sign of it. But if the paper is held for a moment to the fire then the letters turn brown and the meaning becomes clear. Imagine that the whiskey is the fire and that the message is that which is known only in the soul of a man—then the worth of Miss Amelia's liquor can be understood. Things have gone unnoticed, thoughts that have been harbored far back in the dark mind, are suddenly recognized and comprehended. A spinner who has thought only of the loom, the dinner pail, the bed, and then the loom again—the spinner might drink some on a Sunday and come across a marsh lily. And in his palm he might hold this flower, examining the gold dainty cup, and in him might suddenly come a sweetness as keen as pain. A weaver might look up for the first time and see for the first time the cold, weird radiance of midnight January sky, and a deep fright as his own smallness stop his heart. Such things as these, then, happen when a man has drunk Miss Amelia's liquor. He may suffer, or he may be spent with joy—but the experience has shown the truth; he has warmed his soul and seen the message there.

(10)

In *The Ballad of the Sad Café*, paper does not transmit information between subjects so much as define them as already split within themselves, in communication internally before communication between subjects is understood to have begun. Here we find an abstract "message" and not a poem, to return to Wimsatt and Beardsley, a message composed of a "truth" linked to the "sweetness" of a "marsh lily." This internally communicating subject clearly revises the conception of the ballad as natural. Percy argued that the "rude songs of ancient minstrels" should be understood "not as labours of art, but as effusions of nature." Here, no such distinction abides. In *The Ballad of the Sad Café*, indeed, ballads are already caught up within an internal circuit of communication that makes original expression about natural images mediated information.[19]

This subject within a subject, moreover—this courier communicating within itself—places one body inside another. McCullers's mediated bodies are at the same time pregnant, gendered; like O'Connor's grandmother, they call attention to the female body as conduit. As mediated, that is, the balladeer's body is feminized. Macy's "wet and slimy" phallic eels thus appear to figure babies as well. And the eels coming out of Macy's orifice are glossed by an earlier image in McCullers's novella, an errant fragment of song momentarily erupting from within a "motionless" and "silent night." "Somewhere in the darkness a woman sang in a high wild voice," the narrator interjects in a moment of narrative inaction, "and the tune had no start and no finish and was made up of only three notes which went on and on" (41). In contrast to the chain gang's ballad, which is emitted in unison from sweaty bodies, the lone "high wild voice" of a woman singing "three notes" with "no start or finish" emerges solitary and out of nowhere, disappearing as quickly as it emerges. In its amorphous form and unexpected appearance, the woman's voice resembles the eels, suggesting that those slithery creatures too indicate a "wild" femininity lurking in the male balladeer and his structured song—an unpleasant break that like this voice could erupt randomly from within the wholeness of male song at any moment, a sign of abjection perhaps. That "three notes" sung by a "high wild voice" might also describe the popular improvisatorial forms heard on the radio in earlier decades—that they might refer to jazz—only further troubles the association apparently invoked in McCullers's title between Agrarian "ballets" and her work.

With their portrayals of music as part of the plot in "A Good Man Is Hard to Find" and *The Ballad of the Sad Café*, McCullers and O'Connor invite obvious comparisons between the songs within their stories and the songs that, by virtue of their titles, are their stories. This song-within-a-song frame calls attention to the deeply replicative structure of these short works: McCullers's signaled by its repeated verselike line, emerging at the beginning and then at the end of the story, "You might as well go down to the Forks Falls highway and listen to the chain gang" (4, 70); O'Connor's by an image of the parrot printed on a shirt, for instance, that repeats the characters' general tendency to repeat. The shortness of their works as well allows for tight formal unity. The technical skill for which these authors were lauded qualified each as exemplars of the high literary during the 1950s: I have mentioned that both were anthologized as models of the craft in the New Critical text-book *Understanding Fiction* by Brooks and Warren. The short form and the repetition clearly enabled both O'Connor and McCullers more efficiently to achieve New Critical technical perfection—allowed these authors more easily to make of each work a machine without "bugs," as Wimsatt and Beardsley called it, and to create an expression of what they identified as poetry's meaning "handled all at once."[20] In this sense both the repetition and the shortness of these works should be taken as expressions of New Critical influence emerging in form. But in that very achievement, these women also make of their stories little sound machines, casting their paper as technological media that, along with transistor radios and phonographs, broadcast disembodied voices from Georgia to faraway geographical regions beyond. By designating in their titles an affinity between these internally repeating narratives and vernacular song in the age of rock and roll, McCullers and O'Connor blend literary craft and technical perfection.[21]

The New Critical distinction between art and information thus unravels in these highly crafted stories by women, as ballads and electronic communication converge in the figure of the mother. As for rock and rollers, so for the writers I am examining in *Novel Sounds*: literature cannot be teased apart from technology, not even as music. O'Connor and McCullers explore this problem in relation to the difference gender makes in the New Critical assumption that poetry emerges from bodies that remain intact, even as they seem compromised by sound technology. The figure of the balladeer embeds a conception of femininity, these women suggest, and, noting that appeals to ballads as natural involve assumptions about gender, both O'Connor and McCullers offer portrayals of femininity as technical to trouble the cultural distinctions to which those appeals gave rise. In their story worlds it emerges that the fiddle has always been a machine—was always a technical instrument, one more like the radio than Agrarians would have liked. And Barthes comes under revision in light of these discoveries. For when he noted the "phallic stature" of oral singing, he also lamented its disappearance "under the pressure of the mass long-playing record."[22] We might surmise that if sound media disrupts the phallic cast of the "thrill" in live music, perhaps finding as we do in these stories a link between mothers and balladeers might be understood as a celebration of that disruption—one that is called forth by rock's gleeful affirmations of electricity. In any case, these images of even maternal production as technological craft undo the opposition between literature and rock that was founded on the image of the balladeer, feminizing as it does away with a reliable origin in bodies—an origin rock may have seemed to disrupt.

4.1 Russell Lee, "Negro child playing phonograph in cabin home" (January 1939). Transylvania Project, Louisiana.

Source: Courtesy of Library of Congress, Prints and Photographs Division, FSA/OWI Collection [LC-USF34-031941-D (b&w film nitrate neg)].

4

THE LEAD BELLY THING

William Styron's Records

Now, if I can just work up enough courage to learn how to play a guitar, I might turn professional. There's a wonderful old guitar up here, made in 1880, a sort of Stradivarius among guitars, and I'll have only myself to blame if I don't learn how to use the thing. Incidentally, have you heard Leadbelly [sic]? I heard an album the other day of his, and went overboard for him. He's the Louisiana negro convict who died just recently. If you can get a couple of records of his—especially "Midnight Special" (shine your ever-lovin' light on me) and "Irene, Good Night," I think you'll see what I mean.

—WILLIAM STYRON TO WILLIAM BLACKBURN (JANUARY 13, 1949)

Ultimately the phonograph records are not artworks but the black seals on the missives that are rushing towards us from all sides in the traffic with technology; missives whose formulations capture the sounds of creation, the first and last sounds, judgment upon life and message about that which may come thereafter.

–THEODOR ADORNO, "THE FORM OF THE PHONOGRAPH RECORD" (1934)

William Styron titles his 1960 novel *Set This House on Fire* after a line from one of John Donne's epigraphs.[1] Although he frames his narrative with the words of Cleanth Brooks's poet of choice, Styron ends *Set This House on Fire* with an image that readers of Jonathan Lethem's *Fortress of Solitude* (2003) will perhaps recognize as belonging to a later phase of the American novel. In the final pages of *Set This House on Fire*, the white Lead Belly fan Cass grabs a record out of his crate, puts it on his turntable, and drops a record needle on it:

> In the corner there was an old wooden crate, and in it were a dozen phonograph records, their cardboard jackets frayed and smudged against the ravages of his own hands. He pulled one out. There was no need to look at the label; he knew each by its own faded cover, its own peculiar shadow of greasy-fingered stain and grime. He put the record on the battered phonograph, tested the needle with his thumb, set the record spinning along its course, slightly electric and wobbling. Then, as the needle sputtered and hissed in the first worn gray grooves, he went over to the armchair and sat down.[2]

The presence of this record collector in a Southern novel written while Bob Dylan was learning Lead Belly songs creates a crucial precedent in midcentury Southern fiction for a literary invention that would be more readily legible in the early twenty-first century as the rock nerd. Styron creates his proto-rock-nerd at the end of the decade in which "Rocket 88" sent rock and roll out from Memphis into the world—at a moment when many of rock's most influential pioneers were flaming out. "Elvis in the Army, Buddy Holly dead, Little Richard in the ministry, Jerry Lee Lewis in disgrace and Chuck Berry in jail." So Peter Guralnick puts the situation at the end of the 1950s.[3] As for Lethem's Dylan Ebdus at the moment of rock's death, so for Cass, hatched a half-century earlier at this crucial end of rock's first chapter: for each protagonist, psychological interiority is glossed by the records in his collection, and in each case neurosis is portrayed as intertwined with the electric "hiss" of a record needle. The book collector "lives in" his books, so argued Walter Benjamin in 1931. The rock nerd, we will follow him in observing, lives in his records.[4]

Set This House on Fire is filled with images of Cass's records and their electric sounds, and Styron constellates these around his nerd's psychic development. Styron indeed creates an essential link between Cass's psychological state—*Set This House on Fire* is principally a therapeutic novel—and the "cardboard jackets frayed and smudged," the "battered phonograph," Cass's "thumb" on the "needle," the "sputter" and "hiss," and the "worn, grey grooves" of the 78. As we shall see, these technological images map rock and roll onto Cass's emotional life, compressing the cultural evolution in popular music into the development of a single psyche. Cass "lives in" his "battered phonographs" in the sense that the data they store comprise formative moments in Cass's personal history. The presence of these records also indicates that by 1960 instruments of sound technology have taken on a different meaning in Southern fiction. Rather than electronic hums or radio intruding as referents into images of oral music, sputters and hisses have become available to Southern authors as literary vehicles—as fodder, indeed, for pleasurable literary images.

Returning to Flannery O'Connor's 1953 "A Good Man Is Hard to Find," I note again that whereas the inclusion of the blues song likens her story to rock, her depiction of an actual rock song almost ten years later performs a different task. With Elvis in the military and Chuck Berry in jail, that is, her character Rufus Johnson's performance of "Shake, Rattle, and Roll" in the 1962 "The Lame Shall Enter First" amounts to an objectification of rock rather than a version of its ideological processes —a reification, it could be called, rock as a fait accompli. As we shall see, *Set This House on Fire* resembles "A Good Man Is Hard to Find" in that it too repeats rock's mixtures, bringing Lead Belly's "A Midnight Special" into its form. But in its presentation of the sputter and hiss as accepted features of its story world, Styron's 1960 novel also registers something of the sense that rock's moment has come—something of the objectification we find in Rufus's "rock, rattle, and roll." At the end of

rock's first chapter, that is, even as Styron continues to repeat its processes, records and their machines have gone from influencing figures
of Southern oral forms to becoming themselves an aesthetic resource
for Southern fiction.

Skip forward to 2012, again to rock's death, when Michael Chabon's
Telegraph Avenue made its appearance on the contemporary literary
scene with an album cover for a book jacket. As I have noted elsewhere,
Telegraph Avenue's cover comes complete with a perfectly scaled record
label, offset to appear glued as on a vinyl LP, listing its chapters as if they
were recorded tracks.[5] Along with his rock nerd, Styron's 78s should be
understood as inaugurating the cultural melding of rock and the novel
that Chabon's cover crystallizes half a century later. As strains of the
ballad form and other vernacular music merged into rock during the
1950s, the New Critics' conception of the balladeer was displaced as
overtly technological devices became their principal modes of transmission. It was this shift that the appearance of records and phonographs
in Styron marks, and that culminates in Chabon's 2012 novel, a literary
creation packaged as itself as a record—described by Theodor Adorno
in my second epigraph as a "seal" on technology's "missives."[6]

We have seen that New Critics produce an idea of Lead Belly's singing
mouth as grounding the poetic image—that the inclusion of "Frankie
and Johnny" in *Understanding Poetry* construes poetry as connected to
corporeal wholeness. But by 1966, Elvis Presley had recorded "Frankie
and Johnny" for an album to be released along with his cheesy film
version of *Frankie and Johnny.*[7] Over the 1950s, the balladeer that for
New Critics defined the literary was absorbed into records—entirely
taken into the technological ethos of rock and roll as the lines between
literature and communication became ever more blurred. *Novel Sounds*
has sought to show that Southern novelists in the 1950s tracked this
change, joining Southern practitioners of rock in creating an explicitly
mechanical aesthetic. By the time Elvis's version of "Frankie and Johnny"
delivered Lead Belly in the form of vinyl, I want to suggest, Styron had
incorporated the cultural transactions leading to that development into
portrayals of the human, that central "mirage," as Fredric Jameson once
called it, of the novel.[8]

In the traces of the hand's repeated touching in this passage in *Set This House on Fire*, in the "greasy-fingered stain," the "grime," and the "smudged" covers, we can detect an expression of desire for that which Warren and Brooks earlier reviled: for sound technology's instruments in particular. Styron too raises questions about the divisions upon which we have founded our idea of the literary. Does Styron's depiction of desire for these records register a moment when literature is finally at ease with—even in love with—the tools against which it had been defined?[9] In answer to this question, we note first that these images incorporate the body, suggesting perhaps a nostalgia for the mouth and thus a melancholic alignment with New Critical ideals. The "smudge" and "grease" can be taken as residue of the hand, for example, transferred onto the record cover by the finger. The "hiss" and "sputter" might also be said to recall the thumb as it tests the needle, such that clearly electronic noise becomes an audible "smudge," a signal that the body's sound remains in the record.

We might read the thumb testing the needle as Styron's figure for the singing mouth of the balladeer: the singer's body but displaced onto the collector's—the mouth figured as the information-gathering hand, the hand that collects and "tests," a quasi-tool whose work is a quasi-singing. This weird version of the balladeer's mouth aligns *Set This House on Fire* with the logic advanced in *Understanding Poetry*, in which, as we have seen, sound technology substitutes for the experience of hearing the singing body. In Styron's novel, it seems, records do not just substitute for the voice; they bear its bodily marks. And here we find an affinity in Styron's novel for the work of Sigmund Freud—in particular, for Freud's conception of the fetish. In psychoanalytic terms, these "smudges" would be read as metonymic signs of a disavowal—in Freud, a disavowal of the absent penis; here, of an absented live voice in performance.[10] Cass's attachment to records indeed seems straightforwardly fetishistic. And insofar as Styron presents Cass as "living in" his records in Benjamin's sense, he appears to construe collecting as a psychoanalytic symptom.

As symptoms, the images of sound technology in *Set This House on Fire* emerge as dialectical markers of bodily subjectivity. On this reading, their extrasensory essence paradoxically confirms the sensory subject

Watt—and Fredric Jameson after him—identified as the novel's central contribution. As objects of desire, that is, these images of sound media are inextricable from the fetishistic psyche to which Cass's sensory body has given rise. This would confirm the worry Jameson articulated in *The Political Unconscious*, that the novel advances bourgeois ideology by producing the "mirage" of "the centered subject" (153). On this reading, desire for technology in *Set This House on Fire* would be understood as desire nonetheless—as leading right back to the body.[11] Returning to the images under examination, however, we find that the fetishized records perform another function as well. In particular, they indicate the possibility of halted symbolic value—an absence of symbolic meaning that corresponds with the transparent aesthetic the other authors in *Novel Sounds* create.[12] *Set This House on Fire* depicts this refusal of literary depth as resulting from an evacuation of the human from the scene of musical performance. Records and other images of sound technology are the uninterpretable things against which Cass attempts to cure himself. As fetishes, records appear to affirm the body. But as things, they displace it, disrupting the mirage of subjectivity.[13] Theodor Adorno suggests that this impenetrable quality is endemic to records, arguing in his 1934 "The Form of the Phonograph" that the record as a form becomes meaningful only "once one forgoes considering it as an art object and explores the contours of its thingness" (58). The acceptance during the 1960s of records as literary figures signals an acceptance of "thingness" in Southern fiction.[14]

About midway through *Set This House on Fire*, we find Cass listening to Lead Belly's "The Midnight Special." This scene of hearing a recorded voice does not take place in the present of the narrative but is presented instead as an event Cass recalls during his psychoanalytic confession. The novel's first-person narrator, Peter Leverett, acts as the analyst figure of *Set This House on Fire*, and Cass tells him that he admired his former "noodle specialist," Slotkin, who ran the "psycho ward" (129) at the naval hospital. Cass had been committed to this hospital after the war, as he explains to Peter: "I was sick as a dog inside my soul, and for the life of me I couldn't figure out where that sickness came from" (55). Cass's conversation with Peter is entirely made up of the search in his psyche for the "elusive fact" of "raging importance" (432) that might cure this "sickness," a misery that still plagues him in the narrative present. As part of this therapeutic discourse, Cass describes a "record player I'd picked up at the Flea Market," recalling for Peter that the phonograph "played loud as hell":

> It was a scratchy hoarse monster but I had a few records: *The Magic Flute* and *Don Giovanni* and some early Haydn and Christian Bach and the *St. Matthew Passion* and a Palestrina mass and—oh yes, I had an ancient Leadbelly [sic] album with about every record held together by Scotch tape. Old Leadbelly. Every time I heard "The Midnight Special" I got right back to Carolina.
>
> (255)

Here, in the narrative present, Styron portrays Cass recounting for Peter a past event in Italy in which an "ancient" Lead Belly record "got" him "right back to Carolina."[15] In the memory he relays in the present, the loud-as-hell voice coming from the "scratchy hoarse monster" transports Cass to his origin in North Carolina. And Cass's present speech too—his own voice talking to Peter—is a conduit "back." But while Cass's voice in the present therapeutic discourse "gets" him back just as the Lead Belly record does, it is not to his childhood North Carolina but to Sambuco, the town in Italy where he met Peter, to the time and place in which he heard "The Midnight Special" and from there "got right back to Carolina." Here as elsewhere in the novel, Styron collapses Italy and North Carolina, rendering both crucial origins in Cass's psychoanalytic searching.

Lead Belly's voice emerges here amid the "scratchy" electric sounds of a "loud" record player, and the inclusion of sound technology in this scene of listening too suggests that the mouth has disappeared, no longer conforms to the image of the balladeer presented in *Understanding Poetry*. But there is a mouth in the scene: not Lead Belly's but Cass's, the mouth invoked by his confessional analytic speech. In the memory, Cass goes "right back"; Lead Belly's electrified voice transports Cass from his present place and time immediately. By contrast, the long sections of Cass's talking in the narrative present move the story back to Sambuco at an excruciatingly slow pace. Styron's depiction of Cass's speaking voice creates a sense of near-stagnation in the narrative present, the feeling that readers of *Set This House on Fire* are stuck along with Cass in the sludge of his repeating, alcohol-impaired psyche. This slowness is achieved in part by all the dialogue but also by the novel's retrospective structure: Styron portrays almost everything that happens in *Set This House on Fire* as a memory by disclosing the story's "awesome and shocking" main events at the beginning of the novel. "Lest . . . I be accused at the outset of sounding too portentous," Peter says in the opening pages, "I will say that these events were a murder and a rape" (4). Having already revealed the climax at the outset, the narrator can only go back over what has already occurred—can only repeat what happened during the "recent summer" that comprises the novel, a moment before the time of the novel even begins. So, from the opening of *Set This House on Fire* up until the moment the presumed rapist is found dead (241), Peter narrates his own time in Sambuco. Then, at the end of Peter's description of this segment of time, the novel takes readers back to the moment narrated at the beginning of the novel one more time: for the next 160 pages Cass goes over the same period of time in Sambuco once again (241–402). Just after the novel was published, Louis D. Rubin identified this as *Set This House on Fire*'s "grievous structural flaw." But the novel's repetitive structure, I want to suggest, helps Styron achieve the slow pace of the oral confession.[16]

Lead Belly's electrified voice thus contrasts Cass's oral one. The immediate return to the South the record enables is juxtaposed with the slowness of Cass's return to Sambuco in the novel's psychoanalytic speech. The depiction of therapeutic talk in *Set This House on Fire* performs a function that resembles the ballad in *Understanding Poetry*: it serves as an oral remedy for sound technology's troubling reproductions—it is a reference to the human body, the mouth, that grounds the literary in bodily "experience." Cass's analytic conversation with Peter takes him "back" just as the Lead Belly record does, but slowly, according to a narrative time frame that approximates the temporal pace of oral speech and allows for a corresponding interpretive depth. The musicologist Mark

Katz creates the term "phonographic effect" to designate "responses to differences between live and recorded music"; as he points out, records make music "unstuck in time," such that the "dead can speak to the living." Acknowledging that all media "can store 'phantasms of the living' for playback after bodily death," John Durham Peters argues that the phonograph made a special contribution to media's capacity to create a ghostly experience. In his words, the phonograph "changed the meaning of sound, music and the voice" by producing the conditions in which music "no longer required a live performer; sound could be produced without bodily labor."[17] These formulations of the phonograph help us see the Lead Belly performance in *Set This House on Fire* as precisely "unstuck in time." The "form of the phonograph" indeed allows Cass to experience Lead Belly's song as paradoxically both immediate—it takes him "right back"—and "ancient." By contrast, the slow pace of the narrative depicted as spoken sticks novelistic events in time so thoroughly that the plot barely moves forward. Cass's analytic voice seems to compensate for Lead Belly's recorded one, and in rendering the narrative of *Set This House on Fire* therapeutic, Styron appears to cast his novel as itself a species of oral discourse. We have seen that Brooks and Warren portray the authenticating mouth as the balladeer's in the era of race records. In the rock era, it seems, Styron gives it to the novel.

But novels are not oral at all. Or, at least, their life in and as paper stands as a central preoccupation for Southern authors at the birth of rock. Three years before the publication of *Set This House on Fire*, as I have noted, Ian Watt expressed a similar view when he defined novels as essentially "connected with the medium of print," arguing that the novel is distinguished from other literary forms precisely in that it was never oral.[18] The apparent alignment between the novel and Cass's mouth is belied as well by the similarity Styron creates between Cass's voice and Lead Belly's, a link that emerges in Cass's description of his own therapeutic speech as a version of "singing the blues" (129). Here, we can identify an eruption of the blackface that Black Arts leaders argued Styron's later *The Confessions of Nat Turner* (1967) more clearly enacts, the whitening that afflicted rock and roll as it turned into what was called, after the release of Bob Dylan's "Like a Rolling Stone," New

Rock.[19] In recounting his experience of listening to Lead Belly, Cass also creates the suggestion of a parallel between the two moments and two places to which he gets back: North Carolina, to which "The Midnight Special" gets him "right back"; and Sambuco, to which his own analytic discourse takes him. There is a contrast, to be sure, between these two instances of return through the voice. But Styron creates a doubling in the same images, so that even as the "scratchy hoarse monster" making hisses and sputters contrasts Cass speaking to his "analyst" Peter, the record player also emerges as a version of Cass's body.

In describing his narrative as "singing the blues," moreover, Cass takes Lead Belly's voice as his own, and Styron casts this incorporation of black voice into white as that which defines him as a Southerner—that which can take him "right back to Carolina." In collapsing the voice that emerges from his white body with Lead Belly's from the "hoarse monster," the narrator also turns the analysand's memories into black sounds emitted from a sound machine. And as the white voice becomes black, "the South" becomes entirely virtual, an "immersive" experience of the South in Cass's mind. In this process, the African American voice from the South disappears, becomes a buried truth in the unconscious of a self-centered white man. These figural collapses in the novel allegorize what was audible in the American soundscape as Styron was writing—Lead Belly's voice in Cass's the fictional expression of Crudup's in Elvis's, a novelistic tracking of Nashville's transformation to "Music City, U.S.A."

Describing the phonograph as "hoarse" clearly integrates vocal sound into scratchy electric sputters, and again we observe the body's smudge coming into Cass's experience of sound technology, the phonograph along with the records becoming his fetish. But the transformation of these sound media into signs of Cass's body works the other way around as well. Just as Cass's desire infuses his records with human life (as Freud describes the fetish) electricity comes into the apparently oral speech of the analysand too, so that the self in analysis seems to have derived from a thing. Cass as Styron's novelistic character, that is, resembles the images Styron gives Cass's psyche but in an inverse form. In Cass's fetishizing unconscious, sound technology becomes bodily. But as body blends into machine, Cass is shown to have already incorporated what

Adorno calls the phonograph's "thingness." We will recall here that the narrative returns twice to the events already disclosed at the outset of the novel, repetitively circling around the murder and rape—absent because they transpired before the novel opens. This repetition, we have seen, creates a narrative slowness that mimics the analytic speaking. In a setting containing so many records, however, Cass's therapeutic narrative repetition seems as much technical glitch as symptom—as much skipping record, we might say, as unconscious snare. That which indicates the novel's oral dimension, the simulation of the temporal pace of a speaking voice, is paradoxically achieved in likening the narrative to a scratched record. As with Cass's hand on the needle, the throat in the phonograph construes Cass as interiorizing sound technology by making it an object of his desire. But like McCullers's balladeers, whose voices appear in the end as broadcast "voices in the void," Styron's image of the analysand emerges in *Set This House on Fire* as inextricable from the electronic singing coming out of his phonograph. The body invoked in the fetishizing of records emerges as itself a technological instrument enabling reproduced sounds on shellac.

When Cass unravels a series of dreams involving racial guilt, the Freudian method seems at first confirmed. He and Peter engage in typical psychoanalytic dream analysis, employing *The Interpretation of Dreams* in all its deep symbolic analytics. But as Cass makes his way through this analytic interpretation, the "elusive fact"—in analytic terms, the formative event—disappears. Slotkin "kept wanting to dig" into "my being an orphan," Cass tells Peter, explaining that he knew his analyst "was barking up the wrong tree" (363). And as things turn out, Cass is right: in the world of *Set This House on Fire*, introspection does not follow the Freudian model. Recall that it is to Sambuco and not North Carolina that Cass "gets back" in his analytic discourse; to remember his home Cass must apparently listen again to "The Midnight Special." Cass is delivered to his geographical origin in the South, that is, not by slow interpretation but by the reproduced sound of a human voice on a 78. In the setting Styron gives us here, unearthing the repressed causes of present symptoms is reformulated in terms of the literature-rock nexus that had been developing since Lead Belly went to the MLA—from the era, that is, in which microphones replaced acoustic horns. "Getting back" to the "elusive fact" of "raging importance" is here presented as simulation, a virtual effect of what is actually an unyielding phonographic thing.

So, Cass explains to Peter that the dreams can be interpreted to refer back to "something wretched and horrible I had done when I was about fifteen years old—something really dreadful" (370). Along with Lonnie, a white "assistant manager of a Western Auto store" where Cass was employed as a teen, Cass helps vandalize an impoverished African American man's cabin to "redeem a defaulted radio from a Negro farmer" (373). Cass recalls the "stench" in the cabin, a smell of "dirt and sweat and rancid fat cooked up a multitude of times and of too many human bodies in one place, of bathless crotch and armpit" (375). Here, we find an image of bodily surplus—the smell of "too many bodies in one space." The "too many bodies in one space" marks the psychoanalytic search for the origins of neuroses, glosses the interpretive therapy as a hope for just this, bodily surplus. With the assertion of so many black bodies in particular, bodies in a past discovered by listening a recording of "The Midnight Special," we can identify quite clearly the racial dimension of the balladeer's mouth. At the same time, the hyperbole here, the "too many," is asserted in a portrayal of absence: in fact, there are no black bodies in the cabin when Lonnie and Cass arrive. I want to suggest that the suggestion of excess in smell—of "bathless crotch and armpit"—refers to a void at the interpretive origin of sound: in particular, the voided voice of Lead Belly in the phonograph, that paradigmatic voice bringing the body into the New Critics' literary balladeer. The scene in the "Negro farmer's" cabin does not so much provide an interpretive referent for Cass's present symptomatic repetitions as create a fantasy of bodies to remedy the virtual South created by his experience of the 78. And the fantasy of bodies comes along with the simulation of referential stability—it is only because they can be interpreted from Cass's oral analytic speech that these bodies exist.

But since Styron portrays the bodies as not actually present, the intense racial violence in the scene occurs in a realm that resembles the virtual. Lonnie unleashes his wrath not on black bodies, that is, but on the objects that "store 'phantasms of the living' for playback after bodily death" (142), to return to John Durham Peters's formulation. So, Lonnie and Cass find a "pathetic radio—white, plastic, already cracked, not much larger than a box of salt or rice" (375), and a photograph of the family who live in this cabin. Cass remembers that the photograph conveyed a "sweetly gentle, calm-visaged mood of solidarity and pride and love." As Peter explains:

> He remembered too, how this dissolved—or splintered, rather, right before his eyes—as Lonnie (spying the crack on the radio's plastic side he let out a wounded yell which broke in on Cass's reverie like the sound of broken glass) in a frantic swing of rage and frustration and unstoppered resentment thrust his hand violently forward, sweeping with his arm every jar and bottle and can of beans off the shelf above the stove, the momentum carrying him on so that in a sort of final flick or encore of wrath he lighted upon the photograph and sent it spinning across the room, where it tore apart—frame, glass, and all—into two raggedly separated pieces. "Shit!" Cass heard him cry, in a voice pitched near hysteria.
>
> (376)

As Cass reaches to pick up the picture, Peter explains, he is "fetched up short by Lonnie's voice again: 'Well, we'll see about who breaks what!'" (376). The "wounded yell," the "voice pitched near hysteria" that "fetches" Cass "up short": Styron portrays Lonnie's racial violence in an image of vocal potency, and here the hyperbole of "too many human bodies" emerges as indeed a phallic voice. This exaggerated bodily voice is set against the radio and the photograph, images of mediation that draw attention to the absence of bodies in the cabin. The "splintering" photograph frame that begins as a "dissolving" and effaces the "solidarity and pride and love" "right before" Cass's "eyes" clarifies that we are meant to understand Lonnie's violent act as nothing more than a media operation, an impotent assertion of white dominance where the distinguishing features of Southern identity are up for grabs. And although the dominating voice is emitted from a violent white body—

though it is potent enough to "fetch" Cass "up short"—the white voice too is "wounded" and "hysterical," and so its display of racial superiority is undercut in the "dissolving" atmosphere of mediation. The bodily kernel at the origin of the dream turns out to be the sound of a voice, and as sound, the "elusive fact" is immaterial, virtual, nothing. Aurality and virtuality "have much in common," argues the media theorist Frances Dyson: "being neither visible nor tangible, sound is never quite an object, never a full guarantor of knowledge."[20] And so interpretation fails. The oral discourse of the analysand founders at the impenetrable surface of the phonograph as thing.

Early in the novel as well Styron produces bodily potency in the human voice, in an image of the father. The loathsome wealthy heir Mason Flagg is accused of raping a young girl while he is away at prep school with Peter, and the girl's father travels to Mason's home to take his revenge while Peter is there on a visit. Peter explains that he and Mason overhear the man talking to Mason's mother in a "countrified voice, guttural, faintly Negroid—almost Elizabethan" (89). Mason's father sends this man away, as Peter puts it, in "a display of sheer annihilating authority, of will" (91):

> The voice sounded again: Hold! It was Mr. Flagg. Barefooted and in pajamas he emerged from a corridor—it seemed miles away across the hall—and padded noiselessly toward us. Was it the baritone parade-ground voice which alone was so commanding? Or indeed some pure presence, some compelling quality of power and authority which transmitted itself almost instantly to everyone in the place and caused each to stop, transfixed petrified in separate attitudes of anguish and wrath and flight? Whatever the case, as he spoke and came across those infinite distances toward us it was as if by sudden legerdemain we had all been frozen like statues in our tracks.
>
> (91)

The "annihilating authority" of this father's voice is "pure presence," another hyperbolic image of phallic bodily surplus in the defense of an act of male violence. At the same time, however, Mr. Flagg's ability to "transmit" this "authority" "almost instantly," as well as the suggestion that the voice travels "miles" and "infinite distances," likens this oral experience of the paternal voice to radio broadcast. Mason's father thus seems an older version of Cass, oral, yet also defined in terms of the sound technology from which the "pure presence" of his voice is meant to distinguish him. As with the scene of vandalizing, here again a potent white voice is linked to a racialized violence: Mr. Flagg justifies Mason's rape by refusing the rebuke of the girl's father, a man with a "faintly Negroid" voice. But in this scene too white dominance is undercut by a virtual milieu in which "Negroid" voices merge into "Elizabethan" ones, undoing the very basis of the racial distinction Donald Davidson found codified in the authenticating mouths of folk balladeers. Cass is an orphan, and the story situates Mason's father as also Cass's father, nuancing Cass's sense that Slotkin had been "barking up the wrong tree." The therapeutic narrative traces Cass to a father, that is, just not to his own. Or rather, the father at the origin is Cass's, but he only belongs to Cass because he belongs to everyone. He is a broadcast voice, that is, a no one. And as virtual father, it seems, the radio voice at the origin makes orphans of all rock's Southern white boys.[21]

Lonnie's pronouncement about "breaking" things—"we'll see about who breaks what!"—raises the question of how to understand the cracked radio in *Set This House on Fire* as heir to the radio Lytle suggested we "throw out" in 1930. I want to suggest that Styron positions two broken forms of media in this space to clarify that by 1960 "taking down the fiddle from the wall" does not allow for throwing out the radio. Lytle's clarion call had become entirely futile. It was just two years after the publication of *Set This House on Fire*, we will recall here, that the new edition of *I'll Take My Stand* would go to press, and it was in the introduction to that edition that Rubin observed, "Andrew Lytle's suggestion . . . has not been followed; instead the radio has been replaced by the television set." The problem for Lytle was that human expression was cheapened by sound media. But by the early 1960s, as this scene in *Set This House on Fire* makes clear, the absence of media was not understood as returning humanity to the world via acoustic fiddle or balladeer's voice. The voice was now feminized as "hysterical" and erratic, even when emitted from the father. In *Set This House on Fire* throwing out the radio is shown to illuminate the music's status as thing, bringing to light the "historical ambiguity," as Bill Brown has described it, between persons and things created by slavery.[22] The radio Lonnie seeks to repossess "brought witchery in the night," as Peter puts it, "and tinny bright sounds of singing and laughter" (375). But its crack removes this magic, reduces the radio's status to that of the other things Lonnie destroys in the cabin. Breaking the radio is like throwing it out, as Lytle would have us do. But in this world throwing out the radio only transforms it from an instrument of technological "witchery" into a useless hunk of plastic.

The other medium in the scene, the photograph, similarly loses its "witchery" as it breaks apart. But the bodies of the African American family do not suddenly reappear when these media, understood as substitutes for them, break. Rather, in their absence the cabin becomes filled with even more "raggedly" and "separated" things. Cass and Lonnie are fictional versions of John Lomax entering the prison—like Lomax, seeking something of themselves in a black space resembling Angola's. Styron's narrative retroactively glosses Lomax's discovery as a hope to find bodily surplus in the person of Huddy Ledbetter during an earlier moment of anxiety about white dominance.[23] This "Negro cabin" is where white boys go in search of a radio, and it allegorizes entry into the spaces Lomax construed as authentic spaces of musical discovery. But here, rather than oral music, white collectors find a dizzying number of things in black spaces: "china cups and plates and saucers"; "gimcrack mementos as had brought to this place color and loveliness—china dolls, a plaster bulldog brightly enameled, picture postcards . . . a pennant . . . which read University of Virginia" (376–77). Along with these, the paradigmatic "thing" for which they have come, the "pathetic radio," appears to define them all, and in the end it is as if these objects are all little broken radios—all useless, enduring plastic things littering the bodiless cabin. Without the radio, Styron suggests, we find neither fiddle nor voice but things, the disappointing alternative, ultimately, to what Styron portrayed—even as civil rights were approaching codification—as "too many" black bodies.

In Peter's description of driving to Sambuco early on in the novel, he begins to sing as he experiences "a rowdy euphoria and a sudden love for the Italian night":

> for the remarkable stars above, for the towns silhouetted on the hill-tops, for the wind—smelling of countryside, of earth, of manure and vegetation—which cooled me off and set the sleeves of my garments, piled up behind me, to chattering like pennants. I had the top down; I drove fast, because the highway was straight and empty, and I bawled out songs on the wind.
>
> (25)

Peter's euphoria soon flips, and his delight driving through the hilltops and singing "on the wind" becomes an experience of "infinite dark-ness." Peter explains that his "expansive mood began to fade" (26), and the smells "of earth, of manure" give way to an experience that seems extraterrestrial, as if this trip abroad has meant leaving the earth, leaving humanity, entirely. "For miles at a stretch," he explains, "I could see nothing at all on either side of me—no homes, no humans, no growing things" (26). As Peter begins "to feel strictly alone," he stops singing and turns on the radio:

> Then abruptly I was in cliff country, ascending the flanks of gaunt, wounded hills where nothing grew and no one lived, a wilderness of dried-up riverbeds and parched ravines, the hangout of thieves. I turned on the radio, and found only chill comfort: a woman's voice announcing "*Un po' di allegria negli Spike Jones*"; then off in Monte Carlo a faint, windy snatch of Beethoven, which soon dimmed away, becoming silent altogether. The American Army station in Germany was signing off in a hubbub of noise, with a program called the Hillbilly Gasthaus. There was something in this liaison of tongues and in the harmony of guitars and banjoes and fiddles, moaning among these forsaken hills, which gripped me with anxiety.
>
> (26)

The Italian mountainside is transformed into the Southern hills by these "banjoes and fiddles," but the absence of "humans" and "growing things" following upon Peter's singing suggests that to return to the South via reproduced music is not to return at all. For Donald Davidson, recall, cultural decline could be indexed in the "shop-girl" who listens to "a jazz record while she rouges her lips."[24] For Davidson, a "shop girl" might be restored to health by getting rid of her record player and listening to ballads preserved in "mountain fastness." Styron brings Davidson's valorization of firsthand encounters with Southern ballads as cure forward into rock's moment, like Davidson portraying in the oral ballad a remedy rooted in the Southern landscape. But here, where mountain fastness has dissolved into a static-filtered "liaison of tongues," the "harmony of guitars and banjoes and fiddles" takes Peter nowhere: singing stops as he traverses a dark space with no "homes," no humans, nothing.

Lead Belly's powerful influence in rock and roll could not be more legible. There is Dylan's line, as we have seen, "Here's to Cisco an' Sonny and Lead Belly too," from one of the first songs he ever wrote, and Dylan also played harmonica on Harry Belafonte's 1961 version of Lead Belly's "The Midnight Special"—Dylan's first professional recording session.[25] On a live recording made at Threadgill's Bar and Grill in Austin, Texas, in 1962, Janis Joplin can be heard belting out "CC Rider" and "Careless Lover," both apparently learned from versions by Lead Belly.[26] On *Led Zeppelin III*, Robert Plant screams his way through "Gallows Pole," Led Zeppelin's 1970 version of Lead Belly's 1939 "The Gallis Pole," and Nirvana's live performance of Lead Belly's 1933 "Where Did You Sleep Last Night" for their release *MTV Unplugged* (1994) features a cursing Kurt Cobain introducing the song by complaining that he cannot afford to buy a guitar once owned by Lead Belly, whom he describes as his "favorite performer."[27]

Novel Sounds has sought to explain why Lead Belly is to be found in literary domains as well, from the 1934 MLA to *Set This House on Fire* and beyond. I end this chapter by returning to the shellacked things that qualify Cass as an early rock nerd. In the scene with which I began, Cass is listening to Wolfgang Amadeus Mozart and not, as Lethem's Dylan Ebdus will be, to Syl Johnson, or the Meat Puppets, or Lucinda Williams. Cass's album collection does include the Lead Belly record along with his recordings of classical music by Mozart, Bach, and Haydn. But how does this scene in 1960, in which Cass's hand caresses the cover of a classical record, preview the one in 2003 in which Dylan Ebdus's angry girlfriend tosses his classics of soul, blues, rock, and alternative country, in CD format, onto the floor? My first epigraph shows that Styron was a Lead Belly fan early on, and indeed he saw fit to recommend Lead Belly to his writing mentor at Duke University, William Blackburn. In 1999, just four years before Lethem published *The Fortress of Solitude*, Styron explained in an interview with the *Paris Review* that he had been "in love with hillbilly music" as a child and that this credential of his literary stature extended even into the 1990s. "In the proper mood," he explained, "I have been as deeply moved by a ballad sung by Emmylou Harris as by the *Missa Solemnis*."[28] Styron's view, apparently unchanged over fifty years, draws *Understanding Poetry* forward into Lethem's moment, like the 1938 volume authenticating literary status by tying it to vernacular music. When Styron made these comments, Emmylou Harris's most recent solo album was the 1995 *Wrecking Ball*, an album that featured Lucinda Williams, one of the artists whose CD ends up on Dylan Ebdus's floor in Lethem's 2003 novel.[29] Cass's crate includes classical music along with his Lead Belly record for the same reason Styron titles a novel featuring Lead Belly after a line from John Donne: because it makes vivid the company high-cultural masters keep. *Set This House on Fire* is thus in the end more like "A Good Man Is Hard to Find" than like "The Lame Shall Enter First." Even in spite of the novel's evolved embrace of sound technology, *Set This House on Fire* does not, as the later O'Connor story did, reify rock. Styron's incorporation of "The Midnight Special" repeats that of the white rockers like Led Zeppelin, who bring Lead Belly's canonizing imprimatur into what, it must be acknowledged, are high-cultural endeavors after all.

c.1 Bob Dylan in book store, Greenwich Village, 1964.

Source: Courtesy of Douglas R. Gilbert.

CODA

NOBEL SOUNDS

Bob Dylan's Novel Prize

t was hardly news when *Billboard* named Bob Dylan's 1965 "Like a Rolling Stone" the greatest rock and roll song of all time. But when the bard of rock also walked away with the Nobel Prize in Literature, people tuned in.[1] That he who conceived the cut earning this musical distinction would in 2016 win the most prestigious literary prize in the world repeats in the first decades of the twenty-first century the kinship *Novel Sounds* traces. A surprising reciprocity between the musical form best known for its irreverence and serious literature turns out to have commenced at the birth of rock, and I have sought to tell the story of how they were intertwined. I want to end *Novel Sounds* by filling in some gaps between rock's birth and its death, in particular attending to a few key texts published in the 1970s. These works help us understand how Dylan's win, which the *New Yorker* editor David Remnick described as an "astonishing and unambiguously wonderful thing," brings Lytle's call in 1930 to take down the fiddle from the wall into the contemporary moment.[2]

There are other notable instances of rock's cultural legitimation at the millennium, of course, for example in 2012 when the Rock and Roll Hall of Fame and Museum opened its library and archives—the largest archive of rock and roll music in the world—or when, during that same year, Robert Plant could be glimpsed standing reverent in his tuxedo during the National Anthem, poised to receive on behalf of Led Zeppelin the Kennedy Center Honors for "lifetime contributions to American culture through the performing arts."[3] Then there was Michael Chabon's 2013 lecture entitled "Rock and Roll," delivered at the American Academy of Arts and Letters and published later that year as "Let It Rock" in the *New York Review of Books*. The Pulitzer Prize winner Chabon took it upon himself to bring rock out on both platforms, delivering this message to America's anointed literati: "I don't think I could have learned more about the joy and sensuous appeal of alliteration, assonance, and consonance from any poem of Gerard Manley Hopkins than I did from Warren Zevon's wonderful line in 'Werewolves of London': '*Little old lady got mutilated late last night.*'"[4]

So what happened? Can we arrange these events at the end of a developmental narrative, a linear history whose apotheosis came in October 2016? Rock was so potent that it was finally able to overcome the arbitrary strictures put in place by high culture's lame institutions? So cool have we all become that the Nobel Prize in Literature can now go to one of the pioneers of rock and roll? "Let's not torture ourselves," advises Remnick, "with any gyrations about genre and the holy notion of literature to justify the choice of Dylan."[5] There are detractors from the idea that Dylan was writing literature, to be sure.[6] But rather than wading into those tepid waters—after all, who fucking cares?—I want to ask, are these events the culmination of an evolving ease with countercultural art forms? A groovy attunement with low culture? Dylan, Chuck Berry, and James Brown had already taken the Kennedy Center Honors when Led Zeppelin came up—in 1997, 2000, and 2003 respectively—and Ray Charles was deemed worthy as far back as 1986.[7] Should we view these awards as earlier moments in our march toward an evolved sense of cool? As the music writer David Hajdu put it just after Dylan took the Nobel, the "old categories of high and low art, they've been collapsing for a long time, but this is it being made official."[8]

Undoing the claim that rock and literature are anathema was a particularly relevant project in 1975, when Greil Marcus published his pioneering *Mystery Train*. In this widely read work of first-wave rock criticism, Marcus suggested that rock and roll expressed nothing less

than the American Jeremiad. Other early rock writers sought to legitimate rock and roll by describing its aesthetic, but it was Marcus who
first plugged rock and roll into American literary history, presenting
Pilgrim's Progress by John Bunyan as a portal into the development of
The Band, for example, and suggesting that the paradigmatically American theme of prophets crying in the wilderness should be understood
as a way to grasp Elvis Presley's life story, which Marcus cleverly calls
"The Presliad."[9] In *Mystery Train*, rock and roll was credited with being
a legitimate American art form, but more than that, Marcus made it a
version of American literature itself.

So, perhaps *Mystery Train* marks the pivotal shift, the first move
toward expansion: American letters includes Harmonica Frank and so
world literature encompasses "Like a Rolling Stone." It was not until 1979
that AC/DC released their monster hit, but perhaps our journey down
this highway to hell began in 1975 when Marcus—is he the rock era's
Worldly Wiseman?—set us against the holy notion of literature.[10] It was
after all Marcus who made the suggestion that, close reading aside, Walt
Whitman's *Democratic Vistas* should be understood as an injunction to
bring forgotten progenitors of rock like Robert Johnson into legitimacy.
And at *Mystery Train*'s end, Marcus's gesture is revealed to be just that—a
democratic move, a way to draw marginalized persons into civic life by
expanding the literary canon to include rock and its forebears.

Along with toppling literary shibboleths, Marcus therefore succeeds
in archiving for us a number of under-recognized figures from rock's
prehistory. Among these, he includes as prime movers the Prisonaires,
a doo-wop group consisting of five African American musicians who
in 1953 were allowed leave from the state penitentiary in Nashville
to record "Just Walkin' in the Rain" with Sam Phillips, which they
accomplished under the watch of armed guards.[11] The group gets only
a brief mention in *Mystery Train*, but because they again enter the
literary domain in 2003, I cite them here as a point of comparison.
In the later appearance, which occurs in Jonathan Lethem's *The Fortress of Solitude*, the Prisonaires are deployed to play a more structural
role. "The Prisonaires" is indeed the title of the third section of Lethem's rock novel, and as *Mystery Train* had several decades earlier, *The*

118 CODA: NOBEL SOUNDS

Fortress of Solitude also keeps the Prisonaires within literary sights, following a democratizing impulse that resembles Marcus's.[12] But in naming the third section of *The Fortress of Solitude* after the group, Lethem accomplishes something else as well, making use of the history of rock to provide a real-world referent for his protagonists' tragically racialized ends. Like *Mystery Train*, *The Fortress of Solitude* presents the Prisonaires as emissaries of mass culture in a literary domain, a domain whose apparently white record needs to be set straight. But as the inspiration for the racial injustice that ends up overtaking his characters, popular music also becomes a crucial organizing element in his Lethem's novel—a construal of rock and roll as nothing less than the novel's historical principle. In tying his characters to early rock and roll figures, Lethem connects rock's racial past to his own whitened media form, portraying this familiar gesture in rock as a transaction endemic to the novel as well.

We could place *Mystery Train* and *The Fortress of Solitude* along our imagined progressive development to show that the march of rock into the literary had advanced over the thirty years between them. Along with Lethem, we could argue, the novels of Lorrie Moore, Michael Chabon, and all the others explicitly incorporate rock and roll into their fiction, melding into one two forms of expression that in 1975 Marcus still had to insist belonged in the same category at all. To take it back slightly earlier, we might consider the infamous dueling banjoes in James Dickey's *Deliverance* (1970), the filmic version of which constitutes an earworm for all time. The novel emerged a decade after *Set This House on Fire* and five years before *Mystery Train*, neatly bridging the construal of ballads in the 1970s to the musical novel at the birth of rock and roll. Before the city-dwelling Southern protagonists of Dickey's novel make their weekend trip to rural Georgia, the character Lewis describes the culture they will soon enter: "There's lots of music, it's coming out of the trees. Everybody plays something: the guitar, the banjo, the autoharp, the spoons, the dulcimer." Along with their facility with ballads, these folks are prone to incest and murder: "They don't think a whole lot about killing people up here," says Lewis.[13] Dickey's suburban Southerners intend to slum in these hills.

The backwoods horrors that ensue in *Deliverance* suggest that by 1970 the cultural meaning given to ballads by Lytle and Davidson had gone quite awry. Dickey would draw from Agrarian traditions to construe ballads as naturally occurring in the mountains—as indeed "coming out of the trees"—but to show that the ballad has mutated into a musical sign of genetic malfunction. Ballads here signal that the musical guarantee of whiteness is in fact inbreeding by hyperbolically isolated, monstrous Southerners. Davidson's mountain fastness was now a setting for horror, and the ballad's corporeal wholeness was unrepentant phallic violence. We might argue that Marcus makes claims about rock as literature, then, because the Agrarian notion of ballads had by 1970 come full circle, in Dickey's moment indicating not cultural salve but national damage. Such a construal invites us to add Robert Altman's film *Nashville* (1975) to our linear history and to identify Shelley Duvall's character LA Joan as yet another sign that literary ground zero no longer was, had become a faded Nashville more diffuse even than Music City, U.S.A. Any cultural value to be found in the city of Nashville is entirely lost on LA Joan, allegorized away in this character's utter apathy about her dying Nashville relative. This Nashville is a later iteration of Isaac Sumpter's Nashville, not a locus for close reading but a sinkhole collapsing divisions between high and low formerly ensured by Vanderbilt.

And so perhaps there was a great rift in the 1970s, a cultural meltdown that made room for *Mystery Train*. This might explain the appearance of Don DeLillo's fictionalization of Bob Dylan in *Great Jones Street* (1973), that first foray by an acclaimed American novelist into deep rock territory.[14] And surely these works mark a departure from stricter lines set in earlier decades. Didn't Clement Greenberg begin his seminal 1939 essay "Avant-Garde and Kitsch" by announcing the very divide Marcus flouts? "One and the same civilization," Greenberg lamented, "produces simultaneously two such different things as a poem by T. S. Eliot and a Tin Pan Alley song."[15] In 1947 Brooks too pressed the point, noting the difference between John Donne's "The Canonization," a "massive poem" in his account, and the "flimsy little lyric" of a Tin Pan Alley song.[16] In his 1950 "Listening to Popular Music," the sociologist David Riesman analyzed the "trashy output" of the "music industry," warning that "its song-pluggers, its juke-box outlets," and its "radio grip" had the power to "mold popular taste and to eliminate free choice by consumers."[17] Certainly the divide between high and low culture was stricter at the birth of rock than it was at its death.

And yet. If instances of overlap in the twenty-first century have followed a neatly evolving continuum toward looser boundaries between high and low, how do we explain the presence of rock's mongrel forms in ballad fiction at the moment rock came into existence? After all, the undeniably institutional formation that was Southern fiction emerged just as Ike Turner and Sam Phillips were cooking up what Guralnick called their "alchemy." A breach can therefore be detected even at the moment these institutional divisions were being erected. What I have sought to show in *Novel Sounds* is that each moment of apparent bleed also replicates and extends an institutional occurrence that goes back much further—to the inception of rock and roll, yes, but to traditions that can be dated to epochs prior as well. Dylan's prize and Chabon's speech mark historical progress forward, but they also repeat understandings of the vernacular that go back to ancient times.

Just a couple of years before *Mystery Train*'s publication, there emerged an anthology called *American Literature: The Makers and the Making* (1973). The contents of this book clarify what Southern fiction at the birth of rock has already shown us. Alongside poetry by Emily Dickinson and Walt Whitman, in particular, the editors of this volume include the lyrics to Lead Belly's "The Midnight Special."[18] Who put this anthology together? Not Greil Marcus. His foray into the terrain of bona fide literary anthologies would have to wait until 2009, when Harvard University Press would bring him in as coeditor along with Harvard's own Werner Sollors for *A New Literary History of America*.[19] The 1973 anthology in question, which like Marcus's *Mystery Train* would include important vernacular artists, was edited by three purveyors of the high literary on faculty at Yale University at the time: Robert Penn Warren, Cleanth Brooks, and R. W. Lewis. Warren, Brooks, and Lewis find notable Lead Belly's role in generating "the first sustained white, urban interest in black blues." "As such," they argue, "it was the beginning of the decisive blues influence that was to form the white folk-rock-blues music of the 1960s."[20] Lead Belly, Robert Johnson, and Bessie Smith all find entries in Warren and Brooks's 1970s anthology; even the Rolling Stones and Bob himself rate a mention.[21] So what should we make of Warren and Brooks's inclusion of these rock and rollers and their blues forebears in the 1973 *American Literature: The Makers and the Making*? Had the gatekeepers of high culture finally learned how to rock? Had Creedence Clearwater Revival's 1969 cover of "The Midnight Special" (on their album *Willy and the Poor Boys*) blown their literary minds? Or could it be the other way around? Did the members of Creedence find in Lead Belly that which Robert Penn Warren had taught them to seek?[22]

When in *Mystery Train* Marcus asserted that vernacular artists belonged in literary domains, it turns out that they were already there. For Warren and Brooks to bring Lead Belly into their 1973 anthology was not new, after all, and the later inclusion indicates the persistence of that which motivated them to do so in 1938. We could keep rolling the narrative back, keep searching for the point when literature hated popular music, but then we would encounter Francis James Child—or, going back further still, Thomas Percy and Sir Walter Scott. Just how far back would we have to go? Medievalists would not have us stop at Geoffrey Chaucer's *Canterbury Tales*; nor would Richard Thompson suggest "Sir Patrick Spens" as a starting point. Rather than closing the gap between literature and rock, it seems, *Mystery Train* was tapping into something a culturally astute Greil Marcus was able to sense early on, something that already existed. The kinship between rock and literature that Marcus drew out in *Mystery Train* was also the basis for Lead Belly's appearance at the MLA and, moving ahead again, for rock novels in the twenty-first century.[23] This essential connection is also what explains the conferral of the Nobel Prize in Literature on the man who wrote the greatest rock and roll song of all time.

Far from confirming the institutional divisions literary scholars are accustomed to rehearsing between the high literary and mass culture, then, the literary readings *Novel Sounds* has offered confirm the American novel's deep roots in rock and roll. *Novel Sounds* does not seek to rescue popular music from its status as low, or to declare that the discovery of this subgenre in Southern fiction indicates a scandalous breach between rock and roll and the high literary.[24] Nor does it promulgate the familiar notion that a focus on high-cultural literary works misses rock's low truths. Rather, *Novel Sounds* discovers a genealogical overlap between literature and rock, a nexus in the vernacular from which both rock and literature emerged as apparently opposing modes of expression with irreconcilable histories. In the late 1980s the literary scholar Andreas Huyssen charged that modernist "aesthetic practice" exhibits an "inherent hostility between high and low," asserting that modernism and the avant-garde "defined themselves in relation to two cultural phenomena: traditional bourgeois high culture . . . but also vernacular and popular as it was increasingly transformed into modern commercial mass culture."[25] *Novel Sounds* is an effort to unsettle the common assumptions that lead to this sort of mistake, showing that on the contrary, vernacular forms of expression were never sequestered from institutional designations of the high literary. From the 1920s to the birth of rock, anyway, keepers of "bourgeois high culture" in the United States unfailingly traced literature to vernacular music. It is this practice that explains Bob Dylan's win and that clarifies how a rock and roller could prevail in a contest of who makes better literature even over novelists like Philip Roth and Joyce Carol Oates. Without a clarification of this history, the claim that we are engaged in scandal when we discover rock and roll in high-cultural domains can only repeat endlessly, caught like a needle on scratched vinyl—playing back again and again the shock of the low, infinitely reinscribing the divisions we pretend to overcome. The point here is not to declare, again, that we have finally closed the gap, but to attend to what governs the ascendance of rock into literature at any given moment, given popular music's constant presence within, or perhaps its repeated incursions into, literature's institutions.

NOTES

INTRODUCTION: MINSTREL REALISM AT THE BIRTH OF ROCK

1. Peter Guralnick, *Sam Phillips: The Man Who Invented Rock 'n' Roll* (New York: Little, Brown and Company, 2015), 106. Guralnick provides a detailed account of the car trip that delivered Ike Turner and band to Memphis (104). See also B. B. King and David Ritz, *Blues All Around Me: The Autobiography of B. B. King*, reprint ed. (New York: It Books, 2011). "Jackie Brenston and His Delta Cats" is the name Sam Phillips gave to the Kings of Rhythm, Ike Turner's group. Guralnick reports that Phillips substituted Brenston for Turner as the singer of "Rocket 88" during the recording session, then released the single under the new name unannounced. Guralnick quotes Turner as admitting, "I was kinda teed about it" (107). Nick Tosches argues that there was "no first rock-'n'-roll record any more than" there was a first "modern novel." Acknowledging that "Rocket 88" was a "turning point," however, he allows there was a "newness" that "set it apart from what had come before." Nick Tosches, *Unsung Heroes of Rock 'n' Roll: The Birth of Rock in the Wild Years Before Elvis* (New York: Da Capo, 1999), 139. See also Jim Dawson and Steve Propes, *What Was the First Rock 'n' Roll Record?* (Boston: Faber & Faber, 1992); Charlie Gillett, *The Sound of the City: The Rise of Rock and Roll* (New York: Da Capo, 1984); and Albin Zak, *I Don't Sound Like Nobody: Remaking Music in 1950s America* (Ann Arbor: University of Michigan Press, 2010).
2. Guralnick, *Sam Phillips*, 212–16.
3. On Faulkner's belated success, see Lawrence H. Schwartz, *Creating Faulkner's Reputation: The Politics of Modern Literary Criticism* (Knoxville: University of Tennessee Press, 1988); and Michael Kreyling, *Inventing Southern Literature* (Jackson: University Press of Mississippi, 1998).
4. Andre Millard, *America on Record: A History of Recorded Sound*, 2nd ed. (Cambridge: Cambridge University Press, 2005), 223. Guralnick, *Sam Phillips*, 106. Greil Marcus, *Mystery Train: Images of America in Rock 'n' Roll Music*, 6th rev. ed. (New York: Plume, 2015), 10.

5. Flannery O'Connor also portrays her character Rufus Johnson performing Charles E. Calhoun's "Shake, Rattle, and Roll" in the 1962 "The Lame Shall Enter First." Flannery O'Connor, *The Complete Stories* (New York: Farrar, Straus and Giroux, 1971), 456. "Shake, Rattle, and Roll" was recorded in 1954, both by the blues shouter Big Joe Turner and by Bill Haley and His Comets. Elvis Presley covered the tune in 1956. I explain why "A Good Man Is Hard to Find" tells us more about the relationship between Southern fiction at the birth of rock and roll in note 25 and chapter 3. Zak argues that "Shake, Rattle, and Roll" clarified how blues could be used as "source material" for rock. Zak, *I Don't Sound Like Nobody*, 126, 182.

6. Guralnick has this to say of rock and roll's Southern roots: "Like the blues, jazz, and rock 'n' roll, both its birth and inspiration stem from the South, so that while Solomon Burke, one of the very greatest of soul singers, is a native of Philadelphia, and Garnet Mimms, a little appreciated but nearly equally talented vocalist, made many of his recordings there, the clear inspiration for the styles of both is the Southern revivalism that fueled such diverse figures as Elvis Presley and Hank Williams on the one hand, Little Richard and Ray Charles on the other." Peter Guralnick, *Sweet Soul Music: Rhythm and Blues and the Southern Dream of Freedom* (New York: Harper & Row, 1986), 6.

7. The American studies scholar Jack Hamilton distinguishes between "rock 'n' roll" and "rock," the latter term for him signifying the end of the first wave of rock and roll in the 1950s. For Hamilton, the term "rock" marks a "whitening" of the genre, one that he argues commenced with the release of Bob Dylan's 1965 "Like a Rolling Stone." Hamilton notes that Sam Cooke's "A Change Is Gonna Come," out one year before, was categorized in the clearly demarcated black musical niche "soul" instead of rock. Jack Hamilton, *Just Around Midnight: Rock and Roll and the Racial Imagination* (Cambridge, MA: Harvard University Press, 2016), 79–81. For a rock journalist's take on the whiteness of rock and roll, see Dave Marsh, *The Heart of Rock and Soul: The 1,001 Greatest Singles Ever Made* (New York: Da Capo, 1999). In describing the moment that Hamilton aptly analyzes in racial terms, I use the term "New Rock" rather than "rock," which I employ here as the abbreviated version of "rock and roll." I take the nomenclature for "New Rock" from Shaun Considine, who oversaw the release of Dylan's "Like a Rolling Stone" for Columbia Records in 1965. In a 2004 op-ed he wrote for the New York Times just after *Billboard* named Dylan's song the greatest rock and roll song of all time, Considine explains that, before becoming a hit, "Like a Rolling Stone" fell into "limbo, soon to be dropped" from Columbia "into the dark graveyard of canceled releases." When it was finally released, Considine reports, "'Like a Rolling Stone' remained on the charts for three months, carrying Columbia into what was then called 'the New Rock.'" Shaun Considine, "The Hit We Almost Missed," *New York Times*, December 3, 2004, http://www.nytimes.com/2004/12/03/opinion/the-hit -we-almost-missed.html.

8. This whitening is explained in the arguments advanced by both Hamilton and the anthropologist Maureen Mahon. See Hamilton, *Just Around Midnight*; Mahon, *Right to Rock: The Black Rock Coalition and the Cultural Politics of Race* (Durham, NC: Duke University Press, 2004).

9. *Rolling Stone*, "Chuck Berry: Twenty Essential Songs," http://www.rollingstone.com/music /lists/chuck-berry-20-essential-songs-w472713/maybellene-1955-w472730. Berry was inspired by Wills's 1938 "Ida Red"; Roy Acuff recorded it in 1939. Glenn Altschuler, *All Shook Up: How Rock 'n' Roll Changed America* (New York: Oxford University Press, 2003), 63. For more information on "Maybellene" in a historical context, see Zak, *I Don't Sound Like Nobody*.

10. Karl Hagstrom Miller, *Segregating Sound: Inventing Folk and Pop Music in the Age of Jim Crow* (Durham, NC: Duke University Press, 2010), 15. On rock's interracial origins, see Guralnick, *Sweet Soul Music*; Hamilton, *Just Around Midnight*; Michael Bertrand, *Race, Rock, and Elvis* (Urbana: University of Illinois Press, 2000). Racial crossover in the aesthetic realm obviously did not end racial discrimination in the business of rock. Zak reminds us that it was Alan Freed, the white disc jockey known for inventing the term "rock and roll," who was credited with writing "Maybellene" (*I Don't Sound Like Nobody*, 82). Although racial inequality was generally perpetuated in rock's business practices as well as in those of soul and Motown, within each genre there are also notable examples of African American artists and entrepreneurs taking ownership of their own musical rights—and indeed W. C. Handy, the Father of the Blues, entered into his music career as publisher as well as artist. See Gerald Early, *One Nation Under a Groove: Motown and American Culture*, rev. and exp. ed. (Ann Arbor: University of Michigan Press, 2004); Guralnick, *Sweet Soul Music*; David Robertson, *W. C. Handy: The Life and Times of the Man Who Made the Blues* (Tuscaloosa: University of Alabama Press, 2011).

11. Guralnick, *Sweet Soul Music*, 67. In Guralnick's words, "the two albums yielded four Top 10 pop hits, several more that were in the top 30, and one ('I Can't Stop Loving You') that sold over three million copies." Guralnick, *Sweet Soul Music*, 67. The soul singer Solomon Burke recounts a story about how his similar crossover success led to the perception that he was white. Burke tells Guralnick that he had showed up to a gig in Mississippi where the promoters had hired him on the basis of his 1961 recording of the country song "Just Out of Reach," also recorded by the country singer Patsy Cline. The audience turned out to be members of the Klan. "They got closer and closer. Man, they was 30,000 Ku Klux Klanners in their sheets—it was their annual rally" (86–87).

12. William Faulkner, *The Town* (New York: Vintage, 1961), 76; W. C. Handy, *Blues: An Anthology* (Bedford, MA: Applewood, 2001), 2; W. C. Handy, *Negro Authors and Composers of the United States* (New York: Handy Brothers Music Co., 1938); W. C. Handy, *Unsung Americans Sung* (New York: ASCAP, 1944). W. C. Handy was indeed a professor, hired to teach music at the Alabama Agricultural and Mechanical College for Negroes after working for years as a musician, including as bandleader for the Mahara Colored Minstrels. David Robertson, *W. C. Handy*, 5, 79, 52–73. In 1912, this self-proclaimed "Father of the Blues" published "The Memphis Blues," reportedly the first published song with the word "blues" in its title. Robertson, *W. C. Handy*, 5, 79, 52–73, 18. Bryan Wagner gives an account of Jelly Roll Morton's refutation of the claim that W. C. Handy was "Father of the Blues," citing Morton's angry letter to *Down Beat*, which, as Wagner points out, "attacked Handy's credibility and frankly doubted whether Handy had ever created anything." Bryan Wagner, *Black Culture and the Police Power After Slavery* (Cambridge, MA: Harvard University Press, 2009), 25.

13. Flannery O'Connor, *Mystery and Manners: Occasional Prose* (New York: Farrar, Straus & Giroux, 1969), 35.

14. Kreyling, *Inventing Southern Literature*.

15. Mark McGurl, *The Program Era: Postwar Fiction and the Rise of Creative Writing* (Cambridge, MA: Harvard University Press, 2009), 3.

16. For a succinct account of the influence of various forms of technology on rock's emergence, see Richard A. Peterson, "Why 1955? Explaining the Advent of Rock Music," *Popular Music* 9, no. 1 (January 1990): 97–116. See also "The History of 78 RPM Recordings," https://www.library.yale.edu/cataloging/music/historyof78rpms.htm; David Suisman, *Selling Sounds: The Commercial Revolution in American Music* (Cambridge, MA: Harvard University Press, 2009).

17. Cleanth Brooks, *The Hidden God: Studies in Hemingway, Faulkner, Yeats, Eliot, and Warren* (New Haven, CT: Yale University Press, 1963), 2; Andre Millard, *Beatlemania: Technology, Business, and Teen Culture in Cold War America* (Baltimore, MD: Johns Hopkins University Press, 2012).

18. Cleanth Brooks, *William Faulkner: The Yoknapatawpha Country* (New Haven, CT: Yale University Press, 1963), 3. Among the areas of concern for midcentury intellectuals Mark Greif enumerates was the worry that "human technologies might be outstripping or perverting humane thought and goals." Mark Greif, *The Age of the Crisis of Man: Thought and Fiction in America, 1933–1973* (Princeton, NJ: Princeton University Press, 2015), 11.

19. John Guillory and Richard Godden have given us our best analyses of the institutional uses of this formal difficulty. Guillory explains that for New Critics, literature "presents a united front, in the form of its difficulty, against the artifacts of mass culture." John Guillory, *Cultural Capital: The Problem of Literary Canon Formation* (Chicago: University of Chicago Press, 1993), 173. Godden describes Faulkner's early novels in terms of an "occlusive stylistics," arguing that this "'difficulty' . . . is driven by his penurious habit of secretion—a habit which demands that the reader attend closely in order to recover, from Faulkner's choked, subverted, underarticulated, and yet imperious prose, inferences of a tale that is not being told." Richard Godden, *Fictions of Labor: William Faulkner and the South's Long Revolution* (Cambridge: Cambridge University Press, 1997), 4. As Guillory clarifies, the valorization of difficult literature comes in part from Eliot. Although it was in 1921 that T. S. Eliot made his bid for difficult poetry—"We can only say that it appears likely that poets in our civilization, as it exists at present, must be difficult" (Eliot, *Selected Essays* [London: Faber & Faber, 1999], 248)—New Critics took Eliot's statement as a defining dictum for the postwar years and on that basis helped establish Faulkner as one of America's greatest novelists.

20. Theodor W. Adorno, "Extorted Reconciliation: On Georg Lukács' *Realism in Our Time*," in *Notes to Literature*, ed. Rolf Tieddemann, trans. Shierry Weber Nicholsen (New York: Columbia University Press, 1991), 1:224. Southern fiction of the 1950s thus aligned more closely with the principal object of Adorno's culture industry critiques, popular music, than with "high culture" as such. Adorno advanced a polemic against technology in popular music that can be gleaned in his writings on jazz in the 1930s and 1940s as well as in his 1941 "On Popular Music." Theodor Adorno, Susan H. Gillespie, and Richard D. Leppert, *Essays on Music* (Berkeley, CA: University of California Press, 2002), 437–69. See also Theodor Adorno, *Night Music: Essays on Music, 1928–1962* (New York: Seagull, 2009).

21. Eric Barry identifies "a high-fidelity boom that took off with the introduction of the long-playing record (LP) in 1948." Barry notes that *High Fidelity* magazine was founded in 1951 and grew rapidly over the 1950s to become in 1960, as the newly named *HiFi Review*, the "top-selling magazine in the industry." Eric D. Barry, "High Fidelity Sound as Spectacle and Sublime, 1950–1961," in *Sound in the Age of Mechanical Reproduction*, ed. David Suisman and Susan Strasser (Philadelphia: University of Pennsylvania Press, 2010), 115, 265n3.

22. Here, we might consider the contrast between the postwar fiction *Novel Sounds* examines and that to which Godden refers when he notes that it was to "Vanderbilt students" that the "inexhaustible fullness" of the New Critical icon was directed. Richard Godden, *Fictions of Capital: The American Novel from James to Mailer* (Cambridge: Cambridge University Press, 1990), 153, suggests that the early novels of William Faulkner were installed to rescue college students from "Sears and Roebuck" transparency. My point is that these 1950s works instead partook of this transparency.

23. For a broad view of the tradition to which these novelists understood themselves to be connecting, see Denis Stevens, ed., *A History of Song* (New York: Norton, 1970). Steve Newman gives a rich and detailed account of the ballad traditions informing midcentury American literary scholars. Steve Newman, *Ballad Collection, Lyric, and the Canon: The Call of the Popular from the Restoration to the New Criticism* (Philadelphia: University of Pennsylvania Press, 2007). A small sampling of the uses in rock and roll of medieval ballads includes Simon and Garfunkel's revamped version of the English ballad "Scarborough Fair," British folk rockers Fairport Convention's version of "Sir Patrick Spens," and Bob Dylan's version of "The Daemon Lover" (as "House Carpenter"). I discuss these versions of "Sir Patrick Spens" and "The Daemon Lover" in what follows.

24. See Eric Lott, *Love and Theft: Blackface Minstrelsy and the American Working Class* (New York: Oxford University Press, 1993).

25. Kreyling notes that the Southern literature anthologies of the 1940s and 1950s "generally upheld separate but equal literatures for the races" and discusses the way in which well-meaning revisions to this tendency, in simply including African Americans as Southerners, elide African American writers' noted opposition to being absorbed into a "white" category (*Inventing Southern Literature*, 76–81). It is for this reason that O'Connor's 1953 use of "A Good Man Is Hard to Find" is more relevant to *Novel Sounds* than her portrayal in 1960 of the bona fide rock and roll song "Shake, Rattle, and Roll" in "The Lame Shall Enter First." The inclusion of the Green song in this classic of Southern fiction repeats rock's incorporation of black blues into rock as rock was emerging. The inclusion of "Shake, Rattle, and Roll" in "The Lame Shall Enter First" indicates that rock was by the 1960s residual, a point I elaborate in chapter 4.

26. This fact leads Hamilton to critique the idea that "love and theft" is "transhistorical" and to note that a blanket description of rock and roll as white people stealing black music erases rock's black originators (*Just Around Midnight*, 9).

27. Martyn Bone, William A. Link, and Brian Ward, *Creating and Consuming the American South* (Gainesville: University Press of Florida, 2015), 2.

28. Martyn Bone, *The Postsouthern Sense of Place in Contemporary Fiction* (Baton Rouge: Louisiana State University Press, 2005), 17. See also Scott Romine, *The Real South: Southern Narrative in the Age of Cultural Reproduction* (Baton Rouge: Louisiana State University Press, 2008).

29. Richard King, *A Southern Renaissance: The Cultural Awakening of the American South, 1930–1955* (New York: Oxford University Press, 1980), 3.

30. Greg "Freddy" Camalier, *Muscle Shoals* (Boulder, CO: Ear Goggles Productions, 2013); Richard Younger, *Get a Shot of Rhythm and Blues: The Arthur Alexander Story* (Tuscaloosa: University of Alabama Press, 2000).

31. Of these artists, Reed and Dixon recorded in Chicago, Reed with Vee-Jay, Dixon with Chess. Thomas had recorded with Sam Phillips at Sun Studio but eventually had the first hit for the legendary origin of "Memphis Soul," Stax Records. The song was "'Cause I Love You," which Thomas recorded with his daughter Carla in 1960. See Guralnick, *Sweet Soul Music*, 102–4. On the Rolling Stones's use of material by Southern black artists in the British Invasion, see Peter Guralnick, *Feel Like Going Home: Portraits in Blues and Rock 'n' Roll*, reprint ed. (Boston: Back Bay Books, 1999); Barry Miles, *The British Invasion: The Music, the Times, the Era* (New York: Sterling, 2009).

32. Ralph Ellison, *Invisible Man* (New York: Random House, 1952); James Baldwin, *Go Tell It on the Mountain* [1953], reprint ed. (New York: Vintage, 2013); John Work et al., *Lost*

Delta Found: Rediscovering the Fisk University–Library of Congress Coahoma County Study, *1941–1942* (Nashville: Vanderbilt University Press, 2005); Clark Kimberling, "Three Generations of Works and Their Contributions to Congregational Singing," *The Hymn: A Journal of Congregational Song* 65, no. 3 (Summer 2014): 10–17; James Baldwin, *Going to Meet the Man: Stories* [1965], reissue ed. (New York: Vintage, 1995).

33.   Ellison, *Invisible Man,* 47.

34.   McGurl has argued that postwar literature anthologies "stabilized a set of literary values" (*The Program Era,* 132) emanating from the institution, and Kreyling notes that "the entire history of southern literature is abbreviated in the history of its anthologies" (*Inventing Southern Literature,* 57). As I discuss more fully in chapter 1, *Understanding Fiction,* which McGurl calls "undoubtedly the most important of the postwar fiction textbooks" (133), did not include any African American authors in its pages until 1979.

35.   Baldwin, "Everybody's Protest Novel," 20, 18, 21, 18.

36.   Cleanth Brooks, *The Well Wrought Urn: Studies in the Structure of Poetry* (New York: Harcourt, Brace, 1947), 3–20.

37.   In an interview on CBS radio, Ellison praised Faulkner's experimentation in particular, and argued as well that "no one in American fiction has done so much to explore the types of Negro personality as has Faulkner." Arnold Rampersad, *Ralph Ellison: A Biography* (New York: Knopf, 2007), 274. It should be noted that Ellison's admiration for Faulkner's style did not disable his critique of Faulkner's racial politics. Kenneth Warren cites a letter from Ellison to Albert Murray in which Ellison complains that "Faulkner has delusions of grandeur because he really believes that he invented these characteristics which he ascribes the Negroes in his fiction." Kenneth Warren, *So Black and Blue: Ralph Ellison and the Occasion of Criticism* (Chicago: University of Chicago Press, 2003), 13. In his 1956 "Faulkner and Desegregation," Baldwin likewise pointed out that "after two hundred years in slavery and ninety years of quasi-freedom, it is hard to think very highly of William Faulkner's advice to 'go slow.'" James Baldwin, *Partisan Review* 23, no. 4 (Fall 1956): 568.

38.   Ralph Ellison, "Richard Wright's Blues," in *The Jazz Cadence of American Culture,* ed. Robert O'Meally (New York: Columbia University Press, 1998), 553.

39.   James Baldwin, "Letter from a Region in My Mind," *New Yorker,* November 17, 1962. http://www.newyorker.com/magazine/1962/11/17/letter-from-a-region-in-my-mind.

40.   Amiri Baraka, *Blues People: Negro Music in White America* (New York: Morrow, 1963), ix–x. See also Amiri Baraka, "Jazz and the White Critic," in *The Jazz Cadence of American Culture,* ed. Robert O'Meally (New York: Columbia University Press, 1998), 137–42. Baraka subscribed to the argument that rock and roll was originally a black form—an argument that Hamilton challenges (*Just Around Midnight*)—and Baraka notes that rock and roll, "usually a flagrant commercialization of rhythm & blues," contained strains that remained "interesting" and "vital" in the 1960s. Rock and roll is not, he declares, "emotionally meaningless," as other popularized forms of black music were. Baraka, *Blues People,* 222–23.

41.   W. E. B. Du Bois and Brent Hayes Edwards, *The Souls of Black Folk* (New York: Oxford University Press, 2007), 6.

42.   Mark Goble has drawn our attention to the music in Richard Wright's "Long Black Song" (1938) as well as the music in both *The Great Gatsby* (1925) and *Tender Is the Night* (1934) by F. Scott Fitzgerald. Mark Goble, *Beautiful Circuits: Modernism and the Mediated Life* (New York: Columbia University Press, 2010). *The Great Gatsby* includes a reference to Handy's "Beale Street Blues": "All night the saxophones wailed the hopeless comment of the Beale Street Blues while a hundred pairs of golden and silver slippers shuffled the shining dust."

F. Scott Fitzgerald, *The Great Gatsby*, Scribner trade pbk. ed. (New York: Scribner, 2004), 151. We might also think of ragtime in James Weldon Johnson's 1912 *Autobiography of an Ex-Colored Man*, the female blues singer in Langston Hughes's *Not Without Laughter*, or Zora Neale Hurston's fictional oral balladeer Tea Cake in *Their Eyes Were Watching God* (1936). The pianist in Eudora Welty's "Powerhouse" (1941) qualifies; as does Black Ulysses, the black protagonist of the white folklorist Howard Odum's novelistic trilogy *Rainbow Round My Shoulder* (1928), *Wings on My Feet* (1929), and *Cold Blue Moon* (1931). Also relevant is Wallace Stegner's *The Big Rock Candy Mountain* (1943), his semiauto-biographical novel titled after the 1928 Harry McClintock recording that reached no. 1 on Billboard's "Hillbilly Hits" chart in 1939. For information about the Harry McClintock hit, see http://www.songfacts.com/detail.php?id=22192 and http://www.vwml.org/record /RoudFS/S228838. On Welty's inspiration for "Powerhouse," see Kenneth Bearden, "Monkeying Around: Welty's 'Powerhouse,' Blues-Jazz, and the Signifying Connection," *Southern Literary Journal* 31, no. 2 (March 22, 1999): 65. See also Katherine Biers, "Syncope Fever: James Weldon Johnson and the Black Phonographic Voice," *Representations* 96, no. 1 (2006): 99–125; Lynn Moss Sanders, "'Black Ulysses Singing': Odom's Folkloristic Trilogy," *Southern Literary Journal* 22, no. 1 (1989): 107.

43. Eudora Welty, "Powerhouse," *The Atlantic* (June 1941): 709, 710, 707.

44. McGurl, *The Program Era*, 42. Certainly the link between literature and technology goes back further than the 1950s—at least to the moment of American modernism, its "hyper-trophied opacity," as Goble calls it, notwithstanding (*Beautiful Circuits*, 10). Marshall has argued for a recognition of the "relationship of American novels" generally to a "more continuous material narrative that accompanies the developments in media and the built world." Kate Marshall, *Corridor: Media Architectures in American Fiction* (Minneapolis: University of Minnesota Press, 2013), 2–3. For a related argument about "a poetics of the virtual" in Progressive Era US writers, see Katherine Biers, *Virtual Modernism: Writing and Technology in the Progressive Era* (Minneapolis: University of Minnesota Press, 2013), 1. For work on literature and technology that goes back further, see Richard Menke, *Telegraphic Realism: Victorian Fiction and Other Information Systems* (Stanford, CA: Stanford University Press, 2008); and Mark Seltzer, *Bodies and Machines* (New York: Routledge, 1992).

45. On rock's death, see Chuck Klosterman, *But What If We're Wrong? Thinking About the Present as If It Were the Past* (New York: Blue Rider, 2016); and Jay Ruttenberg, "Fallen Rock Stars in Contemporary Fiction," *New York Times Sunday Book Review*, September 7, 2012, http://www.nytimes.com/2012/09/09/books/review/fallen-rock-stars-in-contemporary -fiction.html.

46. Florence Dore, "The Rock Novel and Jonathan Lethem's *The Fortress of Solitude*," *Nonsite. Org* 8 (January 20, 2013).

47. Jonathan Lethem, *The Fortress of Solitude: A Novel* (New York: Doubleday, 2003). In his 2016 *A Gambler's Anatomy* (New York: Doubleday, 2016), Lethem again turns to rock, bringing us an eccentric rock fan–turned-neurosurgeon trying to bring Jimi Hendrix back from the dead with every surgery he performs.

48. Doyle's *The Commitments* suggests that this globalization was not entirely new at the turn of the twenty-first century.

49. Current work on global novels might thus be meaningfully be analyzed in terms of what Guillory describes as the "school's historical function of distributing, or regulating access to, the forms of cultural capital." He clarifies that claims about the political potency of acts within the institution should be measured against the reality that the "fact of class

determines whether and how individuals gain access to the means of literary production." As he puts it, "acknowledging the existence of admirable and even heroic elements of working-class culture, the affirmation of lower-class identity is hardly compatible with a program for the abolition of want." Guillory, *Cultural Capital*, vii, ix, 13.

50. See "The History of 78 RPM Recordings," https://www.library.yale.edu/cataloging/music /historyof78rpms.htm, for a timeline showing the introduction of electric microphones. On the marketing of race records and hillbilly music along racially divided lines, see Miller, *Segregating Sound*, 206–14.

51. "Proceedings of the Modern Language Association of America," *PMLA* 49 (1934): 1324–25. Lead Belly's trip to the MLA is chronicled in Charles Wolfe and Kip Lornell, *The Life and Legend of Leadbelly*, new ed. (New York: Da Capo, 1999), 130–36.

52. Kenton Jackson, "Two-Time Dixie Murderer Sings Way to Freedom," *Philadelphia Independent*, January 6, 1935, John A. Lomax Papers at the Briscoe Center for American History. Wolfe and Lornell, *The Life and Legend of Leadbelly*, 133–34. Nolan Porterfield, *Last Cavalier: The Life and Times of John A. Lomax, 1867–1948* (Urbana: University of Illinois Press, 1996), 342–43. The Association for Cultural Equity features a timeline of Leadbelly's life that mentions this article: http://www.culturalequity.org/currents/ce _currents_leadbelly_chronology5.php.

53. Built on a plantation whose slaves had come from Angola, the prison came to be known by this name. Anne Butler and C. Murray Henderson, *Angola: Louisiana State Penitentiary: A Half-Century of Rage and Reform* (Lafayette: Center for Louisiana Studies, University of Southwestern Louisiana, 1990).

54. Lead Belly appears to have played at the University of Alabama (Tuscaloosa) and Bryn Mawr in 1934, at New York University in 1935, at Harvard University in 1935, and at others during the 1940s. For a longer list of Lead Belly's performances at colleges and universities, see John Reynolds and Tiny Robinson, *Lead Belly: A Life in Pictures* (Göttingen: Steidl, 2008), 47; Wolfe and Lornell, *The Life and Legend of Leadbelly*, 130–36.

55. John A. Lomax, Library of Congress Music Division, and George Herzog, *Negro Folk Songs as Sung by Lead Belly*, *"King of the Twelve-String Guitar Players of the World," Long-Time Convict in the Penitentiaries of Texas and Louisiana* [printed music] (New York: Macmillan, 1936), xiii. The Smithsonian archivist Jeff Place argues that the story is legend, noting "the warden swears it had nothing to do with Lomax and the music, that he was actually due to get out on good behavior points." Jeff Place, interview by Kim Ruehl, *No Depression: The Journal of Roots Music* (February 17, 2015), http://nodepression.com/interview/digging -lead-bellys-america-interview-smithsonian-folkways-jeff-place.

56. *I'll Take My Stand: The South and the Agrarian Tradition* (New York: Harper and Row, 1962), 229, 244.

57. *I'll Take My Stand*, 35, 36, 55.

58. *I'll Take My Stand*, 205.

59. *I'll Take My Stand*, 264.

60. Donald Davidson, "The Sacred Harp in the Land of Eden," *Virginia Quarterly Review* 10, no. 2 (April 1, 1934): 215. See also Samuel P. Bayard, "George Pullen Jackson," *Journal of the International Folk Music Council* 6 (January 1, 1954): 62–63; Alton C. Morris, "George Pullen Jackson (1874–1953)," *Journal of American Folklore* 66, no. 262 (October 1, 1953); George Jackson, *White Spirituals in the Southern Uplands: The Story of the Fasola Folk, Their Songs, Singings, and "Buckwheat Notes"* (New York: Dover, 1965).

61. Daphne A. Brooks, "'Sister, Can You Line It Out?': Zora Neale Hurston and the Sound of Angular Black Womanhood," *Amerikastudien/American Studies* 55, no. 4 (2010): 623. Analyzing recordings of Hurston singing the songs she excavated in her fieldwork, Brooks argues that Hurston "pounded out the beat of overlooked histories through" her body and that she "utilized folkloric song as the medium through which to assert a kind of modern black womanhood that might shake the foundations of American culture" (625–26).

62. Donald Davidson, "The White Spirituals and Their Historian," *Sewanee Review* 51, no. 4 (December 1943): 589. Cleanth Brooks did not contribute to *I'll Take My Stand*, but in 1935 he wrote *The Relation of the Alabama-Georgia Dialect to the Provincial Dialects of Great Britain* (Baton Rouge: Louisiana State University Press, 1935), which made similar links between the US South and the British Isles.

63. McGinley analyzes Lomax's exercise of white privilege with Lead Belly. See Paige A. McGinley, "'The Magic of Song!': John Lomax, Huddie Ledbetter, and the Staging of Circulation," in *Performance in the Borderlands*, ed. Ramon H. Rivera-Servera and Harvey Young (New York: Palgrave MacMillan, 2011), 128–46; Paige A. McGinley, *Staging the Blues: From Tent Shows to Tourism* (Durham, NC: Duke University Press, 2014). Lead Belly eventually sued John Lomax for unfairly withholding portions of his pay. For a comprehensive account of these legal dealings, see Wolfe and Lornell, *The Life and Legend of Leadbelly*, 178–85. For two readings of Lomax's exploitation of Lead Belly in terms of the violence against African American persons in the post-Reconstruction United States, see Jennifer Lynn Stoever, *The Sonic Color Line: Race and the Cultural Politics of Listening*, reprint ed. (New York: NYU Press, 2016), 180–228; and Erich Nunn, *Sounding the Color Line: Music and Race in the Southern Imagination* (Athens: University of Georgia Press, 2015), 78–105.

64. Steve Newman has also noted the presence of "Frankie and Johnny" in *Understanding Poetry*, arguing that the inclusion requires that the "received wisdom on the New Criticism" requires revision (*Ballad Collection*, 210, 212). In particular, he suggests, "Frankie and Johnny" contradicts the idea that "New Critics tend to find their favorite objects of analysis in the difficulties of elite poetry." Newman observes that the ballad is the "chosen vehicle" for introducing students to the importance of "concrete and dramatic experience."

65. Guillory describes Eliot's desire for a literature that was "unconsciously Christian" (*Cultural Capital*, 152).

66. Brooks, *The Well Wrought Urn*, xi.

67. Cleanth Brooks and Robert Penn Warren, eds., *Understanding Poetry: An Anthology for College Students* (New York: H. Holt and Co., 1938), 32.

68. Brooks, *The Hidden God*, 2, 3.

69. Newman traces the New Critics' ideas about the ballads to Francis Barton Gummere's 1911 *The Democracy of Poetry*, clarifying that the ballad form harkens back to a primitive "dancing throng" whose "cadent feet" are "resonant in poetry's rhythm." In this conception, print culture makes democratic unity impossible because of its isolating effects (*Ballad Collection*, 198).

70. Thomas Percy, *Reliques of Ancient English Poetry, Consisting of Old Heroic Ballads, Songs, and Other Pieces of Our Earlier Poets, Together with Some Few of Later Date* (New York: Dover, 1966), 1. When *Reliques* was reprinted twenty years after its original publication, Percy wrote in his introduction that a number of the ballads had been taken from "an ancient folio manuscript" that "contains compositions of all times and dates, from the ages prior to Chaucer, to the conclusion of the reign of Charles" (7). Cheesman and Rieuwerts describe *Reliques* as "the first ballad book premised on the notion that ballads must go

into books, to be preserved from an extinction brought about by book-culture." Tom Cheesman and Sigrid Rieuwerts, eds., *Ballads Into Books: The Legacies of Francis James Child* (Bern: Peter Lang, 1997), 10.

71.   Francis Child, *English and Scottish Ballads*, 2nd series (Boston: Little, Brown, n.d.), 1:vii. Child discovered that *Reliques* contained only a portion of the ballads in an original folio manuscript. Intrigued that it was incomplete, Child succeeded in acquiring the folio and published the rest in *The English and Scottish Popular Ballads* (New York: Cooper Square, 1965). Michael Cohen argues that Child's anthology was "part of a postbellum literary reconstruction of the United States, which reimagined the Civil War as the origin of a distinct 'American' literature serving a newly united 'American' people." By contrast, Cohen argues, John Greenleaf Whittier's portrayal of balladeers offers a model of a "rural, local culture of poetry" that "necessarily lies outside the institutionally sanctioned, author-centered national tradition that Whittier and his fellow Fireside poets were later imagined to have inaugurated." Michael Cohen, "Popular Ballads: Rhythmic Remediations in the Nineteenth Century," *Meter Matters: Verse Cultures of the Long Nineteenth Century* (2011): 213; Michael Cohen, *The Social Lives of Poems in Nineteenth-Century America* (Philadelphia: University of Pennsylvania Press, 2015), 19–20. Newman's careful study *Ballad Collection* establishes a definitive genealogical link between eighteenth-century ballad ideals and the New Criticism.

72.   Susan Stewart, *Crimes of Writing: Problems in the Containment of Representation* (New York: Oxford University Press, 1991), 104. In Stewart's view, the ballad collectors of the eighteenth century were involved in creating a myth based on these ideas: "this great tautological 'discovery,'" which was in fact a "recovery," she argued, "would center more and more on the ballad and its contingent subjectivity—a ballad most often providing an etiological narrative of a subject 'bound' by history" (107).

73.   In her discussion of the 1771 transcription of "The Bonny Hynd," a ballad Child picked out for *English and Scottish Popular Ballads* from Sir Walter Scott's 1802–1803 edition of *Minstrelsy of the Scottish Border*, McLane finds what appears to be the original transcription of "The Bonny Hynd." In the unremarkable words of "W.L.," the transcriber—"Copied from the mouth of a milkmaid, 1771"—McLane identifies "a media operation, a medial translation" in which what is conveyed is authenticity in the context of print: "this copy here is no copy." McLane describes the transcription as "not simply an empirical trace" but rather a "deeply figural and rhetorical" inscription. In her words, the note "collapses the space between the milkmaid's vocalization and the man's transcription, as if one could truly copy from the mouth, as if this were, as Lacan might say, an encounter with 'The Real.'" In the figure, McLane argues, the "milkmaid's mouth emerges notionally as a transparent vessel, a frictionless orifice of the real." Maureen N. McLane, *Balladeering, Minstrelsy, and the Making of British Romantic Poetry*, reissue ed. (Cambridge: Cambridge University Press, 2011), 35–39.

74.   This according to Fairport Convention's guitarist Richard Thompson, who told me about his sources in my interview with him at the 2016 Novel Sounds conference held at the National Humanities Center, http://nationalhumanitiescenter.org/novel-sounds-american -fiction-in-the-age-of-rock-and-roll/. Ewan MacColl and A. L. Lloyd, *The English and Scottish Popular Ballads*, 9 vols. (Washington Albums, 1952).

75.   The 1969 studio version of "Sir Patrick Spens" (there is a 1969 BBC recording as well) did not make it onto *Liege and Lief* as released, but it is included as a bonus track on a CD reissue of the album from 2002. A later version of "Sir Patrick Spens" appeared on Fairport Convention's fifth album, *Full House* (1970).

76. Percy's influence on Brooks was quite direct. Newman reports that while a Rhodes scholar at Exeter College, Oxford, Cleanth Brooks wrote a thesis that became an edition of Thomas Percy's letters. Newman also found an essay Brooks wrote "either for a tutorial or an exam in fifteenth-century literature" (*Ballad Collection*, 212).

77. Brooks and Warren, *Understanding Poetry*, 32–33.

78. Brooks and Warren, *Understanding Poetry*, 33.

79. Brooks and Warren, *Understanding Poetry*, 33.

80. Stoever's analysis of Lead Belly's reception amid *Life's* pictures of lynched black bodies illuminates the violent context of such an association, in what Stoever calls the "visual discourse of lynching" (*The Sonic Color Line*, 197).

81. The observation that New Critical poetics relied so crucially on the oral revises Walter Ong's observations about the New Critics' "verbal icon." "It is hard to see," Ong argues, "how this visualist-tactile model of a poem or other verbal creation could apply effectively to an oral performance, which presumably could be a true poem. Sound resists reduction to an 'object' or 'icon'—it is an on-going event." The "on-going" oral event, it seems, was conceived as part of the verbal icon from the start. Walter J. Ong, *Orality and Literacy: The Technologizing of the Word* (London: Routledge, 2002), 157.

82. Lomax, Library of Congress Music Division, and Herzog, *Negro Folk Songs as Sung by Lead Belly*, xiii.

83. Esther K. Birdsall, "Some Notes on the Role of George Lyman Kittredge in American Folklore Studies," *Journal of the Folklore Institute* 10, nos. 1/2 (June 1, 1973): 57–66; Roger D. Abrahams, "Mr. Lomax Meets Professor Kittredge," *Journal of Folklore Research* 37, nos. 2/3 (May 2000): 99–118; Porterfield, *Last Cavalier*.

84. "The One Hundred Twenty-Six Presidents," https://www.mla.org/About-Us/Governance/The-One-Hundred-Twenty-Six-Presidents; "AFS Presidents—American Folklore Society," http://www.afsnet.org/?page=Presidents. Kittredge also published an abridged edition of *English and Scottish Popular Ballads* in 1904: Francis Child, George Lyman Kittredge, and Helen Child Sargent, *English and Scottish Popular Ballads: Edited from the Collection of Francis James Child* (Boston: Houghton, Mifflin, and Co., 1904).

85. John Lomax, *Cowboy Songs and Other Frontier Ballads*, new ed. with additions (New York: Macmillan, 1916), xxviii.

86. Lomax, *Cowboy Songs and Other Frontier Ballads*, xxv.

87. Lomax, *Cowboy Songs and Other Frontier Ballads*, xxv.

88. McGurl, *The Program Era*, 94. The first section of *The Program Era* (77–182) is dedicated to a study of this injunction to "write what you know." For McGurl, this becomes what he calls "autopoesis," a way of updating the modernist focus on individual style for a technological, bureaucratic writer in the university.

89. Lomax, *Cowboy Songs and Other Frontier Ballads*, xxiv.

90. Lomax, *Cowboy Songs and Other Frontier Ballads*, xxiv. That they were gathered in prisons or the "unpeopled West" hardly disqualified Lomax's ballads as literary. Indeed, their authenticity seems to have depended on these remote origins.

91. David Suisman (*Selling Sounds*, 210) argues that the Smith recording "heralded the possibility of a new era of African American music." OKeh's Rockwell found John Hurt out scouting for the label's new practice, called "location recording." OKeh pioneered this practice in 1922, taking mobile recording trucks to performers not otherwise available in urban centers. Robert Cantwell, *When We Were Good: The Folk Revival* (Cambridge, MA: Harvard University Press, 1996); Miller, *Segregating Sound*; Philip R. Ratcliffe, *Mississippi*

John Hurt: His Life, His Times, His Blues (Jackson: University Press of Mississippi, 2011): 56–57.

92. "Summary of Leaving Home," http://docsouth.unc.edu/nc/leaving/summary.html.

93. The song existed in print as well. A 1961 folklore dissertation on the history, origin, and geographical distribution of "Frankie and Johnny" indicates that early popular versions of the ballad existed in print as early as 1904. Bruce Redfern Buckley, "Frankie and Her Men: A Study of the Interrelationships of Popular and Folk Traditions," PhD diss., Indiana University, 1962, 35. It "would be an impossible task," Buckley asserts, "to find all the folk and popular versions of 'Frankie and Johnny' that have been sung throughout the world." He notes that he had located almost three hundred (108).

94. Miller, *Segregating Sound*, 245–48. Lead Belly can be heard telling the folklorist Frederic Ramsey of his love for Autry records in a 1948 recording of "Springtime in the Rockies." Leadbelly, *Leadbelly—Leadbelly's Last Sessions* (Smithsonian Folkways Recordings, 1995). See Holly George-Warren, "'Blues Ain't Nuthin' but a Good Man Feelin' Bad': Balladry, the Blues and Appropriation," presented at Novel Sounds II, National Humanities Center, Research Triangle Park, NC, March 3, 2017, http://nationalhumanitiescenter.org/novel-sounds-ii/.

95. Here is a specific instance of the way in which "race pervades the machine aesthetic of modern culture" (Goble, *Beautiful Circuits*, 171). The example of Lead Belly bears out Alexander Weheliye's observation that "black cultures" have been designated as "somehow pre- or anti-technological" and Gustavus Stadler's observation that African American persons are marshaled to give phonographic technologies "a body and a historical referent." Alexander Weheliye, *Phonographies: Grooves in Sonic Afro-Modernity* (Durham, NC: Duke University Press, 2005), 3; Gustavus Stadler, "Never Heard Such a Thing: Lynching and Phonographic Modernity," *Social Text* 28, no. 1 (March 20, 2010): 97–98.

96. *The March of TIME: Folk Legend Leadbelly—Video*, newsreel, 1935, http://content.time.com/time/video/player/0,32068,30862122001_1918195,00.html.

97. David Remnick, "Let's Celebrate the Bob Dylan Nobel Win," *New Yorker*, October 13, 2016, http://www.newyorker.com/culture/cultural-comment/lets-celebrate-the-bob-dylan-nobel-win.

98. Sara Danius, permanent secretary for the Swedish Academy, made this statement about Dylan. David Orr, "After Dylan's Nobel, What Makes a Poet a Poet?" *New York Times*, March 24, 2017, https://www.nytimes.com/2017/03/24/books/review/after-dylans-nobel-what-makes-a-poet-a-poet.html. It is worth noting here that Amiri Baraka reportedly described James Brown as "our number one black poet." Guralnick, *Sweet Soul Music*, 221.

99. Examinations of rock and poetry are under way. See Jim Elledge, *Sweet Nothings: An Anthology of Rock and Roll in American Poetry* (Bloomington: Indiana University Press, 1994); and Daniel Kane, *"Do You Have a Band?": Poetry and Punk Rock in New York City* (New York: Columbia University Press, 2017).

100. Ian Watt, *The Rise of the Novel: Studies in Defoe, Richardson, and Fielding* (Berkeley: University of California Press, 1957), 12. Watt argued that in *Robinson Crusoe*, Defoe made "as defiant an assertion of the primacy of individual experience in the novel as Descartes' cogito ergo sum was in philosophy" (15).

101. Watt, *The Rise of the Novel*, 32. For an analysis of Watt's "formal realism" in a reading of the novel's apparent death at midcentury, see Deak Nabers, "The Forms of Formal Realism: Literary Study and the Life Cycle of the Novel," in *Postmodern/Postwar and After: Rethinking American Literature*, ed. Jason Gladstone et al. (Iowa City: University of Iowa Press, 2016).

102. Watt's assertion that novelistic realism is enabled by technology runs counter to arguments about late-nineteenth-century realism as responding to technological advances. See Eric Sundquist, "Introduction: The Country of the Blue," in *American Realism: New Essays* (Baltimore, MD: Johns Hopkins University Press, 1982); Amy Kaplan, *The Social Construction of American Realism* (Chicago: University of Chicago Press, 1988); Donald Pizer, *Realism and Naturalism in Nineteenth-Century American Literature* (New York: Russell & Russell, 1976).

103. Jay David Bolter and Richard Grusin, *Remediation: Understanding New Media* (Cambridge, MA: MIT Press, 2000), 21.

104. McLane's work on ballads corrects this tendency, and Lisa Gitelman allows for older media in studies of the virtual as well, noting that media history is a unique way to study the past, since a particular medium provides not simply a representation of the past but also an index of the past, evidence in itself of the moment of representation. Lisa Gitelman, *Always Already New: Media, History and the Data of Culture* (Cambridge, MA: MIT Press, 2006), 5. McGurl has noted that the "technologies upon which literature depends were developed so long ago as to have become entirely naturalized, if not simply invisible, hiding from us the truth that a book, no less than a cell phone or PDA, is a kind of meaning-bearing gadget." Mark McGurl, "The Novel, Mass Culture, Mass Media," in *The Cambridge History of the American Novel* (Cambridge: Cambridge University Press, 2011), 688–89. When McGurl describes the book as a "gadget," he presents printed matter as indexical in this way.

105. Goble argues that "much of the newness that is attributed to new media art and culture is understood to render obsolete the sense of modernism and medium specificity (modernism as medium specificity) championed most notably by Clement Greenberg." Goble's point is that new media theory surprisingly contributes to a sense that modernism lives outside of its technologies: "When new media theorists dispense with its aesthetics of medium specificity, what remains of modernism is a concern with the thematics of high technology, which cannot move past a formalism designed to rarefy and obscure the social and political significance of technology itself" (*Beautiful Circuits*, 8–10). My analysis also draws on what John Guillory has identified as the nineteenth-century "media concept." Guillory argues that although the word media can be traced to the Latin *Medius*, there was no concept of "media" before the nineteenth century: "The emergence of the media concept in the later nineteenth century was the proliferation of new technical media—such as the telegraph and phonograph—that could not be assimilated into the older system of the arts." His observations clarify that "media" influenced the literary before the term came into being. John Guillory, "Genesis of the Media Concept," *Critical Inquiry* 35, no. 2 (2010): 321.

106. McGurl coins the term "technomodernism" to preserve what he describes as "the obvious continuity of much postwar American fiction with the modernist project of systematic experimentation with narrative form" and to clarify "a growing acknowledgment of the scandalous continuity of the literary techne (craft) with technology in the grosser sense" (*The Program Era*, 42). See also Maud Ellmann, *The Nets of Modernism: Henry James, Virginia Wolf, James Joyce, and Sigmund Freud* (Cambridge: Cambridge University Press, 2010). For a study of nineteenth-century realism that brings media theory into literary analysis see Seltzer, *Bodies and Machines*; and Menke, *Telegraphic Realism*.

107. Marshall, *Corridor*, 3; Mark Wollaeger, *Modernism, Media, and Propaganda: British Narrative from 1900 to 1945* (Princeton, NJ: Princeton University Press, 2006), xvi; Goble, *Beautiful Circuits*, 3; McGurl, "The Novel, Mass Culture, Mass Media," 688.

108. Jeffrey Sconce, *Haunted Media: Electronic Presence from Telegraphy to Television*, 2nd ed. (Durham, NC: Duke University Press, 2000), 64.

109. Watt, *The Rise of the Novel*, 196. This was roughly the era in which "compulsory education engulfed people in paper." Friedrich A. Kittler, *Gramophone, Film, Typewriter* (Stanford, CA: Stanford University Press, 1999), 8.

1. FUGITIVES AND FUTILITY: AGRARIAN BALLAD NOVELS IN BOB DYLAN'S MOMENT

1. Their travels also included Virginia and West Virginia. Karpeles reports that they spent a total of forty-six weeks in the Appalachian mountains between 1916 and 1919. Cecil J. Sharp, *English Folk Songs from the Southern Appalachians*, ed. Maud Karpeles (Northfield, MN: Loomis House, 2012), 1:xii.

2. For more information about Mary Sands, see Mike Yates and Kriss Sands, "A Nest of Singing Birds," *Musical Traditions* (March 3, 2002), http://www.mustrad.org.uk/articles /m_sands.htm.

3. With the help of the Americans Olive Dame and John C. Campbell, Sharp published the first edition of *English Folk Songs* in 1917 with G. P. Putnam and Son. Karpeles took over the project when Sharp died in 1924, eventually publishing *English Folk Songs from the Southern Appalachians* with Oxford University Press in 1932. Subsequent editions of Sharp's volume came out in 1952 and 2012. See bibliography.

4. Tom Tierney, "House Carpenter: A Song's Journey Through the Archives," http://www .bobdylan.com/us/bobdylan101/house-carpenter-songs-journey-through-archives.

5. Davidson's correspondence suggests that he was seeking to bring out *The Big Ballad Jamboree* with McGraw-Hill during 1953 and 1954 but trails off with no clear indication of why this never came to fruition in a publication. Donald Davidson, letter to Ed Kuhn, 1954, Vanderbilt Special Collections, Nashville, TN.

6. "The Daemon Lover" first appeared in England in 1685; about two hundred years later, the American version, "The House Carpenter," was printed in New York. Alisoun Gardner-Medwin, "The Ancestry of 'The House Carpenter': A Study of the American Form of Child 243," *Journal of American Folklore* 84, no. 334 (December 1971): 415. When Sands performed it for Sharp and Karpeles in 1916, "The Daemon Lover" had already been published in Percy's 1765 *Reliques*, in Sir Walter Scott's 1802 *The Minstrelsy of the Scottish Border*, and in Child's *The English and Scottish Popular Ballads* (1882–1898).

7. Irene Spain wrote "The Death of Floyd Collins" with her stepfather, Reverend Andrew Jenkins—a professional disaster ballad composer. In 1950, Spain explains that the creation of the song was quick and that the "tragic" affect that led to its creation was fueled by the radio broadcast: "After listening to the radio so much, we knew the entire tragic horror of it, so, after getting the telegram, Daddy took his guitar out to the front steps and went to singing. I went to him, wrote it all down, made the musical score, and had it finished and in the mails in a very short time." Dorothy Horstman, *Sing Your Heart Out, Country Boy*, rev. sub. ed. (Nashville, TN: Country Music Foundation, 1996), 76–77. See also David N. Brinson, "Cave & Bat-Inspired Recorded Music and Spoken Word," http:// caveinspiredmusic.com/rubriques/country_music/country_music.html; Tony Russell, Tennessee Country Music Hall of Fame &&Museum, and Bob Pinson, *Country Music Records: A Discography, 1921–1942* (Oxford: Oxford University Press, 2004); Charles Wolfe, "Event

Songs," in *Reading Country Music: Steel Guitars, Opry Stars, and Honky-Tonk Bars*, ed. Cecelia Tichi (Durham, NC: Duke University Press, 1998). For information on Dalhart's career, see Colin Escott, *Lost Highway: The True Story of Country Music* (Washington, DC: Smithsonian Books, 2003); Jack Palmer, Robert Olson, and Hank Thompson, *Vernon Dalhart: First Star of Country Music* (Denver: Mainspring, 2004). H. R. Stoneback has also noticed that *The Cave* is based on "The Death of Floyd Collins." H. R. Stoneback, "The Box, the Glittering Strings, and the Unbearable Hillbillyness of Being: Warren's *The Cave*, Country Music, and Vanderbilt Fugitive-Agrarianism," *RWP: Annual of Robert Penn Warren Studies* 8 (January 2008): 18.

8. Jack Fincher, "Dreams of Riches Led Floyd Collins to a Nightmarish End." *Smithsonian Magazine*, May 1990, 138. Fincher notes that events "took a bizarre turn from sensational melodrama to macabre commercialism" when the body of Floyd Collins was taken out of the spot where Collins had been trapped and put on display in another cave for tourists. The body was eventually removed from the national park containing the cave and interred at the family cemetery (this was the occasion for Fincher's piece in *Smithsonian*), but not until 1989. In 1982, the University of Kentucky Press put out a book on Collins's story, in which the authors Robert K. Murray and Roger W. Brucker describe the entrapment as "one of the most sensational news events of modern times." Robert K. Murray, *Trapped! The Story of the Struggle to Rescue Floyd Collins from a Kentucky Cave in 1925* (New York: Putnam, 1979), 5.

9. Karl Hagstrom Miller, *Segregating Sound: Inventing Folk and Pop Music in the Age of Jim Crow* (Durham, NC: Duke University Press, 2010), 200–204. Miller reports that by the mid-1920s the former mattress salesman had already made a killing, first as a wholesale phonograph dealer and then as the exclusive record distributor for his region at OKeh Records. Brockman got his start selling mattresses door to door, then transformed his grandfather's furniture store into a distribution center for records and phonograph needles.

10. The producer and engineer Ralph Peer wrote in a 1955 *Variety* article that "Dalhart had the peculiar ability to adapt hillbilly music to suit the taste of the non-hillbilly population . . . He was a professional substitute for a real hillbilly." Ralph Peer, "Ralph Peer Sees No Hypo [sic] for Late Jimmy Rodgers; Dalhart Not a Hillbilly," *Variety*, November 2, 1955. Tracy Laird notes that Peer's letter to the editor is a response to the musicologist Jim Walsh's defense of Dalhart's authenticity. Jim Walsh, "Musicologist Jim Walsh on Hillbilly Champs: Dalhart vs. Rodgers et al.," *Variety*, September 21, 1955; Tracey E. W. Laird, *Louisiana Hayride: Radio and Roots Music Along the Red River* (Oxford: Oxford University Press, 2004), 52n45.

11. Billy Wilder had already based his 1951 film *Ace in the Hole* on Collins's ordeal.

12. Cecil J. Sharp, Olive D. (Olive Dame) Campbell, and Maud Karpeles, *English Folk Songs from the Southern Appalachians*, 2nd and enlarged ed. (Oxford: Oxford University Press, 1960), xx.

13. Donald Davidson, *The Big Ballad Jamboree: A Novel* (Jackson: University Press of Mississippi, 1996), 19.

14. Teresa Lenox, "The Carver Village Controversy," *Tequesta* 50 (January 1990): 39–51; Wayne Greenhaw, *Fighting the Devil in Dixie: How Civil Rights Activists Took on the Ku Klux Klan in Alabama*, reprint ed. (Chicago: Chicago Review Press, 2011); Minrose Gwin, *Remembering Medgar Evers: Writing the Long Civil Rights Movement* (Athens: University of Georgia Press, 2013); John Egerton, "Walking Into History: The Beginning of School Desegregation in Nashville," *Southern Spaces* (2009), https://southernspaces.org/2009

/walking-history-beginning-school-desegregation-nashville"; Neil R. McMillen, "Organized Resistance to School Desegregation in Tennessee," *Tennessee Historical Quarterly* 30, no. 3 (September 1971): 315–28.

15. The line is from "Song to Woody" (one of the first songs Dylan ever wrote), released on his 1962 debut album, *Bob Dylan*. Clinton Heylin reports that Dylan later explained his turn to folk in 1958 thus: "The first thing that turned me on to folksinging was Odetta. I heard a record of hers in a record store, back when you could listen to records there in the store. That was in '58 or something like that. Right then and there I went out and traded my electric guitar and amplifier for an acoustical guitar, a flat-top Gibson." Clinton Heylin, *Bob Dylan: Behind the Shades Revisited* (New York: HarperEntertainment, 2003), 33. Dylan's friend John Bucklen explains that Dylan had discovered Lead Belly soon after hearing the Odetta record in the record store, during the summer of 1958. Heylin makes the point that Dylan's "discovery of Lead Belly almost certainly came after he suffered his most crushing expulsion from the world of rock and roll combos," from the group Bobby Vee and the Shadows. Clinton Heylin, *Bob Dylan: Behind the Shades Revisited*, 1st US ed. (New York: William Morrow, 2001), 26. Surely Dylan's step away from rock and toward the music of Lead Belly was motivated by more than this single experience, but Heylin's anecdote gives biographical context to Dylan's interest in folk.

16. Noting that Cecil Sharp had collected "Man of Constant Sorrow" on the 1916 trek, Harvey gives a thorough analysis of Dylan's possible sources for this ballad. Todd Harvey, *The Formative Dylan: Transmission and Stylistic Influences, 1961–1963* (Lanham, MD: Scarecrow, 2001), 65–67. Harvey traces "Pretty Peggy-O" back through the Clancy Brothers to Ewan MacColl as well as to an American variant also discovered by Sharp (88–90).

17. Harvey, *The Formative Dylan*, 15.

18. Gwin, *Remembering Medgar Evers*, 130; "Dream Songs: The Music of the March on Washington," *New Yorker*, August 28, 2013, http://www.newyorker.com/culture/culture-desk/dream-songs-the-music-of-the-march-on-washington.

19. The moment Dylan switched from acoustic guitar to this Stratocaster is known for the disruption it caused among folk purists at the Newport Folk Festival. Greil Marcus, *The Old, Weird America: The World of Bob Dylan's Basement Tapes*, updated ed. (New York: Picador, 2011); Benjamin Hedin, "Newport 1965," in *Studio A: The Bob Dylan Reader* (New York: Norton, 2004); Elijah Wald, *Dylan Goes Electric! Newport, Seeger, Dylan, and the Night That Split the Sixties* (New York: Dey St., 2015). For an account of the electric guitar as a midcentury artifact, see Andre Millard, ed., "The Music: The Electric Guitar in the American Century," in *The Electric Guitar: A History of an American Icon* (Baltimore, MD: Lemelson Center for the Study of Invention and Innovation, National Museum of American History, Smithsonian Institution, 2004).

20. The *Anthology* was put out by Moses Asch, the engineer and record executive responsible for recording a range of folk standards, including Woody Guthrie's "This Land Is Your Land" and Lead Belly's "Good Night Irene." Richard Carlin, *Worlds of Sound: The Story of Smithsonian Folkways* (New York: Collins, 2008); Anthony Olmsted, *Folkways Records: Moses Asch and His Encyclopedia of Sound* (New York: Routledge, 2003). The Library of Congress holds at least two other versions of "The House Carpenter," both recorded by Alan and Elizabeth Lomax. One, from 1937, is sung by Mr. Clay Walters in Salyersville, Kentucky; the other in 1940 by Mrs. Pearl Jacobs Borusky at Antiago, Wisconsin. "Child Ballads Traditional in the United States," issued from the Collections of the Archive of American Folk Song, L57, RBA 04872-04876, r 53000578, r 56000413.

21. The historian David Suisman provides historical background here, pointing out that the *Anthology* claimed as "folk" recordings made in the 1920s and 1930s for commercial purposes. Many defunct recordings of Child ballads, Suisman points out, "made for a niche market" in the 1920s and 1930s, "resurfaced" on the *Anthology* and, in his words, "cast the spell of its archaic songs anew." David Suisman, *Selling Sounds: The Commercial Revolution in American Music* (Cambridge, MA: Harvard University Press, 2009), 275–76. Originally part of an effort to cash in on "the music of the poor, the isolated, and the uneducated," the folklorist David Cantwell adds, these songs came to be understood as "a kind of avant-garde art." Robert Cantwell, *When We Were Good: The Folk Revival* (Cambridge, MA: Harvard University Press, 1996), 190. Both Mississippi John's recording of "Frankie" and Clarence Ashley's of "The House Carpenter" were part of a body of recordings that, as Cantwell explains, derived "from a former generation of entrepreneurs who in the early days of electrical recording had cultivated the ethnic and regional record markets" that would be quashed in subsequent radio and music industry developments (189–90).

22. Cantwell, *When We Were Good*, 189; Marcus, *The Old, Weird America*.

23. Marcus explains that by "the early 1960s the *Anthology* had become a kind of lingua franca, or a password: for the likes of Roger McGuinn, later of the Byrds, or Jerry Garcia, founder of the Grateful Dead . . . it was the secret text of a secret country." The "presence of Smith's music in Dylan's has been a template for the presence of that music in the country," argues Marcus, "and the world, at large." Greil Marcus, "American Folk," https://granta.com/american-folk/.

24. Suisman, *Selling Sounds*, 276.

25. The archivist Todd Harvey describes Dylan's version as an "orally transmitted compilation of the ballad as it existed in the hills and hollows of Greenwich Village" (*The Formative Dylan*, 48). Without venturing too far into the "land of Bob," as David Kinney calls this territory, I will note my affinity for Marcus's assessment in *The Old, Weird America* of Dylan's influence by the *Anthology*. David Kinney, *The Dylanologists: Adventures in the Land of Bob* (New York: Simon & Schuster, 2014). For an opposing take, see Clinton Heylin, *Dylan's Daemon Lover: The Tangled Tale of a 450-Year-Old Pop Ballad* (London: Helter Skelter, 1999). For an archival account of Dylan's recording, see Tierney, "House Carpenter." Heylin argues that Dylan's song "The Man in the Long Black Coat," from the 1989 release *Oh Mercy!*, rewrites the ballad from the carpenter's point of view (*Dylan's Daemon Lover*, 168).

26. Marcus, *The Old, Weird America*, 101.

27. Robert Penn Warren, *The Cave* (Lexington: University Press of Kentucky, 2006), 161, 13.

28. McGurl has argued that Flannery O'Connor "achieves the logical equivalent of ethnic difference" at a moment when "the South was being pressed into conformity with federal law." "Southern writing," he argues, would be "promoted" as "a white minority discourse that resists assimilation into the American mainstream." Mark McGurl, *The Program Era: Postwar Fiction and the Rise of Creative Writing* (Cambridge, MA: Harvard University Press, 2009), 60. Isaac's transformation into a Jewish newspaper reporter suggests that McGurl is right. I would only add that the creation of Southern identity as "minority discourse" that McGurl demonstrates as an institutional formation should also be understood as arising from a newly labile vernacular, the sense of mobility enabled by technology that also produced rock and roll.

29. It would not be until 1969 that Roth's Portnoy would explain that "a self-hating Jew" is the "best kind," but it is notable that we find a version of this in a novel written by an

inveterate Southerner like Warren. Philip Roth, *Portnoy's Complaint*, reprint ed. (New York: Vintage, 1994), 265.

30. Cleanth Brooks, *The Well Wrought Urn: Studies in the Structure of Poetry* (New York: Harcourt, Brace, 1947), xi.

31. I refer here to the media theorist Jussi Parikka's intriguing argument that there is a crucial relation between media and insects, identifying "cultural discourses and practices" that "have hailed the powers of insects as media in themselves, capable of weird affect worlds, strange sensations, and uncanny potentials that cannot be immediately pinpointed in terms of a register of known possibilities." Jussi Parikka, *Insect Media: An Archaeology of Animals and Technology* (Minneapolis: University of Minnesota Press, 2010), xiii.

32. Richard A. Peterson, "Why 1955? Explaining the Advent of Rock Music," *Popular Music* 9, no. 1 (January 1, 1990): 102.

33. Robert Penn Warren, *Who Speaks for the Negro?* (New York: Random House, 1965), 1.

34. Warren, *Who Speaks for the Negro?*, 11.

2. NEW CRITICAL NOISE IN MUSIC CITY: THOMAS PYNCHON'S WILLIAM FAULKNER

1. William Faulkner, *The Town* (New York: Vintage, 1961), 189.

2. Thomas Pynchon, *The Crying of Lot 49* (New York: Perennial Library, 1986), 118.

3. I describe the convergence of "Negro folk" and Donne in *Understanding Poetry* in my introduction. I note there as well that it is Guillory who details Eliot's role in securing Donne's status during the years after World War I. In Guillory's account, it was the retroactive celebration of Eliot's Donne that indicated the New Critics' retrenchment— their attempt to reconsolidate bourgeois class status in "cultural capital," as he calls it, in the residual reading practices of modernism. He argues that Eliot's Arnoldian project of creating "unconsciously Christian" literature to unify culture failed, since literary "sensibility" does not function in culture like Christian belief. John Guillory, *Cultural Capital: The Problem of Literary Canon Formation* (Chicago: University of Chicago Press, 1993), 137–38. In Eliot's own words, he seeks "a literature which should be *unconsciously*, rather than deliberately and defiantly, Christian." T. S. Eliot, *Selected Essays* (London: Faber & Faber, 1999), 392.

4. W. C. Handy appears in a memory from Gavin's childhood. Faulkner, *The Town*, 72–73. Tim A. Ryan mines Faulkner's novels for other mentions of Handy and other African American blues artists. Tim A. Ryan, "'The Faint Plinking of a Guitar': Faulkner's Forgotten Bluesman and the Power of Vernacular in *If I Forget Thee, Jerusalem*," *Faulkner Journal* 27, no. 1 (2013): 3–27.

5. William Faulkner, "A Letter to the North," *Life*, March 5, 1956. See also Philip Weinstein, *Becoming Faulkner: The Art and Life of William Faulkner* (New York: Oxford University Press, 2010), 117.

6. In McGurl's terms, we might say that an examination of these two novels together bears out one of his points about postwar fiction, which is that technological work like *The Crying of Lot 49*, understood as "technomodernism," is the "unmarked, dialectical reversal" of Southern fiction, what he describes as an example of "high cultural pluralism." As white ethnic fiction, Faulkner's *The Town* would be understood to repress the technological in an appeal to identity. My reading clarifies that this novel fails to accomplish that task. Mark

McGurl, *The Program Era: Postwar Fiction and the Rise of Creative Writing* (Cambridge, MA: Harvard University Press, 2009), 62.

7. Marshall McLuhan, *Understanding Media: The Extensions of Man* (Cambridge, MA: MIT Press, 1994), 7.

8. Louis Decimus Rubin, "Introduction," in *I'll Take My Stand* (New York: Harper and Row, 1962), xxvii. His dismay with suburbanization notwithstanding, Rubin hardly gave up on Southern literature. Indeed, he remained a major force in maintaining the field until his death. Rubin founded the *Southern Literary Journal* in 1968, wrote several books on the topic—including *The Faraway Country: Writers of the Modern South* (Seattle: University of Washington Press, 1963) and *The Writer in the South* (Athens: University of Georgia Press, 1972)—and edited *The History of Southern Literature* (Baton Rouge: Louisiana State University Press, 1990).

9. The term is attributed to David Cobb, a radio announcer for Nashville's WSM. Cobb reports that he first began using the phrase in 1950. Craig Havighurst, *Air Castle of the South: WSM and the Making of Music City* (Urbana: University of Illinois Press, 2007); Michael Kosser, *How Nashville Became Music City, USA: 50 Years of Music Row* (Hal Leonard Corporation, 2006); and Colin Escott, *The Grand Ole Opry: The Making of an American Icon* (Hachette Digital, Inc., 2009). On the suburbanization of American literature after World War II, see Catherine Jurca, *White Diaspora: The Suburb and the Twentieth-Century American Novel* (Princeton, NJ: Princeton University Press, 2001).

10. As rock and roll began to gain in popularity, a strain of country music that came to be known as the "Nashville Sound" developed in response. Created at Studio B by Chet Atkins and Jim Reeves, among others, the Nashville Sound rendered Nashville's traditional country music slicker, more pop sounding—and generally more commensurate with rock. Jocelyn Neal, *Country Music: A Cultural and Stylistic History* (New York: Oxford University Press, 2013); Joli Jensen, *The Nashville Sound: Authenticity, Commercialization, and Country Music* (Nashville, TN: Vanderbilt University Press, 1998).

11. Robert Penn Warren, ed., *Faulkner: A Collection of Critical Essays* (Englewood Cliffs, NJ: Prentice-Hall, 1966), 10–11.

12. Joseph Blotner, *Robert Penn Warren: A Biography* (New York: Random House, 1997), xi–xiii.

13. Cleanth Brooks, *William Faulkner: The Yoknapatawpha Country* (New Haven, CT: Yale University Press, 1963), 215–16; Andrew Lytle, "The Town: Helen's Last Stand," *Sewanee Review* 65 (1957): 484; Michael Kreyling, *Inventing Southern Literature* (Jackson: University Press of Mississippi, 1998), 150.

14. Robert Penn Warren, *Who Speaks for the Negro?* (1965).

15. *I'll Take My Stand: The South and the Agrarian Tradition* (New York: Harper and Row, 1962), 205.

16. William Brevda, "Neon Light in August: Electric Signs in Faulkner's Fiction," in *Faulkner and Popular Culture* (Jackson: University Press of Mississippi, 1988), 234.

17. My point here is informed by Guillory's observation that "every poem" was for New Critics "an image of the institutional space in which it is read" (165). The South, I am suggesting, is invoked in New Critical formal practice as well. Leigh Ann Duck ties construals of the South to American cultural identity more broadly, arguing that "U.S. nationalism has tended to code its investments in racial hierarchies as regional traits." Leigh Anne Duck, *The Nation's Region: Southern Modernism, Segregation, and US Nationalism* (Athens: University of Georgia Press, 2006), 14. I am making a similar, if inverse, version of this

claim: that Southerners preserved racist notions by construing them as portable—as rituals, perhaps, that could be practiced in university rooms "up North."

18. Baudrillard describes the hyperreal as the "generation by models of a real without origin or reality," the hyperreal hides nothing, since it begins with no referent. Jean Baudrillard, *Simulacra and Simulation* (Ann Arbor: University of Michigan Press, 1994), 1.

19. H. W. Brands, "Coca-Cola Goes to War," *American History* 33, no. 3 (August 1999).

20. Mauri Skinfill, "The American Interior: Identity and Commercial Culture in Faulkner's Late Novels," *Faulkner Journal* 21, nos. 1/2 (2005): 134.

21. Norman Mailer, *Advertisements for Myself* (Cambridge, MA: Harvard University Press, 1992), 341, 339.

22. Michael Szalay, *Hip Figures: A Literary History of the Democratic Party* (Stanford, CA: Stanford University Press, 2012), 2.

23. Richard Godden, *Fictions of Labor: William Faulkner and the South's Long Revolution* (Cambridge: Cambridge University Press, 1997), 1–4.

24. This is Jonathan Lethem's formulation. Lethem describes Dylan this way and confesses to an affinity for Dylan's reverence for African American vernacular culture. Jonathan Lethem, "The Ecstasy of Influence: A Plagiarism," *Harper's*, February 1, 2007. Theresa Towner is surely right to suggest that Faulkner's later style is inextricable from race: "'Race' and 'art' thus become, in Faulkner's later career, functions of one another" (8). But rather than gleaning in *The Town* evidence of Faulkner's "increasing interest in how racial identity is formed and maintained" (8), as Towner does, I am arguing that racial identity emerges in a new form in the later works. What Lott calls the "panic, anxiety, terror, and pleasure" involved with minstrelsy—what Godden calls "blacks in whiteface"—can of course be identified in early Faulkner too. But race is figured differently in 1957, more in keeping with the "hipsters" for which Szalay provides his analysis.

25. William K. Wimsatt, *The Verbal Icon: Studies in the Meaning of Poetry* (Lexington: University of Kentucky Press, 1954), 4.

26. Fredric Jameson, *Postmodernism; or, The Cultural Logic of Late Capitalism* (Durham, NC: Duke University Press, 1991), 34–35.

27. For analyses of *The Crying of Lot 49* in relation to radio, see Marcus Erbe, "The Transcription of Electronic Music in *The Crying of Lot 49*," *Pynchon Notes* 54–55 (2008): 99–107; and Umberto Rossi, "Acousmatic Presences: From DJs to Talk-Radio Hosts in American Fiction, Cinema, and Drama," *Mosaic: A Journal for the Interdisciplinary Study of Literature* 42, no. 1 (2009): 83–98. For studies of Pynchon in relation to media systems, see David Seed, "Media Systems in *The Crying of Lot 49*," in *American Postmodernity: Essays on the Recent Fiction of Thomas Pynchon*, ed. Ian D. Copestake (Oxford: Peter Lang, 2003); and Bernhard Siegert, *Relays: Literature as an Epoch of the Postal System*, trans. Kevin Repp (Stanford, CA: Stanford University Press, 1999).

3. THE BALLAD'S GENDER: FEMININITY AND INFORMATION IN GEORGIA

1. The song was written by the African American songwriter Eddie Green, who copyrighted it in 1917 and then sold it to W. C. Handy's publishing company a year later. It was first recorded by the white blues singer Marion Harris in 1919. Elva Diane Green, *Eddie Green: The Rise of an Early 1900s Black American Entertainment Pioneer* (Albany, GA: Bear Manor

Media, 2016), 6. The reading that follows privileges Bessie Smith's 1927 version of the recording because of its legendary status, though in her introduction to *Habit of Being*, Sally Fitzgerald notes that O'Connor chose the title after seeing a newsreel in which the song was sung by a seven-year-old girl who had won first prize in an amateur singing contest. Fitzgerald does not disclose whether this "crimped" and "beribboned" child was black or white, only that O'Connor found it amusing. Flannery O'Connor, *The Habit of Being: Letters of Flannery O'Connor*, ed. Sally Fitzgerald, repr. ed. (New York: Farrar, Straus and Giroux, 1988), xiii. Susan Scott Parrish has given details of Bessie Smith's notoriety, noting that when she recorded "A Good Man Is Hard to Find," Smith was filling theaters, selling out for both "whites-only" crowds and black audiences as well. Susan Parrish, *The Flood Year 1927: A Cultural History* (Princeton, NJ: Princeton University Press, 2017), 125. See "Columbia Matrix 144797. 'A Good Man Is Hard to Find' / Bessie Smith—Discography of American Historical Recordings," http://adp.library.ucsb.edu/index.php/matrix /detail/2000034512/144797-A_good_man_is_hard_to_find; "Victor Matrix B-22593. A Good Man Is Hard to Find / Marion Harris—Discography of American Historical Recordings," 2016, http://adp.library.ucsb.edu/index.php/matrix/detail/700007738/B-22593 -A_good_man_is_hard_to_find. On Marion Harris and racial crossings in early blues, see Will Friedwald, *Jazz Singing: America's Great Voices from Bessie Smith to Bebop and Beyond* (New York: Da Capo, 1990).

2. Although Ray Charles has been classified as one of the earliest soul artists to come out of the US South, few if any accounts of rock and roll would deny the hybridization of rock, country, and soul during these years or the influence, in particular, of "I Got a Woman" (1954) or "What'd I Say" (1959) on the development of rock. Peter Guralnick notes that rock and roll developed "in tandem" with soul, subject to cross-fertilization and hybridization. Far "from taking place in a vacuum or developing an aesthetic in splendid isolation from other more corrupt and hybridized strains," argues Guralnick, moreover, soul music "was in fact developing in tandem with rock 'n' roll and country music, was competing, really, for the same dollar." Peter Guralnick, *Sweet Soul Music: Rhythm and Blues and the Southern Dream of Freedom* (New York: Harper & Row, 1986), 6–7. In his 2004 autobiography *Brother Ray: Ray Charles' Own Story* (Cambridge, MA: Da Capo, 2004), Ray Charles distinguished his music from rock and roll: "I never considered myself part of rock 'n' roll," he explained. "When I think of true rock 'n' roll, cats like Chuck Berry and Little Richard and Bo Diddley come to mind." Noting that his "stuff was more adult," Charles dismisses the Beatles' claim that he had influenced them: "I believe them, but I also think my influence on them wasn't nearly as great as these other artists" (177). Jack Hamilton's argument—that soul developed as part of a 1960s ideology that sorted Dylan into white and Cooke into black categories—is nuanced by the emergence of soul in the 1950s as well as by its hybridized development.

3. Cleanth Brooks, *Understanding Poetry: An Anthology for College Students* (New York: H. Holt and Co., 1938), 33; *I'll Take My Stand: The South and the Agrarian Tradition* (New York: Harper and Row, 1962), 244.

4. There has been almost no scholarly attention given to O'Connor's use of Eddie Green's song. The exception is Allison R. Ensor, who in presenting each mention of music in O'Connor's oeuvre observes that Green's song "sums up" the worldview shared by the grandmother and Red Sammy Butts. Allison R. Ensor, "Flannery O'Connor and Music," *The Flannery O'Connor Bulletin* 14 (1985): 9. Scholarship on *The Ballad of the Sad Café* as a ballad has been more extensive. Dawson F. Gaillard, "The Presence of the Narrator in

Carson McCullers' 'The Ballad of the Sad Café,'" *Mississippi Quarterly* 25, no. 4 (Fall 1972), reads the novella in relation to thematic and formal features of the ballad—a concern with "communal life," she argues, and repetition. Gaillard goes so far as to declare that there is an "oral quality" in this novella, noted in a sense of "presence" created in the narrative: "Because of this presence the reader cannot, I feel, distance himself from the emotional impact of the action. Such is the magic of the oral quality in literature" (419, 422). Likewise, Joseph R. Millichap, "Carson McCullers' Literary Ballad," *Georgia Review* 27 (1973), argued that, like a ballad, McCullers's story is a "perfect blend of the literate and colloquial, the objective and the personal, talky observation" (12). Daniel Patrick Barlow, "'And Every Day There Is Music': Folksong Roots and the Highway Chain Gang in *The Ballad of the Sad Café*," *Southern Literary Journal* 44, no. 1 (2011), associates *Ballad of a Sad Café* with folk music, noting that the absence of lyrics leaves readers with an "enigmatic portrait of the American work song" (75).

5. Carson McCullers, *The Ballad of the Sad Café and Other Stories*, 1st Mariner Books ed. (Boston: Houghton Mifflin, 2005), 61.

6. *Understanding Fiction* was first published in 1943. McCullers and O'Connor both landed stories—"A Domestic Dilemma" and "A Good Man Is Hard to Find"—in its two subsequent editions (1959 and 1979). In 1960, Brooks and Warren published a shorter version of *Understanding Fiction*, *The Scope of Fiction*, noting in their preface that the volume is "not in any sense a watering down of *Understanding Fiction*" but rather the "very core of the longer book." Cleanth Brooks and Robert Penn Warren, *The Scope of Fiction* (Englewood Cliffs, NJ: Prentice-Hall, 1960), v. These stories by McCullers and O'Connor both make the cut. For an account of O'Connor's work with Lytle at Iowa Writer's Workshop, see Mark McGurl, *The Program Era: Postwar Fiction and the Rise of Creative Writing* (Cambridge, MA: Harvard University Press, 2009), 154. As editor of the *Sewanee Review*, Lytle published several O'Connor stories, including "The Displaced Person" and "The Lame Shall Enter First." John Crowe Ransom, as well, published O'Connor in the *Kenyon Review*. See Flannery O'Connor, *The Complete Stories* (New York: Farrar, Straus and Giroux, 1971), 551–55.

7. Marshall McLuhan, *Understanding Media: The Extensions of Man*, 1st MIT Press ed. (Cambridge, MA: MIT Press, 1994), 89.

8. Roland Barthes, "The Grain of the Voice," in *Image-Music-Text*, trans. Stephen Heath (New York: Hill and Wang, 1978), 181. For another Lacanian take on the voice, see Mladen Dolar, *A Voice and Nothing More* (Cambridge, MA: MIT Press, 2006).

9. The "voice," Barthes argues, "bears along *directly* the symbolic, over the intelligible, the expressive: here, thrown in front of us like a packet, is the Father, his phallic stature." Barthes, "The Grain of the Voice," 182.

10. McLuhan, *Understanding Media*, 89. In his assertion that electronic communication began as couriers on physical roads, McLuhan was following the work of his colleague Harold Innis, the political economist who introduced McLuhan to the idea that the control of information crucially defines civic organization. The "changing character of the British Empire during the present century," argued Innis, "has been in part a result of the pulp and paper industry and its influence on public opinion." Harold Innis, *Empire and Communications* (Lanham, MD: Rowman & Littlefield, 2007), 25.

11. "Broadcast" as colloquially understood is a twentieth-century invention: "a. Of seed, etc.: scattered abroad over the whole surface, instead of being sown in drills or rows." *OED*. The media scholar John Durham Peters dates to the nineteenth century uses of the word

"communication" that mean something more than physical transfer. It was then that "technologies such as the telegraph and radio refitted the old term 'communication,' once used for any kind of physical transfer or transmission, into a new kind of quasi-physical connection across the obstacles of time and space." John Durham Peters, *Speaking Into the Air: A History of the Idea of Communication* (Chicago: University of Chicago Press, 1999), 5. Mark Goble examines the "shared history" of modernism and "communication" as both "flourished as conglomerating triumphs of the postwar university in the United States." Mark Goble, *Beautiful Circuits: Modernism and the Mediated Life* (New York: Columbia University Press, 2010), 4.

12. Flannery O'Connor, *The Complete Stories* (New York: Farrar, Straus and Giroux, 1971), 120.

13. O'Connor once claimed not to enjoy music of any kind. Writing in 1959 to the correspondent known as "A," she said: "I am a complete musical ignoramus, don't know Mozart from Spike Jones." In 1964, Thomas Stritch sent O'Connor a box of records, and she explained to A: "We are broke out with records now as Thomas has sent me a box full out of his basement. All I can say about it is that all classical music sounds alike to me and all the rest of it sounds like the Beatles." O'Connor, *The Habit of Being*, 566.

14. "No I cannot meet James Baldwin in Georgia," the author said. "It would cause the greatest trouble and disturbance and disunion. In New York it would be nice to meet him; here it would not. I observe the traditions of the society I feed on—it's only fair. Might as well expect a mule to fly as me to see James Baldwin in Georgia. I have read one of his stories and it is a good one." O'Connor, *The Habit of Being*, 329. Scholars have disagreed about whether O'Connor's fiction reiterates racist ideologies. On the one hand, Frederick Crews charged that O'Connor's depiction of a Sambo figure in "The Artificial Nigger" was a "regressive political act." Frederick Crews, "The Power of Flannery O'Connor," *New York Review of Books*, April 26, 1990. On the other, Hilton Als has argued that O'Connor's black characters are "not symbols defined in opposition to whiteness." Hilton Als, "Flannery O'Connor's Revelatory Honesty," *New Yorker*, January 22, 2001. Als argues that "they are the living people who were, physically at least, on the periphery of O'Connor's own world. She was not romantic enough to take Faulkner's Dilsey view of blacks—as the fulcrum of integrity and compassion. She didn't use them as vessels of sympathy or scorn; she simply—and complexly—drew from life." Mark Greif complains about the "liberal reading" of O'Connor, noting that where the author appears to be advocating liberal views on race, she is in fact making those readings "available" to "try to humiliate them." Mark Greif, *The Age of the Crisis of Man: Thought and Fiction in America, 1933–1973* (Princeton, NJ: Princeton University Press, 2015), 220.

15. Brooks, *Understanding Poetry*, 32–33.

16. William K. Wimsatt, *The Verbal Icon: Studies in the Meaning of Poetry* (Lexington: University of Kentucky Press, 1954), 4–5.

17. O'Connor takes "Pitty Sing" from Pitti Sing, one of the "three little maids" falsely blamed for an execution in W. S. Gilbert and Arthur Sullivan's 1885 *The Mikado*. See J. Peter Dyson, "Cats, Crime, and Punishment: The Mikado's Pitti-Sing in 'A Good Man Is Hard to Find,'" *English Studies in Canada* 14, no. 4 (1988): 436–52. O'Connor's decision to name the cat Pitty Sing may also have been influenced by the fact that swing versions of *The Mikado*—"Swing Mikado" and "Hot Mikado," featuring all-black casts—were produced to great acclaim in Chicago and New York in 1938 and 1939. Josephine Lee, *The Japan of Pure Invention: Gilbert and Sullivan's* The Mikado (Minneapolis: University of Minnesota Press, 2010).

18. The media theorist Frances Dyson describes as "reverse transubstantiation" assertions that an unmediated body is ruined by sound technology. Dyson argues rather that "the voice is already a metaphysical instrument, and already caught within particular circuits, switchboards, or machines that both literally and figuratively encode, transmit, and give meaning to vocal acts." Frances Dyson, *Sounding New Media: Immersion and Embodiment in the Arts and Culture* (Berkeley: University of California Press, 2009), 26, 25. The communications theorist Jonathan Sterne similarly contends that "the practices, ideas, and constructs associated with sound reproduction technologies predated the machines themselves." Jonathan Sterne, *The Audible Past: Cultural Origins of Sound Reproduction* (Durham, NC: Duke University Press, 2003), 1. Southern fiction in the 1950s bears out these ideas, presenting the corporeal wholeness presumed in *Understanding Poetry* as ultimately irretrievable.

19. Dyson would perhaps understand McCullers's depiction as driven by an accurate view of the Western metaphysical subject. For Dyson, "I think therefore I am" is crucially spoken and heard. *Cogito ergo sum* contains a "condensation," she says, such that "I think therefore I am" narrates a subject hearing herself speak as other: "Obliterating the distance between the speaker (now thinker) and listener (now thought) enables the fiction of the inner voice to substantiate (literally) a disembodied subjectivity." Dyson, *Sounding New Media*, 25. Dyson's point is that disembodiment is the condition of the voice even before radio: "it is no great leap of faith to suggest that" the voice of Western philosophy is "already abstracted" when it becomes "transformed into electrical impulses, transmitted through wires, and emerge[s] carrying the being, the 'there' of the speaker" (27). Considered in relation to Dyson's philosophy, McCullers's literary depiction of subjects riven by paper in the age of rock and roll might be understood as an acknowledgment, like rock's, of sound technology's essential entanglement with humans.

20. Wimsatt, *The Verbal Icon*, 4.

21. McGurl has identified in the shortness of O'Connor's preferred medium evidence of an allegiance to New Criticism (*The Program Era*, 144, 135). Specifically, he argues, O'Connor's brevity is evidence of a tendency to submit to the emergent institutional discipline of creative writing. For McGurl, O'Connor's obeisance to formal limitation induced her to produce "the same perfectly crafted short story again and again." McGurl's reading of the fiction as paradigmatically institutional raises the question of how we should read the blues song in this context. While surely McGurl is right to read obeisance in O'Connor's aesthetic, I am suggesting that this has the paradoxical effect of likening her works to the mechanical arts held up as anathema to institutional practices.

22. Barthes, "The Grain of the Voice," 182, 189. "It is very tempting," argues Dyson, "to read this grain as something both originary and irreducible: an expression of the body that culture has yet to contain" (*Sounding New Media*, 18). Barthes produces this perception in his comments about sound technology. He distinguishes music that causes this "thrill" from singing voices "lacking in any 'grain'" and suggests that a weak voice "fits well the demands of an *average* culture." Art, in such a culture, "inoculates pleasure," Barthes argues, by "reducing it to a known, coded emotion" and "reconciles the subject to what in music *can be said*." Praising the voice of the Swiss operatic baritone Charles Panzera, Barthes points out that Panzera "does not belong to" the reductive "average culture." For Barthes, his status as culturally superior is a pretechnological condition: "he could not have done, having sung before the coming of the microgroove record" ("The Grain of the Voice," 185). Toward the end of the essay as well, Barthes advances his linguistically

constituted subject as opposing sound technology: listening for a "grain," he argues, applies to all types of music. "As for piano music," he argues, "I know at once which part of the body is playing—if it is the arm, too often, alas, muscled like a dancer's calves, the clutch of the finger tips (despite the sweeping flourishes of the wrists), or if on the contrary it is the only erotic part of the pianist's body, the pad of the fingers whose 'grain' is so rarely heard." Barthes laments that "under the pressure of the mass long-playing record, there seems to be a flattening-out of technique; which is paradoxical in that the various manners of playing are all flattened out *into perfection*" (189). Even as Barthes refuses to allow that the symbolic operations of language might disappear at the moment of musical performance, that the experience of the body might be unaccompanied by prohibitions, he accepts the narrative of a whole body prior to technology and in this way belies his own skepticism about the thrill created by a singing voice.

4. THE LEAD BELLY THING: WILLIAM STYRON'S RECORDS

1. Styron quotes a larger excerpt from this 1622 sermon at the beginning of the novel: "that God who, when he could not get into me, by standing, and knocking, by his ordinary meanes or entring, by his Word, his mercies, hath applied his judgments, and shaked the house, this body, wit agues and palsies, and set this house on fire, with fevers and calentures, and frighted the Master of the house, my soule, with horrors, and heavy apprehensions, and so made an entrance into me." John Donne, *The Major Works: Including Songs and Sonnets and Sermons*, ed. John Carey (Oxford: Oxford University Press, 2009), 319–20.

2. William Styron, *Set This House on Fire* (New York: New American Library, 1960), 453.

3. Peter Guralnick, *Feel Like Going Home: Portraits in Blues and Rock 'n' Roll* (Boston: Back Bay, 1999), 16.

4. Benjamin argued that "inside" the collector "are spirits, or at least little genii, which have seen to it that for a collector—I mean a real collector, a collector as he ought to be—ownership is the most intimate relationship that one can have to objects. Not that they come alive in him; it is he who lives in them. Walter Benjamin, "Unpacking My Library: A Talk About Book Collecting (1931)," in *Illuminations* (New York: Harcourt, Brace, 1968), 67.

5. Florence Dore, "The Rock Novel and Jonathan Lethem's *The Fortress of Solitude*," *Nonsite. Org*, no. 8 (January 20, 2013).

6. Theodor W. Adorno, "The Form of the Phonograph (1934)," in *Essays on Music*, ed. Richard Leppert, trans. Susan H. Gillespie (Berkeley: University of California Press, 2002), 277–82.

7. Elvis Presley, *Frankie and Johnny*, LP (Hollywood, CA: RCA Victor, 1966); Frederick De Cordova et al., *Frankie and Johnny* [videorecording] (Santa Monica, CA: MGM Home Entertainment, 2001).

8. Fredric Jameson, *The Political Unconscious: Narrative as a Socially Symbolic Act* (Ithaca, NY: Cornell University Press, 1981), 153.

9. As Goble has shown, an erotic attachment to machines can be gleaned in modernist literature as well. In what follows I show how desire shifts in the postwar fiction. Mark Goble, *Beautiful Circuits: Modernism and the Mediated Life* (New York: Columbia University Press, 2010).

10. Sigmund Freud et al., "Fetishism," in *The Standard Edition of the Complete Psychological Works of Sigmund Freud* (London: Hogarth Press and the Institute of Psycho-Analysis, 1953), 21:152–59.

11. Jameson nuances this conception of the novel's "mirage," the sensory subject, in *Antinomies of Realism*, reconceptualizing Barthes's "The Reality Effect" (1968) to include thoughts about "affect." Barthes had argued that Flaubert introduces "useless details," like the "barometer" in "A Simple Heart" from *Three Tales*, arguing that the fact that they have "no function" indicates a new moment in realism, one in which pointless objects void of signified meaning come to indicate reality. Roland Barthes, "The Reality Effect," in *The Novel: An Anthology of Criticism and Theory, 1900–2000*, ed. Dorothy J. Hale (Malden, MA: Blackwell, 2006), 230–31. Such objects, Barthes argues, "say nothing but this: *We are the real*; it is the category of 'the real' and not its contingent contents which is then signified" (234). In *Antinomies of Realism* Jameson argues that this change indicates a "transformation of the sensorium" in the middle of the nineteenth century. Fredric Jameson, *The Antinomies of Realism*, repr. ed. (London: Verso, 2015), 32. The change to realist fiction Barthes correctly identified, so Jameson argues, occurred because the way that capitalist subjects experienced their bodies through the senses was changing. Jameson reads Barthes' "reality effect" as only available when "affect"—in his words, "global waves of generalized sensations"—start to take the place of mere "named emotion" (28, 31). Revising his earlier designation of the "mirage" of the centered subject in this later work to include affect, then, Jameson allows that the novel involves a liberatory feeling that escapes the bourgeois mirage. I make no such claim for the impenetrable phonographs in Styron's fiction, though it seems fair to say that rock and roll was involved in a "transformation of the sensorium" such that the relation between bodies and machines changed.

12. This tendency was gleaned by early readers of the novel. Just after *Set This House on Fire* was published, one reviewer, David L. Stevenson, observed that the novel's "materials are everywhere 'un-novelized'": "The odd difficulty in *Set This House on Fire* is that the individual scenes, the individual characterizations, accumulate, but they remain inert, they do not achieve their potential content." I want to suggest that this "inert" quality, taken by Stevenson and other early critics as a defect, should be understood rather as the novel's aesthetic gambit in the age of rock and roll. David L. Stevenson, "Styron and the Fiction of the Fifties," *Critique: Studies in Contemporary Fiction* 3, no. 3 (1960): 51. Things in *Set This House on Fire* have generated much commentary. Tara McLellan, "'Nothing in America Remains Fixed for Long': Examining William Styron's *Set This House on Fire* Through a Postsouthern Lens," *Publications of the Mississippi Philological Association* (2008): 137–38, describes the attention to detail in the novel as "acute," observing the moments when Styron "catalogues each precious item." Radoslav Nenadal, "The Patterning of a Modern Hero in William Styron's *Set This House on Fire*," *Prague Studies in English* 15 (1973): 83, notes the "careful selection of the minutest concrete details" from "the hero's material world." For Stevenson as for many critics, Styron's things are a feature of his beautiful but empty style.

13. Dyson gives primacy to technologies of voice in producing a sense that the body is displaced: "As the first attribute to become disembodied through electronic transmission, the voice has anchored all other transmissions." Frances Dyson, *Sounding New Media: Immersion and Embodiment in the Arts and Culture* (Berkeley: University of California Press, 2009), 8.

14. Styron incorporates records into his fictional scheme as part of Cass's collection. For Susan Stewart, collections are by definition removed from "everyday life" and indeed from the flow of history itself. Unlike fetishes, collections are not, in Stewart's terms, "representational." The collection "presents a hermetic world" containing "both the minimum and the complete number of elements necessary for an autonomous world." Susan Stewart, *On*

Longing: Narratives of the Miniature, the Gigantic, the Souvenir, the Collection (Durham, NC: Duke University Press, 1993), 152. As nonrepresentational items in a collection, the 78s in *Set This House on Fire* might also be understood as "things" in Bill Brown's sense of the term: objects that block "dogged ideation" and "unnecessary abstraction." Bill Brown, "Thing Theory," *Things* (2004): 1. Or we might view these records as lacking what Jonathan Lamb has identified as the "properties of objects of most interest to us"—their "mobility in the world of exchange, expressed as commercial and symbolic value." Jonathan Lamb, *The Things Things Say* (Princeton, NJ: Princeton University Press, 2011), xi.

15. Styron does not specify the format of Cass's phonographs, but in 1960 an "ancient" recording of Lead Belly singing "The Midnight Special" would have been a 78. "Victor Matrix BS-051298. The Midnight Special/Golden Gate Quartet; Leadbelly—Discography of American Historical Recordings," http://adp.library.ucsb.edu/index.php/matrix /detail/200044900/BS-051298-The_Midnight_Special.

16. Louis D. Rubin Jr., "An Artist in Bonds," *Sewanee Review* 69 (1961): 175. On the repetitive structure, see also Cologne-Brookes, who describes *Set This House on Fire* as a "twice-told-tale." Gavin Cologne-Brookes, "Rome to Ravello with *Set This House on Fire*," *Sewanee Review* 122, no. 3 (2014): 485. It should be noted that Rubin makes this comment in an article defending *Set This House on Fire* amid some early negative reviews. In his July 1963 *Esquire* article "Some Children of the Goddess: Norman Mailer vs. Nine Authors," blasting nine of his contemporaries, Norman Mailer called *Set This House on Fire* a "bad maggoty novel," the "magnum opus of a spoiled rich boy who could write like an angel about landscape and like an adolescent about people." It wasn't just Mailer. David Stevenson in "Styron and the Fiction of the Fifties" called the novel a "novel manqué," and Richard Foster, "An Orgy of Commerce: William Styron's *Set This House on Fire*," *Critique* 3, no. 3 (Summer 1960): 59–70, noted that there is "a vacancy at the heart of the book." "Styron is as gifted a stylist as anyone now writing, but apparently he has nothing important to say," says William Van O'Connor, in "John Updike and William Styron: The Burden of Talent," in *Contemporary American Novelists*, ed. Harry T. Moore (Carbondale: Southern Illinois University Press, 1964).

17. Mark Katz, *Capturing Sound: How Technology Has Changed Music*, rev. ed. (Berkeley: University of California Press, 2010), 4; John Durham Peters, *Speaking Into the Air: A History of the Idea of Communication* (Chicago: University of Chicago Press, 1999), 142, 161.

18. Ian Watt, *The Rise of the Novel: Studies in Defoe, Richardson, and Fielding* (Berkeley: University of California Press, 1957), 196.

19. I refer to the 1968 response to *The Confessions of Nat Turner*, in which noted African American authors accuse Styron of portraying Nat Turner's revolt as motivated by overweening desire for a white girl. See John Clarke and Nat Turner, *William Styron's Nat Turner: Ten Black Writers Respond* (Boston: Beacon, 1968). As I have noted, Jack Hamilton sees the release of "Like a Rolling Stone" as the turning point after which rock became "the province of whites." Jack Hamilton, *Just Around Midnight: Rock and Roll and the Racial Imagination* (Cambridge, MA: Harvard University Press, 2016), 3. Shaun Considine describes the next epoch in rock as "New Rock." Shaun Considine, "The Hit We Almost Missed," *New York Times*, December 3, 2004, http://www.nytimes.com/2004/12/03/opinion/the-hit-we-almost -missed.html. See note 7, in the introduction to this volume.

20. Dyson, *Sounding New Media*, 4–5.

21. To return to the idea of the fetish here, we will note that Mr. Flagg's radio voice appears perfectly to bear out a Freudian reading: the "pure presence" of his voice

carries the force of the disavowal; his power compensates for that loss. And while "pure presence" here seems to indicate something of the phallic "thrill" Barthes identifies, in collapsing it with radio Styron prevents any sense of the distinctions on which Barthes ultimately insists.

22. Bill Brown has argued that things in the American novel indicate the "American uncanny," the historical ambiguity between persons and things that haunts American capitalism. For Brown, the American uncanny alerts us to the possibility that "within things we will discover the human precisely because our history is one in which humans were reduced to things (however incomplete that reduction)." Bill Brown, "Reification, Reanimation, and the American Uncanny," *Critical Inquiry* 32, no. 2 (January 1, 2006): 207. For Jameson, this cataloguing of things in the "Negro cabin" might be understood in terms of the novel's realism. What makes the novel feel real in the novelistic listing of things, Jameson argues in *Antinomies of Realism* (54–55), is a tension between "antinomies." On the one hand, "enormous lists and catalogues" consolidates the centered subject that has concerned Jameson since *The Political Unconscious*—by positing a consciousness that can classify the listed things. On the other, the "dizzying" result of the cataloguing also undoes this centering work, producing "sensations" in the place of perceptions. "The unexpected result," Jameson argues, "is far from enriching representational language with all kinds of new meanings, the gap between words and things is heightened."

23. Richard Godden describes anxiety about whiteness in the 1930s as "the primal scene of bound southern labor," a scene in which "the master both recognizes and represses the fact that since his mastery is slave-made, he and his are blacks in whiteface." Richard Godden, *Fictions of Labor: William Faulkner and the South's Long Revolution* (Cambridge: Cambridge University Press, 1997), 3–4.

24. In *I'll Take My Stand: The South and the Agrarian Tradition* (New York: Harper and Row, 1962), 35.

25. Robert Shelton, Patrick Humphries, and Elizabeth Thomson, *No Direction Home: The Life and Music of Bob Dylan*, rev. ed. (Backbeat Books, 2011), 100.

26. Holly George-Warren, "'Blues Ain't Nuthin' but a Good Man Feelin' Bad': Balladry, the Blues, and Appropriation," presented at Novel Sounds II, the National Humanities Center, Research Triangle Park, NC, March 3, 2017, http://nationalhumanitiescenter .org/novel-sounds-ii/. According to Alice Echols, these recordings are captured on the soundtrack for the movie *Janis*. Alice Echols, *Scars of Sweet Paradise: The Life and Times of Janis Joplin* (New York: Henry Holt, 2000), 319; Janis Joplin, *Janis: Soundtrack of the Motion Picture Janis* (Columbia, 1975); Janis Joplin, *Blow All My Blues Away* (Bootleg Recordings), 2015.

27. Led Zeppelin, *Led Zeppelin III* (Atlantic, 1970); Beth McCarthy, Nirvana episode of *MTV Unplugged in New York* (New York: Sony Music Studios, 1993). The list of white rockers goes on: Johnny Rivers had a hit in 1964 with Lead Belly's "The Midnight Special," a live recording of his performance at the Whiskey a Go Go club in Los Angeles, and Creedence Clearwater Revival recorded this same song on their 1969 album *Willy and the Poor Boys*. In 2017, Dan Zanes released *Lead Belly, Baby!* (Smithsonian Folkways, 2017), a compliation of children's songs by Lead Belly. See http://media.smithsonianfolkways.org /liner_notes/smithsonian_folkways/SFW40000.pdf. On Dylan's second release in 1963, *The Freewheelin' Bob Dylan*, he includes a version of an old blues tune Lead Belly recorded with Woody Guthrie in 1944. Dylan's versions of Lead Belly's tunes also appear on early

bootleg recordings as well as on Dylan's 1970 release *Self-Portrait*, which includes two versions of Lead Belly's "Alberta."

28. George Plimpton, "William Styron: The Art of Fiction No. 156," *Paris Review* 150 (1999): 140.

29. Emmylou Harris, *Wrecking Ball*, CD (New Orleans: Elektra, 1995). *Wrecking Ball* won a Grammy Award and also featured Steve Earle and Neil Young.

CODA. NOBEL SOUNDS: BOB DYLAN'S NOVEL PRIZE

1. "Like a Rolling Stone" became *Billboard*'s greatest rock song of all time in 2004. *Billboard* has named multiple rock songs the best "of all time," so the value of the designation is admittedly minimal. *Billboard*'s naming of the Dylan tune did have some impact, however, enough to inspire Columbia Records' director of new releases at the time to relay the fascinating story of "Like a Rolling Stone's" release in 1965. Shaun Considine, "The Hit We Almost Missed," *New York Times*, December 3, 2004, http://www.nytimes.com/2004/12/03/opinion/the-hit-we-almost-missed.html; "500 Greatest Songs of All Time," *Rolling Stone*, http://www.rollingstone.com/music/lists/the-500-greatest-songs-of-all-time-20110407/bob-dylan-like-a-rolling-stone-20110516; "Dylan's 'Rolling Stone' Tops *Rolling Stone*'s Greatest Songs List," *Billboard*, http://www.billboard.com/articles/news/65582/dylans-rolling-stone-tops-rolling-stones-greatest-songs-list. Ben Sisario, Alexandra Alter, and Sewell Chan, "Bob Dylan Wins Nobel Prize, Redefining Boundaries of Literature," *New York Times*, October 14, 2016, https://www.nytimes.com/2016/10/14/arts/music/bob-dylan-nobel-prize-literature.html; David Remnick, "Let's Celebrate the Bob Dylan Nobel Win," *New Yorker*, October 13, 2016, http://www.newyorker.com/culture/cultural-comment/lets-celebrate-the-bob-dylan-nobel-win; Joe Otterson, "Bob Dylan's Nobel Prize Win Seriously Annoys Authors," *The Wrap*, October 13, 2016, http://www.thewrap.com/bob-dylan-nobel-prize-in-literature-authors-backlash/; David Orr, "After Dylan's Nobel, What Makes a Poet a Poet?" *New York Times*, March 24, 2017, https://www.nytimes.com/2017/03/24/books/review/after-dylans-nobel-what-makes-a-poet-a-poet.html.

2. Remnick, "Let's Celebrate the Bob Dylan Nobel Win."

3. "Rock Hall Opening Library and Archives Collection This Week," *Billboard*, http://www.billboard.com/articles/news/511232/rock-hall-opening-library-and-archives-collection-this-week; "Led Zeppelin Get All-Star Tribute at Kennedy Center Honors," *Rolling Stone*, http://www.rollingstone.com/music/news/led-zeppelin-gets-all-star-tribute-at-kennedy-center-honors-20121203.

4. "2013 Blashfield Address—American Academy of Arts and Letters," http://artsandletters.org/2013-blashfield-address/; Michael Chabon, "Let It Rock," *New York Review of Books* 60, no. 12 (July 11, 2013): 27–28.

5. Remnick, "Let's Celebrate the Bob Dylan Nobel Win."

6. Otterson, "Bob Dylan's Nobel Prize Win Seriously Annoys Authors."

7. "The Kennedy Center Honors," http://www.kennedy-center.org/pages/SpecialEvents/honors#yrPast.

8. Sisario, Alter, and Chan, "Bob Dylan Wins Nobel Prize."

9. Greil Marcus, *Mystery Train: Images of America in Rock 'n' Roll Music*, 6th rev. ed. (New York: Plume, 2015). See, for example, Yale University dropout Richard Meltzer's *The Aesthetics of Rock* (1970), a book Greil Marcus claims inaugurated rock and roll criticism.

The book opens with the lyrics of the Trashmen's 1964 "Surfin' Bird," beginning with "A-well-a everybody's heard about the bird," and moves from there to gather into a single claim strains from Plato, Kant, and (who else?) Bob Dylan: "all knowledge has already been stated." Meltzer opens the 1987 Da Capo reissue of the book with an apology for the task he set for early rock nerds seeking to gain enlightenment from his work, noting the "whole enormous sections of text that seem so subarticulate (inarticulate?) that it would take a guided tour (or a supplemental voice-over cassette) to clarify, or even hint at, what I might conceivably have been trying to 'express' in the first place" (vii).

10. AC/DC, *Highway to Hell* (Atlantic, 1979).

11. Marcus, *Mystery Train*, 133. See also Peter Guralnick, *Sam Phillips: The Man Who Invented Rock 'n' Roll* (New York: Little, Brown and Company, 2015), 173–85.

12. Jonathan Lethem, *The Fortress of Solitude: A Novel* (New York: Doubleday, 2003), 307–509.

13. James Dickey, *Deliverance*, repr. ed. (New York: Delta, 1994), 45.

14. Don DeLillo, *Great Jones Street* (New York: Houghton Mifflin, 1973).

15. Clement Greenberg, *The Collected Essays and Criticism*, ed. John O'Brian (Chicago: University of Chicago Press, 1986), 1:5–6.

16. Cleanth Brooks, *The Well Wrought Urn: Studies in the Structure of Poetry* (New York: Harcourt, Brace, 1947), 235.

17. David Riesman, "Listening to Popular Music," *American Quarterly* 2, no. 4 (1950): 361.

18. Cleanth Brooks, R. W. B. Lewis, and Robert Penn Warren, *American Literature: The Makers and the Making* (New York: St. Martin's, 1973), 2752, 2767–70.

19. Greil Marcus and Werner Sollors, *A New Literary History of America* (Cambridge, MA: Belknap Press of Harvard University Press, 2009).

20. Brooks, Lewis, and Warren, *American Literature*, 276–78.

21. Brooks, Lewis, and Warren, *American Literature*. Also see Steve Newman, *Ballad Collection, Lyric, and the Canon: The Call of the Popular from the Restoration to the New Criticism* (Philadelphia: University of Pennsylvania Press, 2007), 215.

22. John Fogerty definitely did not attend Yale. But he evinces an affinity for higher learning in his poignant description his children's college education, all the more impressive, as he explains, given his own unsuccessful stint as a student at Contra Costa Community College. John Fogerty, *Fortunate Son: My Life, My Music*, repr. ed. (New York: Back Bay, 2016), 90.

23. My argument here was enriched by the wonderful keynote discussion I was privileged to orchestrate with Jonathan Lethem, Greil Marcus, and Richard Thompson at Novel Sounds I (October 15, 2016): http://nationalhumanitiescenter.org/novel-sounds-american-fiction -in-the-age-of-rock-and-roll/.

24. Fredric Jameson, *Postmodernism; or, The Cultural Logic of Late Capitalism* (Durham, NC: Duke University Press, 1991), argues that postmodernism represents an "effacement" of "the older (essentially high-modernist) frontier between high-culture and so-called mass or consumer culture" (2). McGurl has invited revision to these ideas by noting that the observation of continuities between "high" and "low" forms of art in the postwar moment does not "disable the distinction" but instead widens our view on a system in which this distinction "floats everywhere." Mark McGurl, *The Program Era: Postwar Fiction and the Rise of Creative Writing* (Cambridge, MA: Harvard University Press, 2009), 42. For McGurl, insurgent outsider status is just one of the many features of high modernism that gets refurbished in the bureaucratic Program. To such a comprehensive and compelling argument *Novel Sounds* adds only

that rock and roll becomes a particular and potent *other* for American literature within this system and that postwar ballad fiction perhaps marks a point of origin for this designation.

25. Andreas Huyssen, *After the Great Divide: Modernism, Mass Culture, Postmodernism* (Bloomington: Indiana University Press, 1986), viii–ix.

BIBLIOGRAPHY

Abrahams, Roger D. "Mr. Lomax Meets Professor Kittredge." *Journal of Folklore Research* 37, nos. 2/3 (May 2000): 99–118.

Adorno, Theodor W. "Extorted Reconciliation: On Georg Lukacs' *Realism in Our Time*." In *Notes to Literature*, ed. Rolf Tieddemann, trans. Shierry Weber Nicholsen, 1:216–40. New York: Columbia University Press, 1991.

——. "The Form of the Phonograph (1934)." In *Essays on Music*, ed. Richard Leppert, trans. Susan H. Gillespie, 277–82. Berkeley: University of California Press, 2002.

——. *Night Music: Essays on Music. 1928–1962.* Seagull Books, 2009.

Adorno, Theodor, Susan H. Gillespie, and Richard D. Leppert. *Essays on Music.* Berkeley, CA: University of California Press, 2002.

Als, Hilton. "Flannery O'Connor's Revelatory Honesty." *New Yorker*, January 22, 2001. https://www.newyorker.com/magazine/2001/01/29/this-lonesome-place.

Altschuler, Glenn. *All Shook Up: How Rock 'n' Roll Changed America.* New York: Oxford University Press, 2003.

Baldwin, James. "Everybody's Protest Novel." In *Notes of a Native Son.* Boston: Beacon, 1984.

——. "Faulkner and Desegregation." *Partisan Review* 23, no. 4 (Fall 1956): 568–74.

——. *Go Tell It on the Mountain.* 1953. New York: Vintage, 2013.

——. *Going to Meet the Man: Stories.* 1965. New York: Vintage, 1995.

——. "Letter from a Region in My Mind." *New Yorker*, November 17, 1962. http://www.newyorker.com/magazine/1962/11/17/letter-from-a-region-in-my-mind.

Baraka, Amiri. *Blues People: Negro Music in White America.* New York: W. Morrow, 1963.

——. "Jazz and the White Critic." In *The Jazz Cadence of American Culture*, ed. Robert O'Meally, 137–42. New York: Columbia University Press, 1998.

Barlow, Daniel Patrick. "'And Every Day There Is Music': Folksong Roots and the Highway Chain Gang in *The Ballad of the Sad Café*." *Southern Literary Journal* 44, no. 1 (2011): 74–85.

Barry, Eric D. "High Fidelity Sound as Spectacle and Sublime, 1950–1961." In *Sound in the Age of Mechanical Reproduction*, ed. David Suisman and Susan Strasser, 115–40. Philadelphia: University of Pennsylvania Press, 2010.

Barthes, Roland. "The Grain of the Voice." In *Image-Music-Text*, trans. Stephen Heath, 179–90. New York: Hill and Wang, 1978.

——. "The Reality Effect." In *The Novel: An Anthology of Criticism and Theory, 1900–2000*, ed. Dorothy J. Hale. Oxford: Blackwell, 2006.

Baudrillard, Jean. *Simulacra and Simulation*. Ann Arbor: University of Michigan Press, 1994.

Bayard, Samuel P. "George Pullen Jackson." *Journal of the International Folk Music Council* 6 (January 1, 1954): 62–63.

Bearden, Kenneth. "Monkeying Around: Welty's 'Powerhouse,' Blues-Jazz, and the Signifying Connection." *Southern Literary Journal* 31, no. 2 (March 22, 1999): 65.

Benjamin, Walter. "Unpacking My Library: A Talk About Book Collecting (1931)." In *Illuminations*, 59–69. New York: Harcourt, Brace, 1968.

Bertrand, Michael. *Race, Rock, and Elvis*. Urbana: University of Illinois Press, 2000.

Biers, Katherine. "Syncope Fever: James Weldon Johnson and the Black Phonographic Voice." *Representations* 96, no. 1 (2006): 99–125.

——. *Virtual Modernism: Writing and Technology in the Progressive Era*. Minneapolis: University of Minnesota Press, 2013.

Birdsall, Esther K. "Some Notes on the Role of George Lyman Kittredge in American Folklore Studies." *Journal of the Folklore Institute* 10, nos. 1/2 (June 1, 1973): 57–66.

Blotner, Joseph. *Robert Penn Warren: A Biography*. New York: Random House, 1997.

Bolter, Jay David, and Richard Grusin. *Remediation: Understanding New Media*. Cambridge, MA: MIT Press, 2000.

Bone, Martyn. *The Postsouthern Sense of Place in Contemporary Fiction*. Baton Rouge: Louisiana State University Press, 2005.

Bone, Martyn, William A. Link, and Brian Ward. *Creating and Consuming the American South*. Gainesville: University Press of Florida, 2015.

Brands, H. W. "Coca-Cola Goes to War." *American History* 33, no. 3 (August 1999).

Brevda, William. "Neon Light in August: Electric Signs in Faulkner's Fiction." In *Faulkner and Popular Culture*, 214–42. Jackson: University Press of Mississippi, 1988.

Brinson, David N. "Cave & Bat-Inspired Recorded Music and Spoken Word." *Floyd Collins Ballads: Song Background*, n.d. http://caveinspiredmusic.com/rubriques/country_music /country_music.html.

Brooks, Cleanth. *The Hidden God: Studies in Hemingway, Faulkner, Yeats, Eliot, and Warren*. New Haven, CT: Yale University Press, 1963.

——. *The Relation of the Alabama-Georgia Dialect to the Provincial Dialects of Great Britain*. Baton Rouge: Louisiana State University Press, 1935.

——. *The Well Wrought Urn: Studies in the Structure of Poetry*. New York: Harcourt, Brace, 1947.

——. *William Faulkner: The Yoknapatawpha Country*. New Haven, CT: Yale University Press, 1963.

Brooks, Cleanth, R. W. B. (Richard Warrington Baldwin) Lewis, and Robert Penn Warren. *American Literature: The Makers and the Making*. New York: St. Martin's, 1973.

Brooks, Cleanth, and Robert Penn Warren. *Understanding Fiction*. New York: Appleton-Century-Crofts, 1943.

——. *Understanding Fiction*. 2nd ed. New York: Appleton-Century-Crofts, 1959.

——. *Understanding Fiction*. 3rd ed. Englewood Cliffs, NJ: Prentice-Hall, 1979.

——. *Understanding Poetry: An Anthology for College Students*. New York: H. Holt and Company, 1938.

Brooks, Daphne A. "'Sister, Can You Line It Out?': Zora Neale Hurston and the Sound of Angular Black Womanhood." *Amerikastudien/American Studies* 55, no. 4 (2010): 617–27.

Brown, Bill. "Reification, Reanimation, and the American Uncanny." *Critical Inquiry* 32, no. 2 (January 1, 2006): 175–207.

——. "Thing Theory." *Things* (2004): 1.

Buckley, Bruce Redfern. "Frankie and Her Men: A Study of the Interrelationships of Popular and Folk Traditions." PhD diss., Indiana University, 1962.

Butler, Anne, and C. Murray Henderson. *Angola: Louisiana State Penitentiary: A Half-Century of Rage and Reform*. Lafayette: Center for Louisiana Studies, University of Southwestern Louisiana, 1990.

Cantwell, Robert. *When We Were Good: The Folk Revival*. Cambridge, MA: Harvard University Press, 1996.

Carlin, Richard. *Worlds of Sound: The Story of Smithsonian Folkways*. New York: Collins, 2008.

Chabon, Michael. "Let It Rock." *New York Review of Books* 60, no. 12 (July 11, 2013): 27–28.

Charles, Ray, and David Ritz. *Brother Ray: Ray Charles' Own Story*. 3rd ed. Cambridge, MA: Da Capo, 2004.

Cheesman, Tom, and Sigrid Rieuwerts, eds. *Ballads Into Books: The Legacies of Francis James Child*. Bern: Peter Lang, 1997.

Child, Francis. *English and Scottish Ballads*. 2nd series. 8 vols. Boston: Little, Brown, n.d.

——. *The English and Scottish Popular Ballads*. New York: Cooper Square, 1965.

Child, Francis, George Lyman Kittredge, and Helen Child Sargent. *English and Scottish Popular Ballads: Edited from the Collection of Francis James Child*. Boston: Houghton, Mifflin and Company, 1904.

"Chuck Berry: 20 Essential Songs." *Rolling Stone*. http://www.rollingstone.com/music/lists/chuck -berry-20-essential-songs-w472713/maybellene-1955-w472730.

Clarke, John, and Nat Turner. *William Styron's Nat Turner: Ten Black Writers Respond*. Boston: Beacon, 1968.

Cohen, Michael. "Popular Ballads: Rhythmic Remediations in the Nineteenth Century." *Meter Matters: Verse Cultures of the Long Nineteenth Century* (2011): 196.

——. *The Social Lives of Poems in Nineteenth-Century America*. Philadelphia: University of Pennsylvania Press, 2015.

Cologne-Brookes, Gavin. "Rome to Ravello with *Set This House on Fire*." *Sewanee Review* 122, no. 3 (2014): 484–94.

Considine, Shaun. "The Hit We Almost Missed." *New York Times*, December 3, 2004. http:// www.nytimes.com/2004/12/03/opinion/the-hit-we-almost-missed.html.

Crews, Frederick C. "The Power of Flannery O'Connor." *New York Review of Books*, April 26, 1990. http://www.nybooks.com.libproxy.lib.unc.edu/articles/1990/04/26/the-power-of-flannery -oconnor/.

Davidson, Donald. *The Big Ballad Jamboree: A Novel*. Jackson: University Press of Mississippi, 1996.

——. "The Sacred Harp in the Land of Eden." *Virginia Quarterly Review* 10, no. 2 (April 1, 1934): 203–17.

——. "The White Spirituals and Their Historian." *Sewanee Review* 51, no. 4 (December 1943): 589–98.

Dawson, Jim, and Steve Propes. *What Was the First Rock 'n' Roll Record?* Boston: Faber & Faber, 1992.

DeLillo, Don. *Great Jones Street*. Boston: Houghton Mifflin, 1973.

Dickey, James. *Deliverance*. Reprint ed. New York: Delta, 1994.

Dolar, Mladen. *A Voice and Nothing More*. Cambridge, MA: MIT Press, 2006.

Donne, John. *The Major Works: Including Songs and Sonnets and Sermons*. Ed. John Carey. Oxford: Oxford University Press, 2009.

Dore, Florence. "The Rock Novel and Jonathan Lethem's *The Fortress of Solitude*." *Nonsite.Org* 8 (January 20, 2013).

Doyle, Roddy. *The Commitments*. New York: Vintage, 1989.

——. *The Guts: A Novel*. Reprint ed. New York: Penguin, 2015.

"Dream Songs: The Music of the March on Washington." *New Yorker*, August 28, 2013. http://www .newyorker.com/culture/culture-desk/dream-songs-the-music-of-the-march-on-washington.

Du Bois, W. E. B., and Brent Hayes Edwards. *The Souls of Black Folk*. New York: Oxford University Press, 2007.

Duck, Leigh Anne. *The Nation's Region: Southern Modernism, Segregation, and US Nationalism*. Athens: University of Georgia Press, 2006.

"Dylan's 'Rolling Stone' Tops Rolling Stone's Greatest Songs List." *Billboard*. http://www.billboard .com/articles/news/65582/dylans-rolling-stone-tops-rolling-stones-greatest-songs-list.

Dyson, Frances. *Sounding New Media: Immersion and Embodiment in the Arts and Culture*. Berkeley: University of California Press, 2009.

Dyson, J. Peter. "Cats, Crime, and Punishment: The Mikado's Pitti-Sing in 'A Good Man Is Hard to Find.'" *English Studies in Canada* 14, no. 4 (1988): 436–52.

Early, Gerald. *One Nation Under a Groove: Motown and American Culture*. Rev. and exp. ed. Ann Arbor: University of Michigan Press, 2004.

Echols, Alice. *Scars of Sweet Paradise: The Life and Times of Janis Joplin*. New York: Henry Holt, 2000.

Egerton, John. "Walking Into History: The Beginning of School Desegregation in Nashville." *Southern Spaces* (2009), https://southernspaces.org/2009/walking-history-beginning -school-desegregation-nashville.

Eliot, T. S. *Selected Essays*. London: Faber & Faber, 1999.

Elledge, Jim. *Sweet Nothings: An Anthology of Rock and Roll in American Poetry*. Bloomington: Indiana University Press, 1994.

Ellis, Bret Easton. *Less Than Zero*. New York: Simon and Schuster, 1985.

Ellison, Harlan. *Spider Kiss*. Jackson: University of Mississippi Press, 1996.

Ellison, Ralph. *Invisible Man*. New York: Random House, 1952.

——. "Richard Wright's Blues." In *The Jazz Cadence of American Culture*, ed. Robert O'Meally. New York: Columbia University Press, 1998.

Ellmann, Maud. *The Nets of Modernism: Henry James, Virginia Wolf, James Joyce, and Sigmund Freud*. Cambridge: Cambridge University Press, 2010.

Ensor, Allison R. "Flannery O'Connor and Music." *Flannery O'Connor Bulletin* 14 (1985): 1–13.

Erbe, Marcus. "The Transcription of Electronic Music in *The Crying of Lot 49*." *Pynchon Notes* 54–55 (2008): 99–107.

Escott, Colin. *The Grand Ole Opry: The Making of an American Icon*. Hachette Digital, Inc., 2009.

——. *Lost Highway: The True Story of Country Music*. Washington, DC: Smithsonian Books, 2003.

Faulkner, William. *Go Down, Moses*. New York: Vintage, 1990.

——. "A Letter to the North." *Life*, March 5, 1956.

——. *The Town*. New York: Vintage, 1961.

Fincher, Jack. "Dreams of Riches Led Floyd Collins to a Nightmarish End." *Smithsonian Magazine*, May 1990.

Fitzgerald, F. Scott. *The Great Gatsby*. New York: Scribner, 2004.

——. *Tender Is the Night*. New York: Scribner, 2003.

Fogerty, John. *Fortunate Son: My Life, My Music.* Reprint ed. New York: Back Bay, 2016.

Foster, Richard. "An Orgy of Commerce: William Styron's 'Set This House on Fire.'" *Critique* 3, no. 3 (Summer 1960): 59–70.

Freud, Sigmund, Anna Freud, Charles E. (Charles Edmund) Kistler, Carrie Lee Rothgeb, and James Strachey. "Fetishism." In *The Standard Edition of the Complete Psychological Works of Sigmund Freud,* 21:152–59. London: Hogarth Press and the Institute of Psycho-Analysis, 1953.

Friedwald, Will. *Jazz Singing: America's Great Voices from Bessie Smith to Bebop and Beyond.* New York: Da Capo, 1990.

Gaillard, Dawson F. "The Presence of the Narrator in Carson McCullers' 'The Ballad of the Sad Café.'" *Mississippi Quarterly* 25, no. 4 (Fall 1972): 419–27.

Gardner-Medwin, Alisoun. "The Ancestry of 'The House Carpenter': A Study of the American Form of Child 243." *Journal of American Folklore* 84, no. 334 (December 1971): 414–27.

George-Warren, Holly. "'Blues Ain't Nuthin' but a Good Man Feelin' Bad': Balladry, the Blues and Appropriation." Presented at Novel Sounds II, the National Humanities Center, Research Triangle Park, NC, March 3, 2017. http://nationalhumanitiescenter.org/novel-sounds-ii/.

Gillett, Charlie. *The Sound of the City: The Rise of Rock and Roll.* New York: Da Capo, 1984.

Gitelman, Lisa. *Always Already New: Media, History and the Data of Culture.* Cambridge, MA: MIT Press, 2006.

Goble, Mark. *Beautiful Circuits: Modernism and the Mediated Life.* New York: Columbia University Press, 2010.

Godden, Richard. *Fictions of Capital: The American Novel from James to Mailer.* Cambridge: Cambridge University Press, 1990.

——. *Fictions of Labor: William Faulkner and the South's Long Revolution.* Cambridge: Cambridge University Press, 1997.

Gooch, Brad. *Flannery: A Life of Flannery O'Connor.* New York: Little, Brown, 2009.

Green, Elva Diane. *Eddie Green: The Rise of an Early 1900s Black American Entertainment Pioneer.* Albany, GA: BearManor Media, 2016.

Greenberg, Clement. *The Collected Essays and Criticism.* 4 vols. Ed. John O'Brian. Chicago: University of Chicago Press, 1986.

Greenhaw, Wayne. *Fighting the Devil in Dixie: How Civil Rights Activists Took on the Ku Klux Klan in Alabama.* Reprint ed. Chicago: Chicago Review Press, 2011.

Greif, Mark. *The Age of the Crisis of Man: Thought and Fiction in America, 1933–1973.* Princeton, NJ: Princeton University Press, 2015.

Guillory, John. *Cultural Capital: The Problem of Literary Canon Formation.* Chicago: University of Chicago Press, 1993.

——. "Genesis of the Media Concept." *Critical Inquiry* 35, no. 2 (2010): 321–62.

Guralnick, Peter. *Feel Like Going Home: Portraits in Blues and Rock 'n' Roll.* Reprint ed. Boston: Back Bay, 1999.

——. *Sam Phillips: The Man Who Invented Rock 'n' Roll.* New York: Little, Brown, 2015.

——. *Sweet Soul Music: Rhythm and Blues and the Southern Dream of Freedom.* New York: Harper & Row, 1986.

Gwin, Minrose. *Remembering Medgar Evers: Writing the Long Civil Rights Movement.* Athens: University of Georgia Press, 2013.

Hagedorn, Jessica. *The Gangster of Love.* New York: Penguin, 1997.

Hamilton, Jack. *Just Around Midnight: Rock and Roll and the Racial Imagination.* Cambridge, MA: Harvard University Press, 2016.

Handy, W. C. *Blues: An Anthology.* Bedford, MA: Applewood, 2001.

——. *Negro Authors and Composers of the United States*. New York: Handy Brothers Music Co., 1938.

——, ed. *Unsung Americans Sung*. New York: ASCAP, 1944.

Harvey, Todd. *The Formative Dylan: Transmission and Stylistic Influences, 1961–1963*. Lanham, MD: Scarecrow, 2001.

Havighurst, Craig. *Air Castle of the South: WSM and the Making of Music City*. Urbana: University of Illinois Press, 2007.

Hedin, Benjamin. "Newport 1965." In *Studio A: The Bob Dylan Reader*. New York: Norton, 2004.

Heylin, Clinton. *Bob Dylan: Behind the Shades Revisited*. 1st US ed. New York: William Morrow, 2001.

——. *Bob Dylan: Behind the Shades Revisited*. New York: HarperEntertainment, 2003.

——. *Dylan's Daemon Lover: The Tangled Tale of a 450-Year-Old Pop Ballad*. London: Helter Skelter, 1999.

Horstman, Dorothy. *Sing Your Heart Out, Country Boy*. Rev. sub. ed. Nashville, TN: Country Music Foundation, 1996.

Hughes, Langston. *Not Without Laughter*. New York: Scribner Paperback Fiction, 1995.

Hurston, Zora. *Their Eyes Were Watching God*. New York: HarperCollins, 2000.

Huyssen, Andreas. *After the Great Divide: Modernism, Mass Culture, Postmodernism*. Bloomington: Indiana University Press, 1986.

I'll Take My Stand: The South and the Agrarian Tradition. New York: Harper and Row, 1962.

Innis, Harold. *Empire and Communications*. Lanham, MD: Rowman & Littlefield, 2007.

Jackson, George. *White Spirituals in the Southern Uplands: The Story of the Fasola Folk, Their Songs, Singings, and "Buckwheat Notes."* New York: Dover, 1965.

Jackson, Kenton. "Two-Time Dixie Murderer Sings Way to Freedom." *Philadelphia Independent*, January 6, 1935. John A. Lomax Papers at the Briscoe Center for American History.

Jameson, Fredric. *The Antinomies of Realism*. Reprint ed. London: Verso, 2015.

——. *The Political Unconscious: Narrative as a Socially Symbolic Act*. Ithaca, NY: Cornell University Press, 1981.

——. *Postmodernism; or, The Cultural Logic of Late Capitalism*. Durham, NC: Duke University Press, 1991.

Jensen, Joli. *The Nashville Sound: Authenticity, Commercialization, and Country Music*. Nashville, TN: Vanderbilt University Press, 1998.

Johnson, James Weldon. *The Autobiography of an Ex-Colored Man*. Courier Corporation, 2012.

Jurca, Catherine. *White Diaspora: The Suburb and the Twentieth-Century American Novel*. Princeton, NJ: Princeton University Press, 2001.

Kane, Daniel. *"Do You Have a Band?": Poetry and Punk Rock in New York City*. New York: Columbia University Press, 2017.

Kaplan, Amy. *The Social Construction of American Realism*. Chicago: University of Chicago Press, 1988.

Katz, Mark. *Capturing Sound: How Technology Has Changed Music*. Rev. ed. Berkeley: University of California Press, 2010.

Kimberling, Clark. "Three Generations of Works and Their Contributions to Congregational Singing." *The Hymn: A Journal of Congregational Song* 65, no. 3 (Summer 2014): 10–17.

King, B. B., and David Ritz. *Blues All Around Me: The Autobiography of B. B. King*. Reprint ed. New York: It Books, 2011.

King, Richard. *A Southern Renaissance: The Cultural Awakening of the American South, 1930–1955*. New York: Oxford University Press, 1980.

Kinney, David. *The Dylanologists: Adventures in the Land of Bob*. New York: Simon & Schuster, 2014.

Kittler, Friedrich. *Gramophone, Film, Typewriter*. Stanford, CA: Stanford University Press, 1999.

Klosterman, Chuck. *But What If We're Wrong?: Thinking About the Present As If It Were the Past*. New York: Blue Rider, 2016.

Knausgård, Karl. *My Struggle*. Vol. 1: *Death in the Family*. London: Harvill Secker, 2012.

Kosser, Michael. *How Nashville Became Music City, USA: 50 Years of Music Row*. Hal Leonard Corporation, 2006.

Kreyling, Michael. *Inventing Southern Literature*. Jackson: University Press of Mississippi, 1998.

Kunzru, Hari. *White Tears: A Novel*. New York: Knopf, 2017.

Kureishi, Hanif. *The Black Album*. London: Faber and Faber, 2009.

Laird, Tracey E. W. *Louisiana Hayride: Radio and Roots Music Along the Red River*. Oxford: Oxford University Press, 2004.

Lamb, Jonathan. *The Things Things Say*. Princeton, NJ: Princeton University Press, 2011.

Lee, Josephine. *The Japan of Pure Invention: Gilbert and Sullivan's The Mikado*. Minneapolis: University of Minnesota Press, 2010.

Lenox, Teresa. "The Carver Village Controversy." *Tequesta* 50 (January 1990): 39–51.

Lethem, Jonathan. *A Gambler's Anatomy: A Novel*. New York: Doubleday, 2016.

———. *Chronic City: A Novel*. New York: Doubleday, 2009.

———. "The Ecstasy of Influence: A Plagiarism." *Harper's Magazine*, February 1, 2007.

———. *The Fortress of Solitude: A Novel*. New York: Doubleday, 2003.

———. *Motherless Brooklyn*. New York: Vintage, 2000.

Lomax, John A. *Cowboy Songs and Other Frontier Ballads*. New ed. with additions. New York: Macmillan, 1916.

Lomax, John A., Library of Congress Music Division, and George Herzog. *Negro Folk Songs as Sung by Lead Belly, "King of the Twelve-String Guitar Players of the World," Long-Time Convict in the Penitentiaries of Texas and Louisiana* [printed music]. New York: The Macmillan Company, 1936.

Lott, Eric. *Love and Theft: Blackface Minstrelsy and the American Working Class*. New York: Oxford University Press, 1993.

Lytle, Andrew. "The Town: Helen's Last Stand." *Sewanee Review* 65 (1957): 475–84.

MacColl, Ewan, and A. L. Lloyd. *The English and Scottish Popular Ballads*. 9 vols. Washington Albums, 1952.

Mahon, Maureen. *Right to Rock: The Black Rock Coalition and the Cultural Politics of Race*. Durham, NC: Duke University Press, 2004.

Mailer, Norman. *Advertisements for Myself*. Cambridge, MA: Harvard University Press, 1992.

———. "Some Children of the Goddess: Norman Mailer vs. Nine Authors." *Esquire*, July 1963.

Marcus, Greil. "American Folk." Granta.com, January 9, 2002. https://granta.com/american-folk/.

———. *Mystery Train: Images of America in Rock 'n' Roll Music*. 6th rev. ed. New York: Plume, 2015.

———. *The Old, Weird America: The World of Bob Dylan's Basement Tapes*. Updated ed. New York: Picador, 2011.

Marcus, Greil, and Werner Sollors. *A New Literary History of America*. Cambridge, MA: Belknap Press of Harvard University Press, 2009.

Marsh, Dave. *The Heart of Rock & Soul: The 1,001 Greatest Singles Ever Made*. New York: Da Capo, 1999.

Marshall, Kate. *Corridor: Media Architectures in American Fiction*. Minneapolis: University of Minnesota Press, 2013.

McCarthy, Beth. "Nirvana" episode. *MTV Unplugged in New York*. New York: Sony Music Studios, 1993.

McCullers, Carson. *The Ballad of the Sad Café and Other Stories*. Boston: Houghton Mifflin, 2005.

McGinley, Paige A. "'The Magic of Song!': John Lomax, Huddie Ledbetter, and the Staging of Circulation." In *Performance in the Borderlands*, ed. Ramon H. Rivera-Servera and Harvey Young, 128–46. New York: Palgrave Macmillan, 2011.

——. *Staging the Blues: From Tent Shows to Tourism*. Durham, NC: Duke University Press, 2014.

McGurl, Mark. "The Novel, Mass Culture, Mass Media." In *The Cambridge History of the American Novel*. Cambridge: Cambridge University Press, 2011.

——. *The Program Era: Postwar Fiction and the Rise of Creative Writing*. Cambridge, MA: Harvard University Press, 2009.

McLane, Maureen N. *Balladeering, Minstrelsy, and the Making of British Romantic Poetry*. Reissue ed. Cambridge: Cambridge University Press, 2011.

McLellan, Tara. "'Nothing in America Remains Fixed for Long': Examining William Styron's *Set This House on Fire* Through a Postsouthern Lens." *Publications of the Mississippi Philological Association* (2008): 129–45.

McLuhan, Marshall. *Understanding Media: The Extensions of Man*. Cambridge, MA: MIT Press, 1994.

McMillen, Neil R. "Organized Resistance to School Desegregation in Tennessee." *Tennessee Historical Quarterly* 30, no. 3 (September 1971): 315–28.

Menke, Richard. *Telegraphic Realism: Victorian Fiction and Other Information Systems*. Stanford, CA: Stanford University Press, 2008.

Miles, Barry. *The British Invasion: The Music, the Times, the Era*. New York: Sterling, 2009.

Millard, Andre. *America on Record: A History of Recorded Sound*. 2nd ed. Cambridge: Cambridge University Press, 2005.

——. *Beatlemania: Technology, Business, and Teen Culture in Cold War America*. Baltimore, MD: Johns Hopkins University Press, 2012.

——, ed. "The Music: The Electric Guitar in the American Century." In *The Electric Guitar: A History of an American Icon*. Baltimore, MD: Lemelson Center for the Study of Invention and Innovation, National Museum of American History, Smithsonian Institution, 2004.

Miller, Karl Hagstrom. *Segregating Sound: Inventing Folk and Pop Music in the Age of Jim Crow*. Durham, NC: Duke University Press, 2010.

Millichap, Joseph R. "Carson McCullers' Literary Ballad." *Georgia Review* 27 (1973): 329–39.

Moore, Lorrie. *Birds of America: Stories*. New York: Vintage, 2010.

Morris, Alton C. "George Pullen Jackson (1874–1953)." *Journal of American Folklore* 66, no. 262 (October 1, 1953): 302.

Murray, Robert Keith. *Trapped! The Story of the Struggle to Rescue Floyd Collins from a Kentucky Cave in 1925*. New York: Putnam, 1979.

Nabers, Deak. "The Forms of Formal Realism: Literary Study and the Life Cycle of the Novel." In *Postmodern/Postwar and After: Rethinking American Literature*, ed. Jason Gladstone, Andrew Hoberek, and Daniel Worden. Iowa City: University of Iowa Press, 2016.

Neal, Jocelyn. *Country Music: A Cultural and Stylistic History*. New York: Oxford University Press, 2013.

Nenadal, Radoslav. "The Patterning of a Modern Hero in William Styron's *Set This House on Fire*." *Prague Studies in English* 15 (1973): 83–96.

Newman, Steve. *Ballad Collection, Lyric, and the Canon: The Call of the Popular from the Restoration to the New Criticism*. Philadelphia: University of Pennsylvania Press, 2007.

Nunn, Erich. *Sounding the Color Line: Music and Race in the Southern Imagination*. Athens: University of Georgia Press, 2015.

O'Connor, Flannery. *The Complete Stories*. New York: Farrar, Straus and Giroux, 1971.

——. *The Habit of Being: Letters of Flannery O'Connor*. Ed. Sally Fitzgerald. Reprint ed. New York: Farrar, Straus and Giroux, 1988.

——. *Mystery and Manners: Occasional Prose*. New York: Farrar, Straus & Giroux, 1969.

O'Connor, William Van. "John Updike and William Styron: The Burden of Talent." In *Contemporary American Novelists*, ed. Harry T. Moore. Carbondale: Southern Illinois University Press, 1964.

Odum, Howard Washington. *Cold Blue Moon, Black Ulysses Afar Off*. Productivity Press, 1931.

——. *Rainbow Round My Shoulder: The Blue Trail of Black Ulysses*. Bloomington: Indiana University Press, 1928.

——. *Wings on My Feet: Black Ulysses at the Wars*. Bloomington: Indiana University Press, 2007.

Olmsted, Anthony. *Folkways Records: Moses Asch and His Encyclopedia of Sound*. New York: Routledge, 2003.

Ong, Walter J. *Orality and Literacy: The Technologizing of the Word*. London: Routledge, 2002.

Orr, David. "After Dylan's Nobel, What Makes a Poet a Poet?" *New York Times*, March 24, 2017. https://www.nytimes.com/2017/03/24/books/review/after-dylans-nobel-what-makes-a-poet -a-poet.html.

Otterson, Joe. "Bob Dylan's Nobel Prize Win Seriously Annoys Authors." *The Wrap*, October 13, 2016. http://www.thewrap.com/bob-dylan-nobel-prize-in-literature-authors-backlash/.

Palmer, Jack, Robert Olson, and Hank Thompson. *Vernon Dalhart: First Star of Country Music*. Denver: Mainspring, 2004.

Parikka, Jussi. *Insect Media: An Archaeology of Animals and Technology*. Minneapolis: University of Minnesota Press, 2010.

Parrish, Susan. *The Flood Year 1927: A Cultural History*. Princeton, NJ: Princeton University Press, 2017.

Peer, Ralph. "Ralph Peer Sees No Hypo [*sic*] for Late Jimmy Rodgers; Dalhart Not a Hillbilly." *Variety*, November 2, 1955.

Percy, Thomas. *Reliques of Ancient English Poetry, Consisting of Old Heroic Ballads, Songs, and Other Pieces of Our Earlier Poets, Together with Some Few of Later Date*. New York: Dover, 1966.

Peters, John Durham. *Speaking Into the Air: A History of the Idea of Communication*. Chicago: University of Chicago Press, 1999.

Peterson, Richard A. "Why 1955? Explaining the Advent of Rock Music." *Popular Music* 9, no. 1 (January 1, 1990): 97–116.

Pizer, Donald. *Realism and Naturalism in Nineteenth-Century American Literature*. New York: Russell & Russell, 1976.

Jeff Place, interview by Kim Ruehl, *No Depression: The Journal of Roots Music* (February 17, 2015): http://nodepression.com/interview/digging-lead-bellys-america-interview-smithsonian -folkways-jeff-place.

Plimpton, George. "William Styron: The Art of Fiction No. 156." *Paris Review* 150 (1999).

Porterfield, Nolan. *Last Cavalier: The Life and Times of John A. Lomax, 1867–1948*. Urbana: University of Illinois Press, 1996.

"Proceedings of the Modern Language Association of America." *PMLA* 49 (1934): 1295–1336.

Pynchon, Thomas. *The Crying of Lot 49*. New York: Perennial Library, 1986.

Rampersad, Arnold. *Ralph Ellison: A Biography*. New York: Knopf, 2007.

Ratcliffe, Philip R. *Mississippi John Hurt: His Life, His Times, His Blues.* Jackson: University Press of Mississippi, 2011.

Remnick, David. "Let's Celebrate the Bob Dylan Nobel Win." *New Yorker,* October 13, 2016. http://www.newyorker.com/culture/cultural-comment/lets-celebrate-the-bob-dylan-nobel-win.

Reynolds, John, and Tiny Robinson. *Lead Belly: A Life in Pictures.* Göttingen: Steidl, 2008.

Riesman, David. "Listening to Popular Music." *American Quarterly* 2, no. 4 (1950): 359–71.

Robertson, David. *W. C. Handy: The Life and Times of the Man Who Made the Blues.* Tuscaloosa: University of Alabama Press, 2011.

Rolling Stone. "500 Greatest Songs of All Time." http://www.rollingstone.com/music/lists/the-500 -greatest-songs-of-all-time-20110407/bob-dylan-like-a-rolling-stone-20110516.

Romine, Scott. *The Real South: Southern Narrative in the Age of Cultural Reproduction.* Baton Rouge: Louisiana State University Press, 2008.

Rossi, Umberto. "Acousmatic Presences: From DJs to Talk-Radio Hosts in American Fiction, Cinema, and Drama." *Mosaic: A Journal for the Interdisciplinary Study of Literature* 42, no. 1 (2009): 83–98.

Roth, Philip. *Portnoy's Complaint.* Reprint ed. New York: Vintage, 1994.

Rubin, Louis D., Jr. "An Artist in Bonds." *Sewanee Review* 69 (1961): 174–79.

——. *The Faraway Country: Writers of the Modern South.* Seattle: University of Washington Press, 1963.

——. *The History of Southern Literature.* Baton Rouge: Louisiana State University Press, 1990.

——. "Introduction." In *I'll Take My Stand.* New York: Harper and Row, 1962.

——. *The Writer in the South: Studies in Literary Community.* Athens: University of Georgia Press, 1972.

Rushdie, Salman. *The Ground Beneath Her Feet.* London: Jonathan Cape, 1999.

Russell, Tony, Tennessee Country Music Hall of Fame & Museum, and Bob Pinson. *Country Music Records: A Discography, 1921–1942.* Oxford: Oxford University Press, 2004.

Ruttenberg, Jay. "Fallen Rock Stars in Contemporary Fiction." *New York Times Sunday Book Review,* September 7, 2012. http://www.nytimes.com/2012/09/09/books/review/fallen -rock-stars-in-contemporary-fiction.html.

Ryan, Tim A. "'The Faint Plinking of a Guitar': Faulkner's Forgotten Bluesman and the Power of Vernacular in *If I Forget Thee, Jerusalem.*" *Faulkner Journal* 27, no. 1 (2013): 3–27.

Sanders, Lynn Moss. "'Black Ulysses Singing': Odom's Folkloristic Trilogy." *Southern Literary Journal* 22, no. 1 (1989): 107.

Schwartz, Lawrence H. *Creating Faulkner's Reputation: The Politics of Modern Literary Criticism.* Knoxville: University of Tennessee Press, 1988.

Sconce, Jeffrey. *Haunted Media: Electronic Presence from Telegraphy to Television.* 2nd ed. Durham, NC: Duke University Press, 2000.

Scott, Sir Walter. *Minstrelsy of the Scottish Border: Consisting of Historical and Romantic Ballads, Collected in the Southern Counties of Scotland; with a Few of Modern Date, Founded Upon Local Tradition.* 2nd ed. Edinburgh: Printed by J. Ballantyne for Longman and Rees, and sold by Manners and Miller, 1803.

Seed, David. "Media Systems in *The Crying of Lot 49.*" In *American Postmodernity: Essays on the Recent Fiction of Thomas Pynchon,* ed. Ian D. Copestake. Oxford: Peter Lang, 2003.

Seltzer, Mark. *Bodies and Machines.* New York: Routledge, 1992.

Sharp, Cecil J. *English Folk Songs from the Southern Appalachians.* Vol. 1. Ed. Maud Karpeles. Northfield, MN: Loomis House, 2012.

Sharp, Cecil J., Olive D. (Olive Dame) Campbell, and Maud Karpeles. *English Folk Songs from the Southern Appalachians*. 2nd and enlarged ed. Oxford: Oxford University Press, 1960.

Shelton, Robert, Patrick Humphries, and Elizabeth Thomson. *No Direction Home: The Life and Music of Bob Dylan*. Rev. and updated ed. New York: Backbeat, 2011.

Siegert, Bernhard. *Relays: Literature as an Epoch of the Postal System*. Trans. Kevin Repp. Stanford, CA: Stanford University Press, 1999.

Sisario, Ben, Alexandra Alter, and Sewell Chan. "Bob Dylan Wins Nobel Prize, Redefining Boundaries of Literature." *New York Times*, October 14, 2016. https://www.nytimes.com/2016/10/14 /arts/music/bob-dylan-nobel-prize-literature.html.

Skinfill, Mauri. "The American Interior: Identity and Commercial Culture in Faulkner's Late Novels." *Faulkner Journal* 21, nos. 1/2 (2005).

Spiotta, Dana. *Eat the Document: A Novel*. New York: Scribner, 2006.

Stadler, Gustavus. "Never Heard Such a Thing: Lynching and Phonographic Modernity." *Social Text* 28, no. 1 (March 20, 2010): 87–105.

Stegner, Wallace. *The Big Rock Candy Mountain*. Lincoln: University of Nebraska Press, 1983.

Sterne, Jonathan. *The Audible Past: Cultural Origins of Sound Reproduction*. Durham, NC: Duke University Press, 2003.

Stevens, Denis, ed. *A History of Song*. New York: Norton, 1970.

Stevenson, David L. "Styron and the Fiction of the Fifties." *Critique: Studies in Contemporary Fiction* 3, no. 3 (1960): 47–58.

Stewart, Susan. *Crimes of Writing: Problems in the Containment of Representation*. New York: Oxford University Press, 1991.

——. *On Longing: Narratives of the Miniature, the Gigantic, the Souvenir, the Collection*. Durham, NC: Duke University Press, 1993.

Stoever, Jennifer Lynn. *The Sonic Color Line: Race and the Cultural Politics of Listening*. Reprint ed. New York: NYU Press, 2016.

Stoneback, H. R. "The Box, the Glittering Strings, and the Unbearable Hillbillyness of Being: Warren's *The Cave*, Country Music, and Vanderbilt Fugitive-Agrarianism." *RWP: Annual of Robert Penn Warren Studies* 8 (January 2008): 9–24.

Styron, William. *Selected Letters of William Styron*. New York: Random House, 2012.

——. *Set This House on Fire*. New York: New American Library, 1960.

Suisman, David. *Selling Sounds: The Commercial Revolution in American Music*. Cambridge, MA: Harvard University Press, 2009.

Sundquist, Eric. "Introduction: The Country of the Blue." In *American Realism: New Essays*. Baltimore, MD: Johns Hopkins University Press, 1982.

Szalay, Michael. *Hip Figures: A Literary History of the Democratic Party*. Stanford, CA: Stanford University Press, 2012.

Thompson, Richard. "Novel Sounds Keynote: Richard Thompson, Greil Marcus, and Jonathan Lethem." Interview by Florence Dore, October 15, 2016. http://nationalhumanitiescenter.org /novel-sounds-american-fiction-in-the-age-of-rock-and-roll/.

Tierney, Tom. "House Carpenter: A Song's Journey Through the Archives." *Official Bob Dylan Site*. http://www.bobdylan.com/us/bobdylan101/house-carpenter-songs-journey-through-archives.

Time. *The March of TIME: Folk Legend Leadbelly—Video*. Newsreel, 1935. http://content.time .com/time/video/player/0,32068,30862122001_1918195,00.html.

Tosches, Nick. *Unsung Heroes of Rock 'n' Roll: The Birth of Rock in the Wild Years Before Elvis*. New York: Da Capo, 1999.

Wagner, Bryan. *Disturbing the Peace: Black Culture and the Police Power After Slavery*. Cambridge, MA: Harvard University Press, 2009.

Wald, Elijah. *Dylan Goes Electric! Newport, Seeger, Dylan, and the Night That Split the Sixties*. New York: Dey St., 2015.

Walsh, Jim. "Musicologist Jim Walsh on Hillbilly Champs: Dalhart vs. Rodgers et al." *Variety*, September 21, 1955.

Warren, Kenneth. *So Black and Blue: Ralph Ellison and the Occasion of Criticism*. Chicago: University of Chicago Press, 2003.

Warren, Robert Penn. *The Cave*. Lexington: University Press of Kentucky, 2006.

——, ed. *Faulkner: A Collection of Critical Essays*. Englewood Cliffs, NJ: Prentice-Hall, 1966.

——. *Segregation: The Inner Conflict in the South*. New York: Random House, 1956.

——. *Who Speaks for the Negro?* New York: Random House, 1965.

Watt, Ian. *The Rise of the Novel: Studies in Defoe, Richardson, and Fielding*. Berkeley: University of California Press, 1957.

Weheliye, Alexander. *Phonographies: Grooves in Sonic Afro-Modernity*. Durham, NC: Duke University Press, 2005.

Weinstein, Philip. *Becoming Faulkner: The Art and Life of William Faulkner*. New York: Oxford University Press, 2010.

Welty, Eudora. "Powerhouse." *Atlantic*, June 1941.

Whitehead, Colson. *John Henry Days: A Novel*. New York: Anchor, 2002.

——. *Sag Harbor: A Novel*. New York: Doubleday, 2009.

Wimsatt, William K. *The Verbal Icon: Studies in the Meaning of Poetry*. Lexington: University of Kentucky Press, 1954.

Wolfe, Charles. "Event Songs." In *Reading Country Music: Steel Guitars, Opry Stars, and Honky-Tonk Bars*, ed. Cecelia Tichi. Durham, NC: Duke University Press, 1998.

Wolfe, Charles, and Kip Lornell. *The Life and Legend of Leadbelly*. New ed. New York: Da Capo, 1999.

Wollaeger, Mark. *Modernism, Media, and Propaganda: British Narrative from 1900 to 1945*. Princeton, NJ: Princeton University Press, 2006.

Work, John, Samuel C. Adams, Robert Gordon, Lewis Wade Jones, and Bruce Nemerov. *Lost Delta Found: Rediscovering the Fisk University–Library of Congress Coahoma County Study, 1941–1942*. Nashville, TN: Vanderbilt University Press, 2005.

Yates, Mike, and Kriss Sands. "A Nest of Singing Birds." *Musical Traditions*, March 3, 2002. http://www.mustrad.org.uk/articles/m_sands.htm.

Younger, Richard. *Get a Shot of Rhythm and Blues: The Arthur Alexander Story*. Tuscaloosa: University of Alabama Press, 2000.

Zak, Albin. *I Don't Sound Like Nobody: Remaking Music in 1950s America*. Ann Arbor: University of Michigan Press, 2010.

DISCOGRAPHY

AC/DC. *Highway to Hell*. LP. Atlantic, 1979.

Alexander, Arthur. "Anna (Go to Him)." 45. Dot, 1962.

Animals. "We Gotta Get Out of This Place." 45. MGM Records, 1965.

Beatles. *Please Please Me*. LP. Parlophone (UK), 1963.

——. "She Loves You." 45. Swan, 1963.

Belafonte, Harry. "The Midnight Special." *The Midnight Special*. LP. RCA Victor, 1962.

Berry, Chuck. "Maybellene." 45. Chess, 1955.

Bill Haley and His Comets. "Shake, Rattle, and Roll." 45. Decca, 1954.

Carson, Fiddlin' John. "The Death of Floyd Collins." OKeh 9053, April 1925.

Charles, Ray. "Hey Good Lookin'." *Modern Sounds in Country and Western Music*. LP. ABC, 1962.

Cooke, Sam. "A Change Is Gonna Come." 45. RCA Victor, 1964.

Creedence Clearwater Revival. *Willy and the Poor Boys*. LP. Fantasy, 1969.

Dalhart, Vernon. "Death of Floyd Collins." Victor 33374, September 1925.

Dylan, Bob. "House Carpenter." [1962]. *Bootleg Series Volumes 1–3 (Rare & Unreleased), 1961–1991*. CD. Columbia, 1991.

——. *The Freewheelin' Bob Dylan*. LP. New York: Columbia, 1963.

——. *The Times They Are a-Changin'*. LP. Columbia, 1964.

——. "Like a Rolling Stone." 45. Columbia, 1965.

——. *The Basement Tapes*. [1967]. LP. Columbia, 1975.

——. *Self Portrait*. LP. Columbia, 1970.

Eno, Brian. *Another Green World*. LP. Island, 1975.

Fairport Convention. *Liege and Lief*. [1969]. CD. Island (UK), 2002.

——. *Full House*. LP. Island (UK), 1970.

Harris, Emmylou. *Wrecking Ball*. CD. Elektra, 1995.

Hurt, Mississippi John. "Frankie." OKeh 400221, 1928.

Joplin, Janis. *Blow All My Blues Away* (bootleg recordings 1962–70). 2012.

——. *Janis*. LP. Columbia, 1975.

Lead Belly. "The Midnight Special." Victor 051298, 1940.

——. *Lead Belly's Last Sessions*. Vol. 2. [1948]. Smithsonian Folkways, 1994.

Led Zeppelin. *Led Zeppelin III*. LP. Atlantic, 1970.

Lomax, John Avery, and Lead Belly. *Frankie and Albert*. Angola, Louisiana, 1934.

Presley, Elvis. "Hound Dog." 45. RCA Victor, 1956.

——. *Frankie and Johnny*. LP. RCA Victor, 1966.

Rivers, Johnny. *At the Whisky à Go Go*. LP. Imperial, 1964.

Rolling Stones. *Sticky Fingers*. LP. Rolling Stones Records (Atlantic), 1970.

Smith, Bessie. "A Good Man Is Hard to Find." Columbia 14250, 1927.

——. "Empty Bed Blues." Columbia 145786, 1928.

Thomas, Rufus, and Carla Thomas. "'Cause I Love You." 45. Stax, 1960.

Trashmen. "Surfin' Bird." 45. Garrett, 1963.

Turner, Big Joe. "Shake, Rattle, and Roll." 45. Atlantic, 1954.

Various. *Anthology of American Folk Music* (edited by Harry Smith). [1952]. CD. Smithsonian Folkways, 1997.

Various. *Broadside Reunion: Broadside Ballads*. Vol. 6. LP. Folkways, 1972.

Various. *People Take Warning! Murder Ballads & Disaster Songs, 1913–1938*. CD. Tompkins Square, 2007.

Wills, Bob, and His Texas Playboys. "Ida Red." 78. Vocalion, 1938.

Zanes, Dan. *Lead Belly, Baby!*. CD. Smithsonian Folkways, 2017.

Zevon, Warren. "Werewolves of London." 45. Asylum, 1978.

FILMOGRAPHY

Altman, Robert, dir. *Nashville*. Paramount Pictures, 1975.
Camalier, Greg "Freddy," dir. *Muscle Shoals*. Magnolia Productions, 2013. Netflix.
De Cordova, Frederick, dir. *Frankie and Johnny*. Metro-Goldwyn-Mayer (MGM), 1966.
Sidney, George, dir. *Viva Las Vegas*. Metro-Goldwyn-Mayer (MGM), 1964.
Wilder, Billy, dir. *Ace in the Hole*. Paramount Pictures, 1951.

INDEX

AC/DC, 117
Adorno, Theodor, 6, 95, 98, 100, 104–5,
  126n20
Agrarians, 17, 23, 46, 62, 78, 84
Alexander, Arthur, 9
Als, Hilton, 144n14
Altman, Robert, 119
American Folklore Society, 24
*American Literature: The Makers and the
  Making* (Brooks, Lewis, and Warren),
  120–21
Animals, 14
"Anna" (Alexander), 9
"Another Green World" (Eno), 14
Anthology of American Folk Music, 36–43,
  138n20, 139n21, 139n23
Antinomies of Realism (Jameson), 148n11
Appalachian folk, 33, 36
Asch, Moses, 138n20
Ashley, Clarence, 42
Atkins, Chet, 141n10
"Avant-Garde and Kitsch" (Greenberg), 119

Baldwin, James, 10–12, 51, 82, 145n14
ballad, 2–3, 5–7; Agrarian novels and,
  33–54; in American fiction before
  rock, 13–14; Brooks on, 19–23; Child
  and, 20–21, 24, 34, 37, 121; Davidson

on, 17–18, 109; Dylan and, 33, 40–42;
Fairport Convention and, 21; "Frankie
and Johnny" and, 19–27, 42–43, 98,
131n64; gender and, 77–93; Hurston
on, 18; Lead Belly and, 16–19; J. Lomax
on, 24–26; Lytle on, 17; as poetry, 19,
22–23, 45; race and, 7–11, 17–19, 43–54,
58–59, 62–63, 81–82, 95; Sharp and, 33;
technological basis and, 24–27, 73–75,
77–93, 95–113; in *Understanding Poetry*,
19–23, 47; Warren on, 19–23, 33–34, 47
Ballad of the Sad Cafe (McCullers), 2, 27,
  76–80, 86, 88–93
Band, The, 117
Baraka, Amiri, 12; on rock and roll,
  128n40
Barthes, Roland, 78, 93, 146n22, 148n11
Basement Tapes (Dylan), 42
Beatles, 5, 9, 12, 20, 57–58, 71–72; Charles
on, 143n2; O'Connor on, 145n13
*Beautiful Circuits: Modernism and the
  Mediated Life* (Goble), 30
Belafonte, Harry, 112
Benjamin, Walter, 97, 99, 147n4
Berry, Chuck, 3, 8, 41, 96, 116, 124n9, 143n2
Big Ballad Jamboree, The (Davidson), 2,
  27, 34–43
Billboard (magazine), 115, 124n7, 151n1

variant, 34; Sands and, 33; in *Understanding Poetry*, 20, 42, 45, 127n23

Dalhart, Vernon, 2, 35
Davidson, Donald, 33–34, 81, 109, 119, 136n5; and "Daemon Lover," 36–43; on *Anthology of American Folk Music*, 36–43; on ballads, 17–18; *Big Ballad Jamboree*, 2, 27, 33–43; on jazz records, 17–18, 112; "white spirituals" and, 18; white supremacy and, 19, 23
"Death of Emmet Till, The" (Dylan), 41
"Death of Floyd Collins, The," 2, 33–36, 47–48, 136n7
DeLillo, Don, 15, 119
Deliverance (Dickey), 118
Democracy of Poetry (Gummere), 131n69
Dickey, James, 118
Diddley, Bo, 143n2
Dixon, Willie, 9, 127n31
"Domestic Dilemma, A" (McCullers), 144n6
Donne, John, 19, 57–58, 61, 69, 74–75, 96, 113
Doyle, Roddy, 15
Duck, Leigh Ann, 141n17
Dylan, Bob, 2, 7, 28, 127n23, 138n15, 151n1; on *Anthology of American Folk Music*, 36–43; on ballads, 33–35, 40–43; *Basement Tapes*, 42; "Daemon Lover," 21, 33, 40; fictionalization of, 119; on folk, 138n15; *Freewheelin'*, 41; going electric, 41–42, 138n19; Lead Belly and, 40, 96–97; Lethem on, 142n24; "Like a Rolling Stone," 103–4, 151n1; Marcus on, 42, 139n23; Meltzer on, 151n9; Nobel Prize in Literature and, 115–16, 122; on Odetta, 138n15; race and, 40–41, 68, 103–4, 124n7; Remnick on, 28, 115–16; rock and roll and, 103–4
Dyson, Frances, 108, 146n18; on Barthes, 146n22; on *Cogito Ergo Sum*, 146n19; on voice, 148n13

Eat the Document (Spiotta), 14
Ed Sullivan Show, The (television), 5, 20

Eliot, T. S., 19, 57, 58, 119; on difficult poetry, 126n19
Ellis, Brett Easton, 15
Ellison, Harlan, 15
Ellison, Ralph, 10–12, 51; on blues, 12; on Faulkner, 128n37; inclusion in *Understanding Fiction*, 53; *Who Speaks for the Negro?*, 52
"Empty Bed Blues" (B. Smith), 13
English and Scottish Popular Ballads (Child), 20–21, 34, 132n71
English Folksongs from Southern Appalachians (Sharp), 33, 36
Eno, Brian, 14
Evers, Charles, 43
Evers, Medgar, 40, 43
"Everybody's Protest Novel" (Baldwin), 11

Fairport Convention, 21, 127n23, 132n75
father, voice of, 108–9
Faulkner, William, 1–2, 6, 13, 27–28, 56, 57, 63–66, 72–74; as balladeer, 60; Brooks on, 6; career of, 61, 62; Ellison, R., on, 128n37; Godden on, 68, 90; *Go Down Moses*, 13; modernism and, 6, 66, 68; as "provincial," 6; *Sound and the Fury*, 62, 66; *The Town*, 1–2, 4, 57–75; vernacular in, 74; Warren on, 59–60
femininity, 77–93. *See also* gender
Ferris, William, 4
fiddle, 17, 23, 27–31, 59, 62, 93, 109–10
Fitzgerald, Sally, 143n1
Fogerty, John, 152n22
Folkway Records, 42, 138n20
"Form of the Phonograph Record, The" (Adorno), 95
Fortress of Solitude (Lethem), 14, 96, 113, 117–18
Frank, Harmonica, 2
Frankie and Johnny (film), 98
"Frankie and Johnny," 19–27, 42–43, 98, 131, 131n64, 134n93
Freed, Alan, 125n10
Freewheelin' Bob Dylan, The (Dylan), 41
Freud, Sigmund, 105; and the record as fetish, 99, 104